DAYS THAT CHANGED THE WORLD

HYWEL WILLIAMS

Quercus

CONTENTS

INTRODUCTION

The currents of history run deep and often unseen beneath the everyday flow of events, and it is the historian's pleasurable task to trace the ebb and flow of those forces in the life of humanity. However, there are moments when these currents rise to the surface – with an effect that is often shattering, occasionally moving, but always transforming – to shed an exceptional light on the meaning of history. The days on which these moments occurred are the subject matter of this book.

The fifty days that I have chosen cover a period of time between the development of Athenian civilization in the fifth century BC, and the current crisis in relations between the Western and Middle Eastern powers. My choices inevitably reflect the experiences of a European author writing in English at the beginning of the twenty-first century. But the fact that history reflects personality does not make it merely subjective, and my fifty days have been chosen because of their undeniable significance and global impact. Each generation stands on its predecessors' shoulders and thinks that it sees further, while also being in debt to its forebears. In our own time we have become increasingly conscious of the inter-relation between the world's continents and the relationship between Asia and Europe, Africa and the Americas is, I hope, illustrated in *Days that Changed the World*.

The stuff of history within these two-and-a-half millennia includes military triumphs and defeats, religious revelations and intellectual controversies, social and political revolutions, assassinations and conspiracies. In some cases, the day's events represent the beginning of a new phase, as with the coronation of Charlemagne. Other days mark the significant end of a great period – as in the fall of Constantinople. But the patterns of world history are also shaped by less obviously dramatic occurrences and by processes whose significance only became apparent much later. So the days that changed history also include events such as the start of Isaac Newton's university education, the publication of Albert Einstein's paper on the special theory of relativity, and the patent for a telephone granted to Alexander Graham Bell.

In the pages that follow there are many examples of human cruelty and tragedy, of violent acts and persistent prejudices. But the history of human beings revealed in this slice through recorded time also shows the resilience of the human spirit and its capacity for justice. Slavery, danger and intolerance coexist with emancipation, creativity and energy in the annals of mankind.

It is a pleasure to record my debt to my agent, Georgina Capel, and to Anthony Cheetham who suggested that I should write this book. Wayne Davies provided me with wise guidance as my editor, while Victoria Huxley brought an acute eye and a fine judgement to the copy-editing of the text. Any remaining errors of judgement or faults of expression rest on the author's shoulders.

Hywel Williams

28 September 480 BC

The Battle of Salamis

The Athenian Navy Destroys the Persian Fleet

*'We have forced every sea and land to be the highway
of our daring, and everywhere, for good or ill, we have left
imperishable monuments behind us.'*

Pericles on the Athenians

The battle of Salamis became the first great sea-battle to be described in recorded history. It was a momentous event in the long story of the wars between the Greeks and the Persian empire. The Greek fleet was able to defeat the much larger Persian navy at the straits of Salamis located between the island of Salamis and the Athenian port of Piraeus. By 480 BC the Persian army led by King Xerxes I had conquered large parts of Greece. The Persian navy consisting of a thousand galleys was threatening to surround and overwhelm the Greek fleet of 370 triremes located in the Saronic Gulf. The eventual victory was the result of some clever Greek trickery – a quality which was always a cause for Hellenic self-congratulation. The Greek commander Themistocles sent Xerxes a false message suggesting that he was preparing to change sides. Lured by the Greeks, the Persians then sailed into the narrow waters of the Salamis straits where the Greek triremes proceeded to launch a ferocious attack, ramming the Persian ships and sinking some 300 of them. The Greeks by contrast lost only about forty of their ships. The remainder of the Persian fleet had to withdraw and Xerxes was forced to postpone any further land campaigns for a year. This provided the Greeks with a crucial breathing space during which the autonomous city states (*poleis*) set aside their customary quarrels. Their united armies, under the command of the Spartan general Pausanias, went on to defeat the Persians at the battle of Plataea in 479 BC.

Salamis represented the union of naval strategy with democratic zeal. In 508 BC, twenty-eight years before the battle, Cleisthenes' legislation gave citizenship to all the free men of Athens – including Themistocles whose father was an aristocrat but whose mother was a non-Athenian concubine. Without Cleisthenes' reform the hero of Salamis would not have been an Athenian citizen. Ten years before Salamis the Greeks had won the great land victory at Marathon when, led by Miltiades, they had defeated the Persians. This had been a victory for the spear-carriers who could afford to buy their own expensive bronze equipment. But the Persians were notoriously well equipped with cavalry and archers – their country's huge plains enabled them to train such forces, an advantage denied the Greeks with their terrain of valleys and mountains. The Persians would be perfectly capable of returning in greater numbers.

Themistocles proposed that the Greeks should exploit the difficulties experienced by Persia and her allies (who included the Phoenicians) in maintaining their naval chain of supply and lines of communication. He therefore campaigned for an expansion of the Athenian fleet, then some seventy strong. But this was a proposal with profound democratic consequences. The rich would have to pay higher taxes. Poorer voters, traditionally pro-democracy, supplied the triremes with rowers. A naval expansion therefore meant increasing the influence, and possibly the numbers, of democratic sympathizers. For the conservative and propertied classes a land campaign was always a safer bet politically since the infantry were drawn from those with more money. The 480s in Athens, despite the Marathon victory, threatened to degenerate into that endemic state of political and social conflict known as *stasis* to the Greeks. Silver helped to resolve the argument. The mines at Sunium, owned by the state, produced a rich extra seam in 483 and Themistocles persuaded the Athenian assembly to spend this surplus on his naval expansion programme so that Athens would have 200 triremes. He also persuaded the Greek states of the Peloponnese, including Sparta with her 150 ships, to form a combined fleet. A Spartan admiral was in command since no Corinthian or Aeginan would serve under an Athenian, but it was Themistocles who guided the strategy.

The fleet first sailed north of Euboea – an audacious move since the Greek traditionally fought near their own coastal mainland. A storm inflicted heavy losses on the Persians but the subsequent battle of Artemisium was inconclusive with heavy losses on both sides. Greek disaster struck on 19 August at the pass of Thermopylae which leads from northern Macedonia into the rest of Greece: here 20,000 Persians defeated 300 Spartans and 700 Thebans. They went on to occupy Attica and destroy Athens. Salamis was a deliverance from this humiliation.

The victories of a citizen army and a citizen navy supplied the basis for the self-confidence of a civilization although many of its distinctive cultural achievements pre-dated Salamis. The Olympic games, testimony to the Greek belief in the *agon* or contest which permeated all of life and not just athletics, were first recorded at Olympia in 776 BC. The *Iliad* and the *Odyssey*, attributed to Homer, were written by the mid-ninth century BC. These epics provided the Greeks with a theology describing the gods who might be angry or blessed, jealous or kindly but always unpredictable. Because the Greek soil was so poor the history of searching for a better territory starts early and by 700 BC such colonists were establishing themselves around the Mediterranean, and southern Italy would become Greek. Parmenides, whose associated school of philosophers were the first true metaphysicians, was born in 515 BC and developed the belief that the universe, although appearing to change, is solid and permanent. By 500 BC Heraclitus was teaching at Ephesus his distinctive view that all of nature and of humanity is in constant flux.

After Salamis the Greeks increasingly defined themselves in conscious opposition to an 'east' which was effete, luxurious, decadent and, above all, undemocratic. Having scored great victories over an empire which was so much larger, and richer, they suspected that they were blessed by the gods. Many Athenians also thought that the development of democratic institutions emphasizing common purpose was the key to their own moral and political superiority. The liveliness of that debate had its counterpart in the Athenian development of critical thought and of a philosophy which examined fundamental ideas about matter and atoms, law and morality, the difference between the subjective belief and objective truth. Informally in the *agora* or market place, more formally in the school or gymnasium as well as in the Athenian assembly, intellectual debates raged. Plato, though an anti-democrat, would describe such exchanges of views as dialectic – the path to truth. This was a relentlessly open society, one in which an *idiot* was, literally, someone who withdrew from the public world of the *polis* in which it was a duty to serve. Their language itself, so the Greeks congratulated themselves, was uniquely equipped to express with precision the fine distinctions and abstract ideas which were debated in the fifth century BC.

Salamis did not remove the Greek sense of exposure to Persian threat. And it's that sense of living on the edge which explains the creative brilliance of the Athenian civilization. Herodotus established the new discipline of history when he set to work describing how but also *why* the Greeks and the Persians came to be at war. He handled evidence critically and drew on the Greek fascination with their own difference from the 'barbarians'. Tragedy was the Athenians' most distinctive literary form – a blend of philosophical speculation, religious ritual and sublime poetry never since equalled in any other world civilization. Ideas about the relation between men and gods, between free will and necessity, acquired a human dimension in the plays of Aeschylus, Sophocles and Euripides which reworked the ancient Greek myths to contemporary effect. But there was also a tragic dimension to the inability of the Greeks, after so brilliant an inauguration, to produce a political order whose unity would reflect their cultural depth. Conflicts within the seventy or so *poleis* were also vicious and ostracism – where one's political opponents were outlawed – was often used in Athens. Themistocles himself was ostracised having failed in his campaign for a further reform of the *Areopagus*, the originally aristocratic central council which governed Athens. Under the reformer Solon in the early sixth century BC the membership of the council had been opened up to all who had certain property qualifications and a rival council, the *Boule*, was established. But Themistocles wanted the democracy to go further and as fast as one of his triremes. He died *c.* 460 while serving, ironically enough, as a governor of some of the Asian Greek cities which were still Persian controlled.

By 438 BC the Parthenon, the temple to Athena goddess of Athens in her role as *parthenos* (virgin), had been completed as a symbolic statement of the city's self-confidence. But seven years later the Athenian empire had embarked on the twenty-seven year conflict with Sparta known as the Second Peloponnesian War. It was a war between two systems of government: between Athenian citizen democracy and Spartan aristocratic militarism. It had also been caused by the rough tactics used by the Athenians when developing their empire and by their imposition on their client states of regimes run by pro-Athenian appeasers. The war, ending in Spartan victory and the dismantling of the Athenian empire, sapped the strength not just of Athens but of all Greece. And the fact that Sparta was financed by Persian gold was a kind of revenge for Salamis. All of Hellas was now vulnerable to the rise of the Macedonian kings of the north – first Philip II and then his son Alexander. Philip's victory at the battle of Chaeronea imposed Macedonian kingship and overlordship over the Greek *poleis*. The end, however, was also a beginning. Alexander, seeing himself as a Homeric hero, was Hellenic culture's best ambassador. He and his successors transmitted Greek values (though not democracy) across the vast areas of Alexander's conquests in the east, including Persia, and down to the Indus. The Roman republic rose to greatness during this Hellenistic period and the Romans themselves, for all their military and political prowess and distinctive achievements in the framing of laws, always knew that culturally they stood on the shoulders of the Greeks' gigantic achievements which were given the space and confidence to develop because of the victory at Salamis.

15 March 44 BC

The Assassination of Julius Caesar

The Death of a Dictator and the End of the Roman Republic

'A certain star during those days appeared in the north towards evening…the majority ascribed it to Caesar, interpreting it to mean that he had become immortal.'

Dio Cassius (c.155-235)

On 15 March, 44 BC, a day known as the Ides of March in the Roman calendar that he had himself recently reformed, the general and politician Gaius Julius Caesar was assassinated in the Senate at Rome as a result of a conspiracy of republican noblemen. On the morning of that day he had stood at the apex of his power as the conqueror of Gaul, the undisputed winner in the civil wars which had consumed the old Roman Republic and then as dictator for life – an office which had survived from earlier Roman history and was now revived. Although warned by one of the numerous street soothsayers to beware that day, Caesar had shown his usual toughness of mind and decided to attend the Senate.

As Caesar entered, the Senate rose as a mark of respect and, after he sat down, the conspirators closed around him. Tillius Cimber approached first under the pretext of a petition on behalf of his brother who had been exiled by Caesar. His colleagues joined in with their own prayers, kissing Caesar's head and feet. The surrounded leader tried to get up but couldn't. His assailants' daggers were now unsheathed. Servilius Casca aimed for Caesar's left shoulder just above the collar bone but missed. Casca's brother then drove his sword into the ribs. Cassius slashed his face and Decimus Brutus pierced him on the side. Some of the conspirators ended up hitting each other in the mêlée. Having been wounded some thirty-five times Caesar's body came to rest at the foot of Pompey's statue.

Caesar had already reformed the Senate by increasing its size and making it more representative of the citizens of Rome. He had also pursued a generous policy of granting Roman citizenship to non-Romans such as the entire population of Cisalpine Gaul north of the River Po. And he had also recreated the two great cities of Carthage and Corinth, destroyed by his predecessors in the course of Rome's implacable rise from city state republic to world power status. In the previous year he had passed a law which established the way in which the *municipia*, the local units of Roman self-government, should be run. All of these measures were taken in order to try and solve the great problem of how to deal with the soldiers of the Roman legions, whether discharged and hungry for land or currently serving but detached from any loyalty to the central Roman institutions. Rather than serving the republic, they chose instead to serve the political ambitions of their own generals and this had caused the decline of that republic's institutions. But it was the evidence of Caesar's ability and ambition which caused his death. Among the conspirators were two former governors of Gaul, Marcus Junius Brutus (widely believed to be his illegitimate son) and Decimus Junius Brutus – members of a family long since associated with the cause of republicanism. Indeed, one of their ancestors was supposed to have helped to expel the Tarquin kings in 509 BC, the event which led to the republic's establishment. Caesar, the dictator, seemed bent on subverting half a millennium of republican institutions and beliefs. The argument for killing Caesar was that it would revive the old Roman way of life – *mos maiorum* or the customs of the ancestors.

War, law and politics had always dominated the Roman state. Roman citizens elected the republic's two senior officials, the consuls who were charged with military affairs. Lesser officials then decided legal disputes,organized the public works and presided over religious festivals and other duties of state. Although all Roman citizens could vote for the candidates, they were divided into three groupings determined by status and wealth. The patricians were a small elite group of families who alone had the right to be elected to certain positions. The equites were non-patricians with enough money and leisure to pay taxes and perform the unpaid duties of state. The remainder were the plebeians. This system, suitable for a medium sized central Italian city-state, came under pressure as a result of Rome's expansion. By c. 290 BC Rome had unified the rest of Italy under her rule and the epic struggle which followed in the next century and a half led to the eventual defeat of the north African city of Carthage – Rome's rival for dominance of the western Mediterranean.

The Rome of the mid-second century was also a world power in the east after the defeat of most of Greece, and in the west, southern Gaul (France) had also been conquered. But the imperial economy would tear the republican system apart. Small peasant land holdings were celebrated in Roman literature as nurseries which taught the virtues of hard work and ancestral piety towards the gods; however, they were no longer viable. Imports of cheap food, especially from the granaries of north Africa, as well as the growth of large estates run by slave labour now dominated the markets and created mass rural unemployment. Migration into Rome also resulted in a huge urban proletariat which was hungry, often unemployed, and therefore ready to sell their votes to those who promised them food, money and lavish spectacles. Successful generals, when seeking office, could also use their own troops to bully their way into power. Money and muscle were therefore the resources needed in order to be elected to the offices of praetor and consul whose traditional perks included the governance of a province. And the clients of a successful Roman noble family, those who gave their patrons political support, could therefore include provincial kings and entire national regions.

The family of the Caesars belonged to the *gens* (or clan) called Julius – one of the ancient patrician nobility. But despite the Julii Caesares' claim to trace their family back to the goddess Venus, they were neither rich nor powerful. The latest of their line would have to make his own way.

From the beginning Caesar's ambition was to reform both the old Roman state and the wider Graeco-Roman world. He showed his radical colours by marrying Cornelia, daughter of Lucius Cornelius Cinna who had supported the revolutionary political campaigns of the general, Gaius Marius. The brief dictatorship of Sulla (82-78) was an early attempt at getting rid of republican rule in the name of a reactionary aristocracy – and Caesar disappeared from Italy to do his military service in the province of Asia and in Cilicia. On his return to Rome he was elected to be one of the military tribunes and, with his new ally Pompey, helped to dismantle the Sullan constitution. By c. 68 he had been elected quaestor – the first major step in a political career and served in the province of Further Spain. He borrowed heavily to provide some spectacular public shows while he was one of the *curule aediles*. In 63 he was elected *Pontifex Maximus* or High Priest and became praetor in 62. As governor of Further Spain in 61-60 he was able to loot in the traditional manner while on a campaign, which enabled him to settle his debts. On his return to Rome in 60, and against Senatorial opposition, he stood successfully for the consulship of the year 59.

In the 'first triumvirate' Caesar created a powerful force by uniting himself with

Pompey and Crassus. He pushed through legislation which would give Pompey's soldiers allotments on Italian public land. He then conquered the remaining, non-Roman, parts of Gaul and it was the prestige he gained from this which gave him the authority to attempt the reordering of Rome herself. The triumvirate had by now foundered due to internal rivalries and in 49 BC Caesar moved on Rome. He crossed the Rubicon, the river that marked the divide between Gaul and Roman soil, without giving up his army. By doing so he broke the law and defied the Roman senate. He defeated Pompey, who was now supporting the senate, at the battle of Pharsalus in southern Thessaly which made Caesar the effective – though disputed – ruler of Rome. After expeditions in Egypt and Asia Minor he returned to Rome where he quelled a mutiny in the Campania, subjugated the rebellious legions in north Africa and then defeated Pompey's sons. Caesar had won – but his victories were so conclusive that he had made permanent enemies of those who believed in, and sentimentalized, the old Roman system.

Caesar was not the tyrant who destroyed the Roman Republic because that system had already self-destructed. The effective authority of the Roman nobility had disappeared because it was a mere oligarchy. Caesar adopted his nephew Octavian as his son and, after Caesar's death, Octavian formed a second triumvirate of like-minded power-hungry politicians, Mark Antony and Marcus Lepidus. This group pursued the assassins of Caesar to their deaths and in 42 BC they deified Caesar and forced the Roman magistrates to uphold Caesar's constitutional changes. Octavian was heir to Caesar's military genius but infinitely more subtle in his political tactics. He dissolved the second triumvirate and established himself as Augustus after the resumption of the Roman civil war. At the battle of Actium in 31 BC he gained a great naval victory over Mark Antony and the Egyptian queen Cleopatra. As a result, Egypt became his personal property and the fabulous wealth he now acquired enabled him to distribute power and property in Rome. In 27 BC he was given the title of Augustus Caesar by the Senate. Realizing that it was the naked display of power which had destroyed his uncle he decided to declare that he was simply restoring the old democratic Roman constitution yet his money meant that it was only his own supporters who had a chance of getting the votes for elected office. Beneath a residual democratic façade Rome had become an empire. Behind this achievement stood Julius Caesar's life-work. By getting rid of the Roman oligarchs who had masqueraded as republicans, Caesar in fact gave Rome a new lease of life.

Strengthened as an autocracy Rome could now stand for another 400 years – at a time when barbarian invaders increasingly threatened from both the north and the west. And Gaul, having been Romanized at a deep level during these centuries, was therefore able to draw on those roots and recover to civilized life after the barbarian tribes had come and gone. Recognition of this common European debt explains the survival of Caesar's family name in the title of Tsar to signify a supreme ruler. But the appeal of republicanism as a political ideal also survived. It would first reappear in the Italian city states of the middle ages. The works of Machiavelli, followed by those of Shakespeare, especially in his play *Julius Caesar*, endowed republicanism with an idealism which was hardly evident in the selfish motives of those who hacked the first and greatest of Caesars to death on that day in Rome.

Good Friday *c.*30 AD

The Crucifixion of
Jesus Christ

The Crucifixion of Jesus Christ took place in the highly charged atmosphere of Jerusalem during the week of Passover, an annual holiday when Jews in their tens of thousands would travel to the city in order to celebrate their past deliverance from captivity in Egypt. Earlier that week Jesus, originally from the town of Nazareth in Galilee and whose name meant 'Jehovah saves', had travelled into the city on a donkey. This had been a conscious recreation of Zachariah's Old Testament prophecy that the Jews would find their king coming to them mounted on a donkey as a sign of his humility. His accompanying followers acclaimed Jesus as 'son of David' – the tenth century BC king who had, it was thought, established a unified Jewish state with its capital in Jerusalem. The word Christos, bestowed on Jesus by his disciples, is the Greek version of the Hebrew *Meshiah* or Messiah, 'the anointed one'. In *c.* 30 AD therefore, both in Jerusalem and more generally in Jewish Palestine, Jesus was seen as an anointed successor to David who would restore Israel.

Following the celebration of a Passover meal with his disciples at which he had blessed the bread and wine calling the bread 'my body' and the wine 'my blood of the Covenant', Jesus withdrew to the Mount of Olives to pray. The gospels describe the betrayal of Jesus by one of his disciples, Judas Iscariot, who guided the armed men dispatched by Caiaphas, the Jewish Chief Priest, who had been alarmed by the evidence of Jesus' threat to public order. When brought before Caiaphas and his council (the *Sanhedrin*) Jesus replied ambiguously when asked whether he considered himself 'son of God'. This was enough evidence of blasphemy for Caiaphas to send Jesus before Pontius Pilate, the Roman governor of Judaea, with a recommendation that he be crucified – the cruellest punishment known to ancient Rome. It is probable that the *Sanhedrin* and Caiaphas also thought that Jesus saw himself as 'king of the Jews'. The gospels' presentation of Pilate as being troubled about what to do next is coloured by the fact that Christianity, by the time of the gospels' composition in the late first century, was a fast growing religion and needed to be on good terms with the Roman authorities. Pilate was as rough and ready a character as any other Roman ruler of a troublesome province. He would eventually be dismissed from his job because of his unwise execution of a number of Samaritans. Ordering the crucifixion of a Jewish troublemaker between two criminals on the local hill of Gethsemane would not have been a problem for him.

Jesus was crucified with the title 'king of the Jews' mockingly posted above his head on which he wore a crown of thorns. It is also probable that right up to the moment of death Jesus believed in the imminence of a divine intervention according to that tradition of Jewish eschatology which his life's work had revived and made so dangerous a threat to the Roman political order. His last recorded words were, 'My God, My God, why have you forsaken me?'

Palestine was part of the Roman empire, and Jewish Palestine, at the time of Jesus' birth some thirty years earlier, was ruled by Rome's client king, Herod the Great. Its position between Syria and Egypt made its stability vital for the Romans in this volatile area. The emperor Augustus took away the southern Palestinian territories of Judaea, Idumaea and the (non-Jewish) area of Samaria from Herod's son and successor, Herod Archelaus, and turned them into the imperial province of Judaea which was governed by his prefect, Pontius Pilate. Herod's other son, Herod Antipas, meanwhile ruled in Galilee, northern Palestine. Based in Caesarea, with only a small army to support him, Pilate avoided Jerusalem except when religious festivals such as the Passover turned the city into a mob of patriotic Jews. He relied on the High Priest and his council to enforce order. Jewish-Gentile relations were tense and the Romans were warily respectful of the vivid Jewish sense of their own cultural opposition to the Graeco-Roman world. Jews resisted any establishment of pagan temples in their towns as well as gymnasia and gladiatorial contests. There would be no colonies in Jewish Palestine until the First Jewish revolt of 66-74 AD made them a necessity for the Roman rulers.

Daily Jewish life in the region was governed by the observance of the *Torah* or Law as set out in the Old Testament. Internal divisions among the Jews made Judaea a turbulent place: learned and pious Pharisees advocated a precise interpretation of the laws, the radical sect of the Essenes were a vigorous fringe movement and the Sadducees were politically influential.

The Synoptic gospels of Matthew, Mark and Luke, so-called because of their similarity to each other, portray a figure who spoke of 'the Kingdom of God' using parables, aphorisms and similes whose language and references drew on agricultural and village life. The gospels also make it clear that Jesus, during a very brief public ministry of probably no more than a year, proclaimed the imminent arrival of the Kingdom of God and anticipated that God would intervene and pass a final judgement before establishing an Israel free of foreign domination. By summoning twelve disciples to follow him Jesus also declared his belief that God would restore the twelve tribes of Israel. The 'Kingdom of God' was twofold. It existed in heaven and would be entered on death, but it was also shown in the words and deeds of the here and now. Being a member of this kingdom was a question of realizing God's will, of being filled with faith and rejecting material possessions. It was also evident that Jesus favoured the outcasts of his own time – not just the poor and lowly but also the sinners who repented. Even tax gatherers and prostitutes could therefore be in the Kingdom. By this proclamation Jesus called on people to follow his example rather than himself personally. He also anticipated the arrival of 'the Son of Man' who would come in clouds of glory. This was an authentic piece of Hebraic prophecy. After the resurrection Christ's followers interpreted the Son of Man as Christ himself.

Jesus therefore was a rabbi who worked in the tradition of the Temple but he was also ready to debate what the Law really required of Jews and to rise above mere formalism. The Law had to be followed, most of all, with the inner self. That was why hatred was as great a sin as murder. This was exceptional teaching but not a reason for the scribes and scholars who interpreted the Law, as well as the Pharisees, to threaten his life. It was Passover week's circumstances which placed Jesus in danger. He had already told his followers that the Temple would be destroyed as part of the fulfilment of God's new Kingdom; he therefore entered its precincts where the annual Temple tax of two drachmas was paid, and overturned the tables. The prediction and the assault were the two reasons for Jesus' Crucifixion. He was not a military threat – which is why his disciples were not killed – but in his own person and message he was undermining a precarious Jewish-Roman agreement on how to keep the peace.

After his death some of Jesus' followers claimed that the tomb in which he had been placed was empty. They also said they had seen the risen Christ not as a spirit but as a body. Language, whether Greek, Latin or the Aramaic spoken by Jesus and his followers, struggled to express this novel idea. Paul in his mid-first-century epistles opted for the awkward phrase 'spiritual body' to describe the risen Christ. But it was this belief which explained why Christianity spread and why people were ready to die for it. Reflection on what Jesus represented and meant had started with his first public appearance when he was baptized by John who was another believer in his own imminent end and judgement. This now continued with the development of a Christian Church – an *ecclesia* or community 'called out' of all the world. The Apostles' Creed developed by the early Church said that Jesus Christ had pre-existed his actual birth and had always existed with God the Father. He had therefore become flesh and been incarnated before finally being resurrected to life eternal. The influence of Greek philosophy would also emphasize that Christ was *logos* – the word made flesh who brought redemptive order to the world.

The idea that God was a person was a scandalous one for pious Jews and laughable to clever Greeks but it spoke to the poor and the marginal. Both the incarnation and the Crucifixion were fresh appealing ways of presenting the idea of God since they showed his vulnerability: first as an infant and then as a man nailed to the cross. Plato had said that the history of the world was the victory of persuasion over force. But in the person of Christ that philosophical insight became embodied in the life of the person who was now acclaimed by his believers as the Son of Man and as *Kyrios* (Lord). Jesus Christ moreover was, for Christians, the only such *Kyrios*. Consequently (and very dangerously), the Roman caesar or emperor was not a lord at all. The belief that the covenant God of the Old Testament had, through Jesus, established a new covenant with humanity was the 'good news' acclaimed in the New Testament.

 In the dynamic theology of St Paul this idea became a universal one so that Christianity was not just a Jewish sect but spoke to all humanity, transcending the boundaries of politics, ethnicity and culture. This exhilarating perspective suddenly made Graeco-Roman culture look very parochial. Paul's emphasis on original sin was a novel introduction to Christianity and part of his personal obsession with the fight between flesh and spirit. Many found it psychologically compelling as an explanation of a flaw in humanity. After Paul, the Greek philosophical claim that acting wrongly was just the result of thinking badly, seemed naïve. For Christians the remedy for sin was the Atonement: the creation of a new humanity reconciled to God through the death and suffering of Christ who was the second Adam. It was this faith which sustained the persecuted and the martyred during the strenuous and dangerous first three Christian centuries.

Christianity became the most global of all the major religions showing an unique capacity to exist among a very wide variety of different cultures in Asia, Africa and the Americas. The process had started as an aspect of European colonization as missionaries followed in the wake of armies but the uniqueness and appeal of Christianity's doctrines, centred around the Crucifixion, contributed to its survival in local soil long after the end of empire.

11 May 330

The Dedication of Constantinople

Constantine the Great Establishes his Capital at Byzantium

'Alone of all the emperors…Constantine was initiated by rebirth in the mysteries of Christ – when the ceremonies were complete he put on bright imperial clothes which shone like light.'

Eusebius (c.260-c.339) describes Constantine's baptism

It was the day on which the Emperor Constantine's new city was to be dedicated to the Virgin Mary at a High Mass celebrated at the church of Saint Eirene. But the classical past could not be avoided even on this most Christian of days. Invocations to Tyche (or Fortune), a goddess associated with the city, merged with the sound of Christian prayers. A statue of the emperor with the figure of Tyche in his outstretched hand was probably paraded in procession through the city which established an annual ritual. On every Founder's Day a statue of Tyche would be paraded with the Christian cross attached to her forehead. As Constantine processed through the city named after him, which would now be the capital of the Roman empire, he could admire the statues and works of art plundered from cities and temples right across Europe and Asia. Four hundred and twenty-seven statues had been brought into the city just in order to stand before the church of Santa Sophia. The most important object of plunder was a relic. At the heart of the city, and at the centre of the imperial vision, was the piece of wood which his aged mother Helena discovered after she set out for Jerusalem in 327. This was acclaimed as the True Cross on which Christ had died. It was now set on top of a cupola supported by four triumphal arches on a building called the Milion or First Milestone and from it were measured all the distances within the empire.

Other places showed the same mixture of pagan allusions set within a Christian dimension. The church of St Eirene itself was built on the site of an ancient shrine to Aphrodite. To the west of the Milion ran a large street called the Mese and it was by the side of this thoroughfare that Constantine had built an oval-shaped forum paved with marble where a one hundred foot column of porphyry from Heliopolis in Egypt had been raised. It now stood on a marble plinth which contained, so these new Byzantine Romans were told, the remains of the loaves used by Christ at the feeding of the five thousand as well as a figure of Athene brought back by Aeneas from Troy. At the top of the column was a statue whose body was a statue of Apollo sculpted by Phidias – the greatest of Athenian sculptors. But the head was a newly sculpted representation of Constantine and above it there was a metal halo. In the statue's right hand was a sceptre, the symbol of his earthly power, but the orb grasped by the left hand contained a fragment cut from that same True Cross, whose arrival here in the new Rome showed that this emperor ruled by divine permission and favour which enabled him to crush his enemies in battle. Evidence of piety mingled with sumptuous effects attended Constantine in this year of 330 AD which was also, happily, his silver jubilee as ruler.

Four years earlier Constantine had held a ceremony to mark the foundation of his new city and had laid the first stone of the western wall which protected this east-facing city on its landward side. Like the older Rome this *Roma Nova* too was built on seven hills – but much more quickly. And, since the new buildings and streets needed to be populated and inhabited, colonists were imported into the city on so massive a scale that the grain fleets of the eastern Mediterranean had to be redirected in order to feed them.

Constantine had chosen to build on the site of the little city of Byzantium because it was so well protected. To the south was the sea of Marmara and Byzantium was on the tip of a triangular promontory which stretched out from the Greek mainland. To the north-west was the deep inlet called the Golden Horn and to the east were the straits of the Bosphorus leading up to the Black Sea. The coast of Asia was visible opposite.

The background to Constantine's reign was one of division within an over-stretched empire. Ever since Diocletian became emperor in 284 the idea had gained ground that the empire was too big and that it needed to be divided up into separate administrative regions. Diocletian based himself at Nicomedia in Bithynia while his colleague Maximian controlled the western territories. In 293 there followed a formal, four-fold, division of the empire into its separate constituent parts, but Diocletian's decision to abdicate in 305 initiated a prolonged period of uncertainty as rival rulers within the empire claimed the throne. Constantine was the son of Constantius I – himself a co-emperor – and both father and son had based themselves in Britain during this period of seemingly imminent imperial dissolution. When Constantius died in York in 306, Constantine was declared emperor by the legions but confined his claim to Britain and Gaul. In the same year Maxentius, Constantine's rival, was declared emperor by the praetorian guard in Rome. In 311 Constantine decided to march on Rome and confront Maxentius. The battle of the Milvian bridge on the Via Flaminia in Rome in 312 was a decisive victory for Constantine who now became undisputed and sole ruler of the Roman empire in the west. But there was another event which was recorded as taking place at the Via Flaminia a few miles to the north-east of Rome either just before or during the battle. Constantine claimed to have been granted a vision. At midday, according to Eusebius (Constantine's official historian), he saw, just above the sun, a cross of light bearing the inscription *in hoc signo vinces* (by this sign you will conquer). The victor undoubtedly fought his battle as a Christian warrior and the consequences were momentous. He would be a Christian ruler and Christianity, having been persecuted as a matter of state policy under Diocletian, would become an official and established religion.

In 313 Constantine met his fellow emperor Licinius, the ruler of the eastern territories, in Milan and issued the edict of Milan which gave Christianity full legal recognition throughout the empire. If there was just one God, it was also now obvious that there could only be just one emperor as well. Constantine first defeated Licinius in a series of battles and then had him murdered so that he now became sole ruler in both the eastern and western empires. Meanwhile, legislation made the empire more Christian. The law of 319 outlawed the murder of slaves and in 321 it was forbidden to do any work on Sunday. Constantine also abolished crucifixion as a punishment as well as the branding of certain criminals. Saints' days were officially established. Paganism continued and its followers were not persecuted though some practices were suppressed. The hope was that paganism would just wither away. Romans, after all, believed in tradition and there were therefore limits to what an emperor, bent on establishing a new one, could do. Christian heresy was a different matter. Arianism, the belief that Christ was the perfect man but not himself divine, was splitting the Church and Constantine used state power against it. He summoned a universal Council of the Church which met at Nicaea and presided over it himself, dressed in his purple imperial robes. It was Constantine who proposed and imposed the insertion into the Creed of a compromise wording. Christ the Son was *homoousios* or of one substance with God the Father. Arius of Alexandria, the chief heretic, was condemned and most of his followers accepted the compromise. One Church, one Ruler and One Creed: these were now meant to unite the whole civilized world and the Nicene Creed is Constantine's most important theological legacy. The ruler, who used the title *isapostolos* to signify his equality with the Apostles at the end of his life, was a sincere, if bloody, Christian. When his son, the Caesar Crispus, became too popular he had him murdered. He elevated his mother to the rank of Augusta and when that made his wife jealous he showed his filial devotion by murdering the unfortunate Fausta.

Constantine wanted to make Rome as Christian a city as Constantinople and built the basilica of St Peter on the Vatican Hill. But residual republican sentiment in Rome, as well as loyalty to the pagan gods, meant that the city never took to Constantine nor he to it. The Senate he established in Constantinople was never quite the equal of the one back in Rome in terms of its prestige, yet in other respects Rome was becoming very provincial. The great intellectual centres were in the east, in Alexandria and Antioch with their celebrated libraries and scholars. Economically too, the Italian peninsula was declining, with the increasing threat of malaria, especially in the campagna near Rome, leading to a consequent drop in the birth rate. Strategically also Constantine had to look east because that was where the main threats to the empire came from – Sarmatians around the lower Danube, Ostrogoths who menaced it just north of the Black Sea, and the Sassanian Empire of the Persians.

The emperor did not get the Church unity he wanted and Arianism continued to be a powerful force. His concern with unity imposed from the top merely aggravated subsequent quarrels about theological doctrines with frequently murderous consequences. The greatest minds of Byzantium would be enraptured by over-subtle theology which is why 'Byzantine' remains an adjective for the needlessly complicated. After Constantine's death in 337, the empire returned to conflict when his two sons fought each other, but the legacy of his victory and the legend that attended it had a greater cultural consequence than any short-term political ones. Constantine himself was more at home in Latin than in Greek but the empire he left behind became more and more Hellenic. The idea of a Christian society fused with the Greek inheritance in the east and, as the Byzantine empire, it continued (with many traumas) for over 1100 years. The Constantinian revolution ensured that the legacy of classical civilization would be harnessed to the cause of Christianity and would, as a result, be re-interpreted but also preserved. Constantine saw division as a sin precisely because of the depth of his personal commitment to Christianity. Yet the idea of a secular ruler who was also spiritually authoritative was an inherently despotic one and the religion of an established Church presided over by a Christian emperor encouraged opportunistic conversions. After 330, surrounded by glory, Christianity in Europe entered the mainstream and therefore lost what it had once had – the dissenting edge of an underground movement.

31 December 406

A Confederacy of German Tribes Crosses the Rhine

The Slow Death of Rome's Western Empire

'…the bright light of all the world was quenched…the Roman empire had lost its head and…the whole universe had perished in one city…'

St Jerome (c.340-420) describes the sack of Rome (410)

The river Rhine, at a spot near Coblenz, had frozen over towards the end of December 406 and the natural eastern boundary of the Roman province of Gaul could therefore be crossed. It was to here that the Germanic tribe of the Vandals had been led by their king, Gunderic. They were not alone. Other German tribes had combined to form a great confederation. Unlike the genuinely nomadic Huns, who were pressing in behind them from the east, these migrating Germans wanted to settle and enjoy a safer life than the one they had escaped from. As agricultural peoples they had also discovered that repeated cultivation of the same territorial soil was more fruitful than just tilling and then moving on. Heavily burdened with carts and livestock, their progress was slow and an average of a mile or so an hour was probably their maximum speed. The Alans who had crossed the Dnieper in *c.* 375 would only reach their final home in the Tagus valley near Lisbon in the 420s after travelling on average about five miles a year.

The December 406 crossing of the Rhine was part of a wider and older pattern of tribal movement. The Vandals belonged to the east German group of tribes which had moved from Scandinavia into the region east of the Elbe. Other members of this group included the Burgundians, Visigoths and Ostrogoths. The Goths had left their settlements in the second century AD and then drifted to the south-east so that by *c.* 400 AD the Visigoths or 'Western' Goths were on the Black Sea coast and the Ostrogoths or 'Eastern' Goths found themselves further east (and therefore very exposed to the Huns) in the Crimea and on the Dnieper steppes.

The success of the tribal push on an increasingly porous border reflected the progressive disintegration of Roman imperial authority since the second half of the third century. Internally, the empire was suffering from a low birth rate and choking bureaucracy as well as high tax and inflation because of the expensive, long-term, business of paying for an army to protect the boundaries. After they crossed the Rhine the tribes spread out over Gaul. The Vandals crossed the Pyrenees in 409, left the Suevi to establish themselves in Galicia (north-west Spain) and then travelled across Iberia to Africa which had also been the destination of Alaric, king of the Visigoths until his death shortly after he sacked Rome. By 429 the Vandals were at the Straits of Gibraltar and in 439 they arrived in Carthage. For over a century the Vandal kingdom of north Africa, an important naval power with bases in Sardinia and the Balearic islands, would be a major military threat in the western Mediterranean.

The southward and western migrations of the Germanic tribes were spread over half a millennium. Their movements included long periods of settlement until patterns of climate and of food supplies, along with internal conflicts among the tribes themselves, forced them on. By the fourth century many German tribes had become settled along the imperial boundaries, and were being paid, by the Roman themselves, as *foederati* pledged to protect the frontiers. The one great constant was the external impact on them, and on Rome itself, of the Huns who, with their great herds of cattle, had been moving towards the west from their homelands on the steppes of central Asia ever since the Chinese had defeated a Hunnic empire in *c.* 36 BC. Armed with bows and arrows, and using the stirrup (which they had invented) to ride their Mongolian ponies, the Huns could achieve long distance raids across thousands of miles in the summer months before returning to their bases. Between the second and fourth centuries those bases had shifted from north of the Caspian Sea towards the area of modern Ukraine – that crucial geographic point of contact between the steppe and Europe. Other differences separated them from the barbarian: the clans of the Germanic tribes were bound together by shared kinship but it was a community of interest which bound together the Hunnish tribes into various 'hordes' such as protection from natural forces and from outsiders. Mentally formed by the wide horizons of the steppes, their aim was the establishment of a world empire.

The German migrations were therefore the result of a chain of events stretching from central Asia to the Atlantic coast. The pattern of European nations today is also the result of interaction between late Roman antiquity and barbarian ambition. Mentally, the Romans drew a sharp dividing line between themselves and the barbarians. Rome stood for written law, administrative records, the settled existence of urban centres and great estates. The Germanic tribes, by contrast, were wholly agrarian, bound by the customs of an oral unwritten law and governed by a general assembly. The kinship loyalties of tribal groups contrasted with two defining Roman notions: loyalty to the emperor and the honourable obligations of citizenship. Religion was another divide. Instead of the Graeco-Roman pantheon of gods worshipped in temples, the barbarians gathered in sacred groves for cult festivals which worshipped their own pantheon such as Wotan, Thor who protected farmers,and fertility goddesses like Freyja. But, though so different, the barbarian tribes could see the advantages of Roman order even in an age of civilized breakdown and their fury was often the result of disappointment when the Romans refused to extend those advantages to include them. Alaric turned towards an anti-Roman offensive when his Visigoths were denied the right to settle in Noricum, now modern-day Austria. Thinly spread Roman forces gave the tribes their chance. Alaric's threat to Constantinople, for example, led to the withdrawal of the Roman legions in Gaul and so by c. 400 AD the Burgundians could move into the territory now named after them.

Another, related, tribal movement was well established by the early fifth century. Tall, red-haired and ferocious, the Celts had attacked Rome in 390 BC and mainland Greece in 279 BC. Established in northern Italy and in the lands to the north and west of the Alps they resisted the Roman advance in the first and second centuries BC. Overwhelmed in Gaul and with some of them travelling further west, they became progressively Romanized and then constituted the native population of Spain, Gaul and Britain. The further impact of the invading Angles and Saxons, especially after the withdrawal of the Roman legions from Britain in 410 AD, pushed into the north and west those Celtic tribes previously settled in the south. They survived in western Scotland, Wales and Ireland and also in Cornwall whose émigrés headed for Brittany and made it Celtic. The Scots, a Celtic people native to Ireland, migrated to Caledonia, subjugated the native Picts and established a Gaelic Scotland.

The Huns had started to move into eastern Europe by c. 360 AD and their king Attila (404-53) unleashed them as a terrifyingly destructive force capable of extracting ever higher tribute money. On the death of the emperor Theodosius I in 395 the Roman empire split definitively into its eastern and western halves. Attila attacked the east and west in two campaigns and the west in another onslaught. His defeat in the battle of the Catalaunian plain in north-east France was the result of a joint Roman-barbarian effort which then pushed him out of Italy before his death in 453 after which the Huns faded as a military threat. The Ostrogoths, under Theoderic, now became the dominant power in Italy. At the same time, Clovis, king of the Salian Franks, went on to create a huge Merovingian kingdom in Gaul.

The barbarian migrations established the contours of the European nations. The Visigoths ruled Spain and absorbed the Suevi. The Ostrogothic kingdom of Italy would be conquered by the east German Langobardi or Lombards and the peninsula was contested between them in the north, Byzantines in the south, and the expansionist Franks who also ensured the collapse of the Avars in the Danube basin. That collapse was the Slav opportunity. Western Slavs crossed the Danube in 551 and colonized areas east of the Elbe vacated by the German tribes: Czechs were established in Bohemia, Slovaks in the southern Carpathians, and, further north, Poland became a distinctive territory. The eastern Slavs, including the Russians, moved north and east into the upper Volga. In doing so they established the divide between Slavic Poles and Slavic Russians. The western Slavs of the north were also now separated from the southern Slavs of the Balkans: Slovenes, Serbs and Croats (settled on the Dalmatian coast) became the agents for the Slavicization of Illyria, Bulgaria and Greece. The Slavic kingdoms could never establish an imperial unity but along with a Persia revived by the Sassanians, they threatened the eastern Roman empire. The Bulgar empire of the eighth and ninth centuries was a major anti-Byzantine power.

Europe had become a mosaic of peoples conquered, absorbed or pushed west. Romanized Celto-Iberians in Spain, Gallo-Romans in Gaul, the Latinized peoples of Italy – all had been subsumed under a Germanic layer. Britain assumed its present shape with a Germanic culture in the east, south and centre, a Celtic one in the west and a mixture of Celtic highlanders with Germanic lowlanders in Scotland. Linguistic vernacular variety reflected the ethnic diversity: the Slavs produced three main groups of Slavonic languages and Latin dissolved into the Romance languages. The western provinces of the empire drifted away into their own self-contained worlds. The reign of the emperor Justinian saw an attempt at restoring Roman authority in the west when his general Belisarius destroyed the Vandal kingdom in north Africa. But his reconquest of Italy from the Ostrogoths exhausted the peninsula's resources and made the north vulnerable to the last of the German invaders – the Lombards. Further non-Germanic migrations from sea-raiding Vikings, from nomadic Magyars who moved into the Hungarian plain by c.900 AD, and from the Mongols, as well as the Moors and Turks, lay ahead.

Europe's nations had evolved out of the maelstrom of ethnic diversity, cultural mingling, and military-political conflict – which would also shape their future.

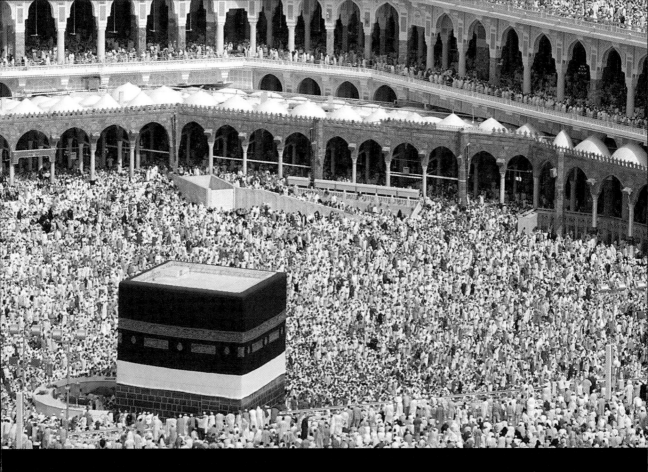

7 December 632

The Death of Muhammad

The Birth of Islam

'In the name of God, the Compassionate, the Merciful.
Recite! Your Lord is the most Bountiful One, who by his pen
taught man what he did not know.'

The mystic, prophet, and former cattle driver Muhammad, founder of the Islamic faith, was born in the Arabian town of Mecca and he returned there in the year of his death. Ten years earlier local reaction against his preaching had forced him to leave Mecca and establish himself in Yathrib some 200 miles to the north – an oasis settlement which would be renamed Medina. This flight (hejira) would be commemorated in Islamic worship and ritual. But since Mecca was where it had all started, and since the Prophet knew that his time had come, he set out on the 'Farewell Pilgrimage'. In the valley of Arafat he delivered the speech which would be his final statement and which became celebrated as the most concise summary of his doctrine. His followers should 'Know that every Muslim is a Muslim's brother, and that the Muslims are brethren.' They should not fight each other but they should fight all others if necessary in order to win universal acceptance of the truth that 'There is no god but Allah'. The poor should be clothed and helped. Muslims had rights with regard to their women but 'they also have rights with regard to you.' 'I have accomplished my mission, and I am leaving you a guide in the shape of the Lord's book and the example of his Messenger... You will not fail if you follow this guide.' When he returned to Medina he lay down in his chamber and said: 'Oh Death, execute your orders.' The community of the faithful that he left behind would be obliged to make its own journey (the Hadj) to Mecca at least once in the lifetime of a believer.

The Arabia which was the springboard for the rapid spread of Islam might have been largely a desert but it was no backwater. It connected Africa with Asia and its various settlements had a lively political tradition of independence which was maintained against Egypt and Abyssinia to the west, India to the east, and Mesopotamia as well as Persia to the north. It had a substantial cultural tradition – especially in Arabic poetry. It was also fringed by the cultural influence of the Roman empire in Egypt and by that of the Sassanian empire in Persia. The decline of both these empires by the time of Muhammad's birth created a power vacuum in the region which would be conquered, and colonized, by the armies loyal to the Prophet's message. Commerce helped the transmission of ideas and influences across Arabia since the peninsula was home to the trade routes which linked the Mediterranean, India and East Africa. Mecca itself was one of the richest of the staging posts on those caravan routes. But the town was also of religious significance with its Kaaba shrine marking the spot where Adam arrived after he had been expelled from the garden of Eden. This then was a good place in which to start a religious, political and military revolution.

The message that Muhammad had preached ever since receiving his vision in c. 610 AD was simple: there was no god but Allah and Muhammad was his prophet. Whoever said those words before witnesses who testified to his sincerity became a Muslim. Allah would judge humanity and he commanded daily religious observance, prayer, and regular fasting. There would be three fundamentals to sustain the faith: the Koran (Qur'an) which was the revelation of God's word to Muhammad by an angel; the Sunna or sayings and traditions ascribed to the Prophet; and the ijma or the common accord of the faithful as they worshipped and prayed. This simplicity contributed to the success of message. The fact that this was a strikingly radical and egalitarian movement was also important. The equality of all Muslims meant that Muhammad was critical of the local Arabian ruling elites. By insisting on the duty of charity that rulers owed their subjects, even on the equality between soldiers and generals, Islam gave a new power and self-confidence to the socially humble. This social dimension is seen in Muhammad's role as an arbiter called upon to solve the frequent inter-tribal disputes which were brought before him in Medina. His judgements are reflected in the Koran with its detailed prescriptions about how to regulate social life, guarantee property rights and protect inheritances.

Initially, Muhammad was received with mockery and suspicion. His was an austere and monotheistic faith unsparing in its rejection of thc local religious practices as mere idolatry. This kind of iconoclasm was dangerous in Mecca, a city which had become a major, and very profitable, centre of pilgrimage. Gradually, however, Muhammad started to convert the various Arab tribes to his faith. In 624 he armed some 300 of his followers and routed an army which had been sent to suppress them. And in 628, at the head of some thousand followers, he rode into Mecca, struck down the idols in the Kaaba and turned it into a shrine which followed the doctrines of the new religion. There then followed a major war of expansion as the Arabian tribes, impelled by the drought that was afflicting their peninsula, pushed their way into the adjacent areas of the Middle East.

After Muhammad's death the next *caliph* (successor) was his own father-in-law Abu Bakr Omar, who succeeded as ruler of the faithful and went on to conquer Syria and Palestine: Damascus fell in 635, followed by Jerusalem in 638. The seizure of Ctesiphon in 637 led to the fall of Persia and the submission of Egypt followed when the Byzantines abandoned Alexandria in 642. In the west Cyrene and Tripoli were captured, and the Arabs now found themselves on the frontiers of Tunisia. A fleet was built to protect Alexandria and the Arabs became the leading Mediterranean naval power.

These had been the victories of a fast moving military force. The next challenge was how to turn nomads into administrators within one generation. Towns such as Baghdad and Fostat (later Cairo) were built and the infrastructure of settled government, of law and taxation, became part of the Islamic dispensation. Initially these missionaries did not enforce conversion on their new subject peoples. Their occupation was a military one and the native religions – including Christianity and Judaism – were respected. After all Muhammad had stressed his line of spiritual descent from Abraham as the founder of a common monotheistic faith and therefore the inspiration behind all three religions.

The personal nature of Arab and Islamic leadership had bound the newly united people together but would also make that leadership vulnerable to chance and challenge. In 644 the caliph Omar was assassinated and his cousin Othman, who succeeded him, lacked Islamic fervour. Islam now wavered. Ali, son-in-law of the Prophet, killed Othman in 656 and inaugurated a new wave of religious conquest. But the establishment of a dynasty was required if these Islamic conquests were to be consolidated as an imperial power. Muawiyah, cousin of the murdered Othman, had been governor of Damascus before becoming caliph and he took a crucial step when, in a break with Arab tradition, he named his son as his successor. The Umayyad dynasty that he founded turned Damascus into an imperial city and the dynasty started to mint coins, to employ Greek and Syrian officials, and to build at the heart of their centre of government the mosque which, named after the family, remains the most beautiful of all the religious buildings of Islam. At the start of the eighth century the dynasty had conquered Transoxania, the Indus valley and Spain – a scale of achievement that rivalled that of Alexander the Great. Less than a century after the death of Muhammad his followers had become masters of the Mediterranean from the Bosphorus to Egypt and from Palestine to Spain.

The Islamic world now comprised a string of cities and towns sustained in each case by the distinctive institutions of the *souk* where goods were bought and sold, by the *madras* where scholars communicated their knowledge, and by the *mosque* where the faith was preached. Islam would also prove to be the crucial means of survival for classical learning since it was the translation of the Greek and Latin texts into Arabic by Islamic scholars which guaranteed their preservation for later generations. If Islam guaranteed religious unity and common social institutions, it was Arabic which gave this society its common language and translation of the Koran was prohibited. This was also a materially rich civilization since it was at the heart of the most advanced economy in the world which was enriched by the trade routes of the east as well as by the corn and gold, the ivory and silk transported along the caravan routes of the Sahara and Turkestan.

Divisions about who was the genuine successor to Mohammad would arise to plague Islam. The followers of Ali, murdered in 661, declared that he was the last legitimate caliph because he was in the blood line of the Prophet. They therefore refused to accept the authority of the new Islamic rulers. Infused by a strong vein of mysticism and an emphasis on hidden meanings within the Koran, this faith became the Shiite branch of Islam, while those who followed the established order of the caliphs became part of what is known as the Sunni tradition. The nature of the caliphate itself as an institution was changing. The Umayyad dynasty was succeeded by that of the Abbasid whose power base in Baghdad became the capital of Islam in 762. It was here that the court ceremonial of the caliphate became increasingly elaborate and influenced by Persian courtly traditions. By the tenth century the caliphate would be restricted to a purely spiritual role and the world of Islam now consisted of a number of independent states governed by their own rulers. The sense, however, of an united and coherent civilization survived these political changes. For Islamic culture remained loyal to the message which had come out of the desert in the early seventh century and to the memory of the Prophet who had lived out his truth.

11 October 732

The Battle of Tours

Charles Martel Defeats the Moors

'As regards the people of the northern quadrant…such as the
Franks – their religious beliefs lack solidity, and this is because
of the nature of cold and the lack of warmth.'

Al-Mas'udi (c.896-c.956) speculates

The victory near Tours of the Frankish army over Arab forces led by Abd ar-Rahman destroyed the expansionist ambitions of the Umayyad dynasty (661-750) which, from its capital in Damascus, had presided over the rapid Islamicization of the southern Mediterranean. The conquest of Carthage had secured the Arab domination of North Africa from Egypt to the Maghreb. An Arab army then crossed the straits of Gibraltar in 711 and destroyed the kingdom of the Visigoths which covered most of the Iberian peninsula. Visigothic Spain had become officially Catholic following the conversion of its ruler Recared I (r. 586-601) from the Arian form of Christianity which denied Christ's divinity. The *Lex Visigothorum*, a legal code binding on both Goths and the Romans, showed how Visigothic Spain aimed to fuse the traditions of the conquerors with those of the conquered. The Visigoth monarchy in Iberia would eventually be replaced by the creation in 756 of the Emirate of Cordoba, an autonomous state administered by the Umayyad dynasty and one whose rule over most of Spain lasted until the eleventh-century onset of the campaign for the re-Christianisation of the Iberian peninsula, known as the *Reconquista*. But the defeat of 732 entailed the loss of the Umayyads' authority in the rest of the Arab empire and led directly to their replacement as the dominant Middle Eastern power by the Abbasid dynasty.

The Arab army which headed north through Spain had hoped to profit from the divisions which had developed in the Frankish kingdom during the seventh century which, now comprising the heartlands of the old Gaul, was nominally ruled by the Merovingian dynasty. By 718 the Arabs had occupied the surviving Visigothic enclave of Septimania, including Narbonne, on the south-west coast of France. From this base North African Berber tribesmen were sent by the Arabs on raiding parties into Gaul. A setback near Toulouse in 721 caused the Arab forces to branch out to the Rhone valley and they pillaged Autun before first returning west to pillage Aquitaine and then turning north towards Tours where they discovered to their cost the deep roots of Frankish civilization.

Between the middle of the third and the fifth centuries AD the tribe of the Franks (from *frekkr*, the Old High German for 'bold' or 'courageous') had expanded from the frontier of the Rhine towards the south-west and the Somme. Their infantry successes were based on each man carrying his own weapons: the shield, the throwing axe which broke the enemy frontline, the bow and spear, the barbed lance and the javelin which were used for long distance combat, while the scramasax (a dagger) and the longsword were used for hand-to-hand combat. Clovis (or Chlodweg, meaning 'path to glory') (r. 482-511) removed what was left of Roman rule in Gaul by his victory over the kingdom of the Roman Dux Syagrius and consequently obtained the land between the Somme and the Loire. Between 496 and 500 he pushed the Alamans in eastern Gaul back towards the upper Rhine. But he realised that in order to gain control of Burgundy and the areas of Aquitaine controlled by the Visigoths he would need the support of their Gallo-Roman inhabitants. And since that population was Catholic Christian a clear divide existed between them and their Arian rulers. Clovis, already married to and influenced by the Burgundian and Catholic Clotilda, was therefore baptized by Bishop Remigus at Rheims. His campaign, which started with the battle of Vouillé and ended at Toulouse, was hailed by the native Catholic Aquitanians as a war of liberation. The consequence was a homogeneous merger of

Franks with Gallo-Romans, just as had happened in the territory north of the Seine which was now called 'Francia'.

The Frankish fusion contrasted with the system of another Germanic invader: that of Clovis' contemporary Theoderic the Great (r.493-526) whose Ostrogothic kingdom in Italy segregated the Goths from the Romans and prohibited inter-marriage. Here the Goths had received a third of the available land in recognition of their services as warriors. Civil administration remained in Roman hands and Italo-Roman civilization was surviving because it had enlisted the invaders as federated allies. Tensions between segregated Catholic Romans and Arian Goths led to the collapse of Ostrogothic Italy in the mid-sixth century and the Byzantines returned to control the south.

All the first generation Germanic settlements, with the exception of the Spanish Visigoths, collapsed in the sixth century. But the Franks belonged to the second generation of invaders – to which the Anglo-Saxons, Alamans, Bavarians and Lombards also belonged – and this group maintained their vital links with the Germanic hinterland. Further Frankish control of the south followed after Clovis' death when the Ostrogoths surrendered Provence. Burgundy was dismembered and partitioned in two campaigns. Further victories over the Thuringians , the Alamans and the Bavarians made the whole of southern Germany subject to Frankish tribute so that Gaul and Germany were now within a common political framework. In the seventh century the Franks could also return to the right bank of the Rhine and colonize a region (Franconia) which still bears their name.

Charles 'Martel' (the hammer), who led the Franks to victory at Tours in 732, was the illegitimate son of the equally formidable Peppin II who had been mayor of the palace or chief retainer of Austrasia and it was his family which restored Frankish unity under the continuing, nominal, suzerainty of the Merovingians. In 687, at the battle of Tertry in western France, Peppin defeated the mayor of the palace of Neustria and then established his authority over the Frisians on the north-east coast. But his authority was non-existent south of the Loire, in the Duchy of Aquitania, and in Burgundy. Charles Martel extended his father's achievements and earned his nickname on account of his bloody suppression of a Neustrian revolt at the battle of Vinchy and because of the blows he inflicted afterwards on the secessionist aspirations of the Frisians, Alamans, Burgundians and Provencals.

At the battle of Tours, fought at a site between Tours and Poitiers, some 15,000 Frankish infantrymen unprotected by armour confronted over 60,000 Arab cavalrymen who were either armoured or wore chainmail – these were history's first true warrior knights. For six days the two forces faced each other – Martel having drawn up his infantry to form a square in a defensive position. He had calculated that the lure of plunder in Tours would eventually force the Arab army into battle. Moving uphill, the Arab army first of all lost its cavalry advantage and it then tried to break up a tightly packed formation of Frankish infantry that was, wrote an Arab chronicler afterwards, 'like a sea that cannot be moved'. Towards the end of one day of fighting the Arab cavalry learnt that Frankish scouts, sent by Martel, were threatening their plunder back at base camp. In the ensuing withdrawal from the site of the battle Abd-ar-Rahman was killed. The next morning the Franks discovered that the entire Arab army had disappeared.

The engagement's consequences were profound. The kingdom of the Franks acquired celebrity as the force which had stopped the Arab advance. It therefore became the most important European power and chief bulwark of the Church.

Clovis and his successors ensured the assimilation of the victors and the vanquished of Roman Gaul within a Romano-Germanic civilization which, although new in form, was also a continuation of Roman imperial unity: the Frankish kings, like other Germanic rulers, assumed the responsibilities of the Roman praetorian prefects and were served by Roman officials. But whereas the Vandals in Africa, the Ostrogoths in Italy and the Visigoths in Spain had established a coexistence with the Roman administration by diplomatic understanding, the Frankish continuation was based on conquest. A zone between the Somme and the Loire was the melting-pot of two civilizations and the Germanic-Latin linguistic frontier which was established there survives as the German-French linguistic divide. Latin had only retreated between 100 and 200 kilometres from the Rhine and the Franks therefore used Latin when they recorded their original legal code: the Salic Law. Both in their culture and religion, Frankish Germanic barbarians became Roman Christians. The Church was the heir to the old Roman order and also to the unity which had characterized *romanitas*. It therefore supplied the Franks with a motive for continued dynamic expansion while at the same time grounding them in Christian culture. Although the Franks were officially converted in *c*.496 the paganism of Gaul was only really extinguished because of the missionary energies of Irish monks who worked among them from the late sixth century onwards. As enthusiasts for the Roman primacy the Irish also moulded the Franks' attachment to the See of Peter. Bishops had already demonstrated their influence during the early barbarian invasions by ransoming members of their flock who had been enslaved and thereby showing how Christianity, literally, set people free. Subsequently, the Irish-inspired establishment of a penitential system, including fasting, for misdemeanours and sins, affected Frankish conduct and the development of a parochial system shaped Frankish administration.

From 737 Charles Martel ruled the Franks without a Merovingian king sitting on the throne. The authority of his son Peppin III (r. 751-68) was confirmed when he was anointed 'king of the Franks' first by Boniface the papal legate and subsequently by Pope Stephen II. The last of the Merovingians, Childeric III, was dethroned and sent to a monastery: the originally pagan dynasty whose charisma had been attested by the long hair of its kings was replaced by the Christian Carolingians whose charisma issued from their consecration. Sacramental power had replaced blood-lineage as the source of authority. The fusion of the Germanic, the Roman and the Christian was now achieved and with explosive results: the military-political threat of Islam had created the matrix for the creation of a Frankish empire and the martial memory of Clovis would inspire the baptism of every French regal Louis.

25 December 800

The Coronation of Charlemagne

The Beginning of the European Idea

'*Let peace, concord and unanimity reign among all Christian people...for without peace we cannot please God...*'

Charlemagne, *The Admonitio* (789)

On Christmas day, 800, Charles I, king of the Franks (r.768-814) and of the Lombards, attended the Mass celebrated in St Peter's, Rome by Pope Leo III .The king, who would be called Charlemagne (from his title of *Carolus Magnus*, Charles the Great), knew Leo well and took a dim view of him. The previous year the Pope had fled to Charlemagne's court at Paderborn seeking protection from the Roman nobility who had rebelled against Leo's rule. The purpose of the king's visit to Rome, where he had been since November, was to restore the Church's government in the city and the associated papal territories. Leo was then able, on 23 December, to purge himself publicly of the charges of misgovernment laid against him. The monarch who now knelt in prayer inside the basilica was a man with an imposing physique and, although he himself could barely write, would inspire the first mediaeval biography of a layman. The historian Einhard in his *Life of Charles the Great* describes a man of unusual height with a broad and strong body. The hair was now grey but full and 'the eyes were lively and rather large.' 'Seated or standing he thus made a dignified and stately impression even though he had a thick, short neck and a belly that protruded somewhat; but this was hidden by the good proportions of the rest of his figure.' He also 'spoke with a higher voice than one would have expected of someone of his build.'

The Mass of the day, attended by the Roman nobility, was always going to be a special event, but as Charlemagne rose from prayer Leo placed a gold circlet in token of an imperial crown on his head and then abased himself before the new emperor in the Roman and Byzantine manner which showed recognition of a protector. The assembled Romans acclaimed the coronation: 'To Charles Augustus, crowned by God, the great and peace-giving Emperor of the Romans, life and victory!' They had special cause to praise the ruler who had subdued the Lombards, their traditional enemies, in the north of Italy. However, the coronation was controversial and it was doubtful whether Leo had the legal right to do it. Einhard's *Life* claims that Charlemagne was taken by surprise. This is unlikely since he had prepared himself by choosing to wear the ancient Roman tunic and *chlamys* or short mantle. These garments symbolized his acceptance of the revived imperial title. Nor was the idea a novelty, for the scholars who had flocked to Charlemagne's court at Aachen had long since campaigned for just such a recognition of their patron.

Ancient Rome lived on in the very fabric of Aachen since the palace Charlemagne had built there was constructed with stones transported from the remains of Roman buildings at Trier and Cologne. Nevertheless a certain bashful humility was appropriate on 25 December. Charlemagne knew the day's events would anger the Greek emperors of Byzantium who considered themselves the sole true heirs to the ancient Roman title, although their claim was weakened by the fact that in 800 they happened to be ruled by a woman, Empress Irene. Leo's action would later be used by the papacy to prove that it had the authority to transfer the Roman *imperium* from the Byzantines to a western ruler. But on that Christmas Day his action was simply the result of his subservience to Frankish interests. Pragmatically, he also needed a powerful protector at a time when the Greek empire was renewing its claim to rule in Sicily and southern Italy. Charlemagne's probable view of his coronation was that it was a personal compliment by a pliant Pope. It's significant that thirteen years later he decided that he himself, not the Pope, should crown his son Louis as co-emperor and eventual successor and that the coronation would take place in Aachen and not in Rome. The Frankish view that they were a chosen race and the heirs to past empires, Persian, Greek and Roman, was deeply held. Popes might be politically convenient but it was God, speaking through the acclamation of the congregated Frankish nobility, who made emperors. Charlemagne knew that his new imperial status would require diplomatic handling. Only the deposition of Irene stopped him from having to take seriously his advisers' suggestion that he should marry her as an act of East-West reconciliation – a risky measure, even for Charlemagne, since she had blinded her own son to secure her throne.

The origins of the Frankish kingdom lay in the region of the Meuse-Moselle on the borders of modern France, Germany, Belgium and the Netherlands. Peppin III, Charlemagne's father, had deposed the Merovingian dynasty and assumed kingship in 751. Charlemagne's own victories created Europe's first Christian superstate: only the British Isles, Southern Italy and the kingdom of Asturias in Spain lay beyond its borders. At its core was Charlemagne's central achievement: the union of the west German tribes of the Saxons, the Alemani, the Bavarians and the Thuringians. Bavaria, conquered in 778, was already Christian but the Saxons, occupying what is now lower Saxony and Westphalia, were pagans. A succession of rebellions by the Saxons from 778 onwards tested the Frankish government and church structure imposed on them at the Diet of Paderborn. Charlemagne had to take his army into battle eighteen times before the Saxons were finally subjugated by 804 and his programme of mass executions and enforced conversions in the territory was an early mediaeval novelty which, even at the time, aroused criticism. He also conquered the Avar kingdom (covering the area of modern Hungary and upper Austria) in three major campaigns and established the Elbe as a frontier against the northern Slavs. His only military defeat came in 778 when he invaded Spain and had to retreat after failing to take Saragossa.

Charlemagne's empire was divided into counties governed by royal counts who were themselves controlled by itinerant royal commissioners. He divided the same territory into twenty-one archbishoprics and charged the Church with the task of educating his subjects. Annual assemblies of ecclesiastics and counts, meeting at court, discussed legal, military and ecclesiastical affairs which, given the missionary and expansionist nature of the empire, were scarcely distinguishable from each other. At these assemblies Charlemagne issued his legislative and administrative decrees. Some of these were recorded in written form as 'capitularies' but many of his judgements were oral and conformed to the Solomonic ideal of early mediaeval kingship with its emphasis on the king's personal declaration of what was right and wrong. Charlemagne's throne at Aachen stood, just like the throne of Solomon, on top of a flight of steps and his numerous concubines and mistresses, who supplemented his five successive wives, also harked back to Solomon's domestic arrangements. Charlemagne was an itinerant monarch until old age forced him to settle in Aachen. The summer months were spent on military campaigning and during the winter he moved between his various palaces demonstrating his personal kingly authority to as many of his subjects as possible.

Charlemagne lends his name to the Carolingian Renaissance which is particularly associated with his palace and court at Aachen. His encouragement of scholars to establish themselves there led to the revival in Europe of the notion of the ruler as a patron of learning. The court library he established contained the texts of ancient classical writers as well as those written by the early fathers of the Church and his court academy was set up to educate young Frankish knights. One script (the Carolingian minuscule), one Church liturgy and one legal code were imposed across his empire: Carolingian civilization was based on the idea that correct thought required accurate expression. The concern with imperial unity and effective lordship flowed from Charlemagne's own view of God as supreme and Christ as a powerful lord. This, ostentatiously orthodox, Christianity was in conscious opposition to a world in which magic and paganism still captivated the minds of the simple and illiterate.

Carolingian unity was always an ideal rather than an enforceable reality. This was an empire without a permanent civil service, a standing army or a navy. Attempts at building up a money-based economy failed and the dominance of agrarian culture would prepare the way for feudal institutions. It's unsurprising that Charlemagne's empire disintegrated after his death. The reign of his unfortunate son Louis the Pious dissolved in the quarrels between the sons of Louis' first and second marriage. But the Treaty of Verdun in 843, agreed between Charlemagne's grandsons, is a momentous event in European history. This threefold division of the old imperial territories of Charlemagne created an East Francia, which comprised the German territories, and a West Francia based on the French ones. In the middle was a separate kingdom extending from what is now Belgium and Holland, through Burgundy, and down to northern Italy. This was the kingdom ruled by Lothar who had succeeded to the imperial title which no longer had a universal significance. The history of France and Germany therefore starts at Verdun as does the Franco-German contest over who should control the land of that middle kingdom. Over a millennium later (1916) Verdun would also be the site of the terrible and prolonged battle caused by that same contest.

Ninth-century Europe, plagued by Vikings from the north and by Saracens to the south, threatened a return to the crushing of states by migrating barbarians. Recovery came in the tenth century with the leadership of the Ottonian dynasty of Saxon princes. In 955 at the battle of Lech, near Augsburg, Otto I defeated a great Hungarian force and then started a vigorous brutal push to conquer the Slavic peoples beyond the Elbe. This inaugurated a German policy of eastern expansion which lasted, intermittently, until 1945. Otto had been chosen as their king by the five German tribes consisting of the Bavarians, eastern Franks, Swabians and Thuringians as well as his own Saxons. His selection, consecration and enthronement as king of the Germans took place, with an appropriate and Carolingian inevitability, at Aachen in 936. On 2 February 962, Otto was crowned emperor by the Pope in Rome. The date signifies the official start of the Holy Roman Empire and from then on the imperial title was especially associated with the German territories. The Saxon bishops, abbots, soldiers and nobles who re-established an imperial order that was sacred and Roman in the tenth and eleventh centuries did so in conscious homage to the Carolingian ideal. Charlemagne's campaign to convert their pagan ancestors at the point of a sword had born remarkable fruit.

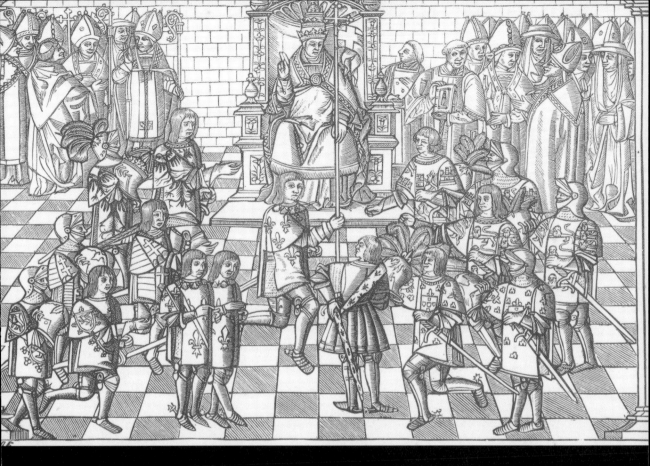

27 November 1095

Pope Urban II Preaches the First Crusade

The Franks Declare Holy War

'Let those who have wearied themselves to the destruction of body and soul now work for the honour of both!'

Pope Urban II (1035-99) at Clermont (1095)

Enthroned on a dais which had been set up on a hillside, Pope Urban II delivered an open-air sermon addressed to a great throng of the French nobility, clergy and common populace assembled at Clermont in the Auvergne. Urban, a Frenchman, described himself as 'chief bishop and prelate over the whole world' – a figure who had to respond to a profound crisis. In March, while holding a synod at Piacenza, he had received renewed and urgent appeals for help from the Greek emperor Alexius I Comnenus. Byzantium had lost all of its territories in Asia Minor, including the holy places of Palestine, to the Seljuk Turks. Alexius wanted his lands back as well as protection against further Turkish advance. Now, eight months later, at the synod he was holding in Clermont, was the time for Urban to announce his response. France, he said, had her own particular problems of over-population and feudal violence as great nobles fought each other but there was a solution. European Christians should stop their internal quarrels and observe the 'truce of God'. Forces would then be available to 'aid Christians in expelling the Turks from regions belonging to our kin'. There was, he said, a danger to Christianity as a whole and not just to the Greeks. In France herself, 'Let robbers become knights'.

The Pope was advocating war of a particular kind, since the First Crusade, like its successors, was also a pilgrimage. Penitential exercises would be performed en route and a Papal decree meant that all those on the crusade would receive full and complete penance for sins committed. Urban had hit the right note. Cries of *Deos Lo Vult* (God Wills It) were heard among the crowds. Papal indulgences which counted as 'satisfaction' (or expiation) for past sins provided excellent crusading motives. As a sign of their intention to crusade thousands now 'took the cross' and the first to do so was Bishop Adhemar of Puy. A holy war, thought Urban, had to be led by a priest and so he appointed Adhemar to be in charge. The Pope fixed 15 August 1096 as the date of departure for the First Crusade and Constantinople would be the rendezvous for a very French adventure. The idea of an anti-Islamic crusade had already been popularized in the contemporary poem *Chanson de Roland*. France was also the home of the great movement of spiritual renewal associated with the abbey of Cluny whose profound impact on the eleventh-century Church in Europe prepared it for a great missionary expansion. Chivalry, basic to the crusading ethic, was a French invention and the country could also supply the necessary manpower in the form of footloose feudal lords. Primogeniture meant that there were also plenty of under-occupied younger sons. This, moreover, was Norman France and the crusades appealed to the old Norse wanderlust which was still there in the bones of these men of the north. In 1095 the Normans had already colonized England and Sicily. Palestine was next on their list.

The crusades started as an ecclesiastical coup, a direction of lay energy towards a Church goal, and a Papal attempt at conducting an independent foreign policy. Feudalism, the codifying of a relationship between lord and vassal, was the basis of eleventh-century territorial order in Europe but it could also lead to private wars between the forces loyal to individual nobles. The Church gave that internecine energy an external outlet and feudalism became the basis of crusading military discipline.

Jerusalem had fallen to the conquering Arabs in 637 and their initial tolerance had allowed Christians to make pilgrimages to the shrines of their faith. After the Turkish victory at Manzikert (1071) such access became much more difficult. But there was an antecedent problem: since 1021 the Greek Church had been the official custodian of the Holy Places and, after the great schism between the Greek and Latin Churches in 1054, the Byzantines interfered regularly with the pilgrimage plans of the Latins. Successes in western Europe made the Latin Christians intolerant of such frustrations. Italy, threatened by the Arab forces in the ninth century, was securely Christian in the tenth century. The thirty years of war waged by the Normans between 1060 and 1090 for control of Sicily ended in Arab defeat while the long *reconquista* of Spain by Christian forces started in the eleventh century and amounted to the great crusade of the west. There were other motives to look east: the Italian towns were keen on establishing their own markets in Palestine in order to trade directly with the region.

There would be six major crusades in the east. The enthusiasm, as well as the violence, unleashed by Urban's call is seen in the spontaneous crusade of the poor which came before the start of the crusade proper. Aroused by the preaching of Peter the Hermit right across France, neo-military divisions of the poor marched in their thousands in the spring of 1096, massacring Jews in the Rhine valley before being themselves slaughtered by Hungarians as they marched east. The official crusade that crossed the Bosphorus consisted of three divisions and a total of some 150,000 men: Godfrey of Bouillon and his brother Baldwin led the crusaders of Lorraine; Raymond IV, count of Toulouse, led the Provencals; Bohemund of Otranto led the Normans.

Syria, initially, proved good terrain: the occupation was tenuous and the conquered natives proved friendly. The crusaders took Nicaea and, after a year's siege, Antioch. Godfrey of Bouillon then asserted his leadership over the quarrelling Bohemund and Raymond. He led the crusaders to Jerusalem which was captured in 1099 and the Latin Kingdom of Jerusalem was established with Godfrey as its first ruler. The Order of the Knights of St John of Jerusalem (the Hospitallers) was founded in the same year. After Godfrey's death in 1100, his brother was crowned as Baldwin I by the newly appointed patriarch of Jerusalem, Dagobert, who was then deposed by the king. The Papacy had wanted a system of church government in Palestine similar to its own administration in central Italy. What it got instead was a feudal kingdom of French noblemen. Antioch, Edessa and Tripoli accepted the new kingdom's suzerainty, Genoese and Norwegian allies helped it to expand. In May 1104 Baldwin seized Acre and by 1110 the kingdom stretched along the coast from Beirut to the Egyptian border. A connection to the Red Sea served its shipping needs. Control of the caravan routes – especially the one from Damascus to Egypt and the Red Sea – gave the kingdom its commercial base.

The fall of Edessa to the Turks led to the proclamation of the Second Crusade in 1145 but Damascus could not be taken in 1148 and the formidable Syrian warrior Nur ad-Din forced the withdrawal of the crusading army. From 1171 Saladin, as sultan of both Egypt and Syria, established a regional unity which robbed the crusaders of an earlier advantage. In 1187 he took Jerusalem. The Third Crusade which followed was a major military expedition of the great powers: England, France and the Hohenstaufen dynasty of German princes. Cyprus now came under Latin rule and would be governed by western Europeans until 1571. But Saladin could not be dislodged and Richard I of England had to negotiate with him on gaining Christian access to Jerusalem.

The Fourth Crusade (1202-04) started as an attempt at re-establishing papal authority, dissolved in internal quarrels and ended in the occupation of Constantinople by the Latins. The Fifth Crusade (1217-21) ended in an ignominious withdrawal from Palestine and the final major crusade (1228-9) was dominated by the quarrel between the Papacy and Emperor Frederick II. As king of Sicily, and as a Hohenstaufen, Frederick ruled in the centralizing manner of his Norman predecessors on that throne and his negotiations with the sultan of Egypt were those of an independent ruler pursuing a secular diplomacy. This resulted in the Christian-Muslim partitioning of Jerusalem and Frederick had himself crowned as king of Jerusalem in 1229. Fifteen years of struggle followed in Jerusalem between Frederick's imperial style and the local feudal nobility before the final loss of Jerusalem to the Ayyubid dynasty of Egypt in 1244. Acre, the last crusader stronghold, fell to their successors, the Mamluks, in 1291. The total evacuation of Syria followed.

Crusades were a pan-European, and not just an eastern, policy. In the thirteenth and fourteenth century the Papacy used them in Italy against the Hohenstaufen threat to the Papal States. The Baltic crusades into north-eastern Germany were led by the Teutonic knights, established in Palestine during the Third Crusade in 1190. These crusades, which were also wars of conversion, lasted into the fifteenth century and pushed German frontiers to the east. Crusades also tried to extinguish Christian heresy: the Albigensian crusade against the Cathars of the Languedoc was launched by Pope Innocent II in 1208. Similar campaigns followed in the thirteenth century against the Cathars of Lombardy and in the 1420s and 1430s against the Hussites in Bohemia.

By 1300 the rulers of European states were preoccupied with building up their own internal authority and the crusading impulse faded away but its consequences were profound. Trade expansion led to urban growth, especially along the great trade routes from Venice, over the Brenner Pass and along the Rhine to Bruges. Paradoxically, this urbanizing side-effect of the crusades undermined the land-based feudalism which had originally sustained them. The missionaries, and the travellers such as Marco Polo, who explored further east, opened up Asia to European discovery and to European curiosity about other cultures. Christian missions to the east studied oriental languages and the greatest historical work of the middle ages is William of Tyre's *Historia Transmarina*. The crusades are also an episode in the history of taste. Sugar and maize, lemons and melons, cotton, muslin and damask, powder, glass mirrors and even the rosary: all made the journey from east to west. European military technology became more sophisticated because of the advanced techniques of fortification and castle building learnt from both the Muslims and the Greeks. And the machinery of government run by European royal households increased in scope and ambition because of the experience of raising taxes to pay for the crusades. The crusades, started on French soil, helped to make France the dominant European power of *c*. 1300. But the Greeks, having asked for the crusades, found themselves trapped between the competing thrusts of the Latin west and the Islamic east.

25 August 1227

The Death of
Genghis Khan

The news of the death of the leader who had unified the various Mongolian tribes spread across an empire which now stretched between the Caspian Sea in the west and the eastern boundaries of China, between Siberia in the north and Tibet along with central China in the south. The background to the achievement of 'Genghis Khan' (whose birth name was Temujin) was one of internecine tribal rivalry. Members of the Tatar tribe poisoned his father, Yesugei. The royal Borjigin clan, to which his father belonged, abandoned the family and the young Temujin was reduced to a life of itinerant privation in which he was forced to eat roots and fish instead of the mare's milk and mutton which formed the staple diet of a Mongol warrior. Toghril, the Khan (or leader) of the Kereit tribe of the western Mongols, decided to help Genghis reunite the tribes which had been previously loyal to his father. Equipped thereby with 20,000 men, Genghis mounted raids against the Tatars, destroyed the Merkit tribe of northern Mongolia who were his chief opponents, and annihilated the nobility of the Jurkin clan. His first followers were men like himself – warriors who lacked powerful connections because their clans had been defeated in battle. Genghis could therefore use them to develop a Mongol army run by officers chosen on the basis of their ability rather than their lineage. Rapid promotion meant that ordinary tribesmen could command units of up to 10,000 men.

The early campaigns established Genghis' typical methods: massacres were regularly used; agents were sent ahead to demoralize and divide the garrison and inhabitants of an enemy city; populations could be slaughtered despite a prompt surrender. Genghis allowed no enemies to survive in his rear as he progressed onto the next campaign and he dealt with the defeated Tatars by killing all those who were taller than the height of a cart axle. After breaking the alliance with his patron Toghril, Genghis dispersed the Kereit tribe whose members became the servants and troops of his own Mongol retinue and army. A dissolution of clan loyalties was basic to his strategy and this led to the bestowal on him of the title Genghis Khan (or Universal Ruler) by the General Assembly of the Mongols held by the River Onon in 1206. As emperor of all the steppes Genghis provided thousands of families with settlements and protectors drawn from his own family and companions in arms. These protectors, and Genghis himself, therefore became the focus of loyalty: feudalism replaced tribalism. Further challenges were brutally dealt with: when the Naiman rulers in the west of Mongolia tried to form an anti-Genghis coalition they were deprived of their kingdoms.

Genghis used his military prowess to advance his political power. The first, more minor, title that he was given, 'Khan of the Mongols', was proposed by the tribes because they were looking for a reliable general to unite them militarily. Next came the support of the Chinese empire which Genghis would subsequently invade and conquer. Relations between the nomadic peoples of the steppe and the settled agrarian and urban civilizations to their south were continuously shifting. Nomads needed staple goods as well as the luxuries produced in China while the Chinese constructed successive alliances among the nomadic tribes according to their own priorities which varied according to the strengths and challenges posed by those tribes. The Liao dynasty for example had formed an alliance with the confederation of 'All the Mongols'. The Chin empire of northern China attacked its former allies the Tatars, and Genghis' attack on the Tatars from their rear led to Chinese recognition of his authority while he was still a minor chieftain building up his power on the steppe.

The unified Mongol nation was an entity organized for continuous warfare. At first the army was exclusively a cavalry force: it did not occupy cities and its focus was the defeat of other nomads. But the conquered societies changed the earlier Mongols profoundly by introducing them to more advanced technology and by spreading literacy among the leaders. Once acquainted with catapults, ladders and burning oil, the Mongol army was able to besiege northern Chinese towns, while in south China the Mongols learnt how to fight from ships. It was his new Chinese advisers in the conquered territories who dissuaded Genghis from turning the cultivated lands of north China into grazing grounds for his army's Mongolian ponies and who also taught him how the taxable goods produced by peasants and craftsmen contributed to state wealth. Mongols, already experienced traders at the time of the conquest of China, became important protectors and guarantors of trade routes. Their original religion, the worship of the 'Eternal Blue Heaven' as a supreme deity, was diffuse enough to allow a religious toleration in which Christianity, Islam and Buddhism could co-exist.

Genghis' anti-Chinese campaign started with an attack on the Tangut kingdom of Hsi Hsia – a state on the north-western Chinese boundaries – and then moved on to an outright attack on the Chin empire. The Chinese tactic of buying Genghis off with booty delayed for just a year his victorious seizure of Beijing in 1215. Afterwards Genghis left one of his generals to oversee the newly conquered China and concentrated on the conquest of the territory of Khwarezm (along the Oxus river) after a caravan of Muslim merchants who had been under his protection was attacked by one of the country's governors. Genghis honoured his agreement in the most savage way possible by destroying three major cities and forcing the survivors to serve as the Mongols' own advance troops. He withdrew from the country in 1223 and his final campaign was waged against Hsi Hsia.

Genghis prepared for his own succession and divided his lands among his sons: Ogodei, the ruler of western Mongolia and northern Sinkiang, was the dominant force. Jochi's western domains extended towards Russia and the Khanate of the Golden Horde which, under Jochi's successor Batu, would control Russia and terrorize eastern Europe. Chagatai ruled northern Iran and southern Sinkiang while Tolui was allocated eastern Mongolia. It was Tolui's son Kublai Khan (r. 1260-94) who became the Great Khan of China during its Mongol occupation under the rulers of the Yuan dynasty, a rule which lasted until the 1367 rebellion which led to the establishment of the Ming dynasty. The Great Khan was based at first in Karakorum, Mongolia, and then from 1267 in Beijing. The Mongol army had conquered all of China by 1279, most of the Middle East by 1260 and all the Russian territories (excluding Novgorod) by 1241. Annam (modern Vietnam) and Burma were invaded as was Java. Japan's defeat in 1281 of the Mongol invasion – helped by a typhoon – was an unusual reversal. The winter of 1236-7 marked the start of the western thrust into Europe: Kiev fell in 1240 and Hungary was invaded in 1241-2 but had to be evacuated as the Mongols retreated to central and southern Russia. The depopulation of Poland and Hungary caused by Mongol attacks accelerated the immigration of Germans who moved east into Silesia, Pomerania and Transylvania.

But the persistent problem of competing authorities on the steppe returned after

Genghis' death and saved Europe and the Middle East from a continuation of the Mongol advance. It was difficult to maintain the initial momentum of rapid expansion and high military morale. Ming Chinese incursions into Mongolia ended the unity established by Genghis Khan. Inner Mongolia, within Chinese boundaries, became progressively Sinicized, and divided from the Outer Mongolia of the steppes. The introduction of Tibetan Buddhism into Mongolia by stages from the fifteenth century onwards provided the Mongols with one of their few sources of unity. The Mughal (or Mogul) dynasty which ruled most of northern India between the early sixteenth and mid-eighteenth centuries, and which tried to integrate Hindus with Muslims, was an important Mongol legacy since Babur (r. 1526-30), the founder of the dynasty, was descended on his mother's side from Chagatai, the second son of Genghis Khan.

Different parts of the Mongol empire acquired their own local identities. The governing class of the Khanate of the Golden Horde in Russia became Muslim and Turkish while ruling over Christian Orthodox-Russian subjects (a division which explains its disintegration). The dynasty ruling the Il-Khanate of Persia (which was subordinate to the Great Khanates in Mongolia and China) had ruled over much of Iraq, north Syria and central Anatolia as well as the Iranian plateau after the occupation (1258) of Baghdad had eliminated the Abbasid dynasty. But the Il-Khanate's rulers became progressively Persian and Islamic as a prelude to the eventual disintegration of their authority. The Great Khanate of China became Sinicized although the native Chinese sense of distance from the barbarians persisted and accounts of Mongols using their own urine in order to wash caused particular offence to Chinese sensibilities. Steppe life survived in central Mongolia but this was the poorest of all the Mongol lands. Here the tribes regained their influence but the re-assertion of rival hereditary power made any political confederation of the tribes a precarious affair. Even the achievement of Timur Lenk (Tamburlaine), who renewed a part of the Mongolian empire, did not survive his death.

Depopulation and disease also hit the Mongols hard. The great constant in Eurasian history since the beginning of the first millennium had been the steady flow of migrants out of the steppe. But plague, the bubonic infection common among the rodents of the steppe, was decreasing the vast region's population levels by the fourteenth century when the disease travelled to western Europe where it would be called the 'Black Death'. In addition military technology had bypassed the bows and arrows of Mongol warriors on horseback. The Mongols had learnt about gunpowder from the Chinese but, whether nomadic or settled, they found it difficult to get the handguns which were arming the western Eurasian powers. The future history of the Mongol steppe would be one of conflict between Russia and China. From the late fifteenth century onwards the Russians were establishing control over the steppe and forests of northern Eurasia and in 1480 Ivan III, grand prince of Moscow, stopped the payment of tribute to the Golden Horde. By 1556 the Russian army controlled the entire length of the Volga and had crossed the Urals. By 1639 it had reached the Pacific and a huge rise in Russian population levels had helped the new settlers to colonize the depopulated areas of Ukraine and Siberia which had once echoed to the sound of the hooves of the Mongols' ponies.

29 May 1453

The Fall of Constantinople

The Ottoman Challenge to Europe

'The spider weaves the curtains in the palace of the Caesars'

A victorious Sultan Mehmed II enters Constantinople's Haghia Sophia and meditates

The city of Constantinople itself was all that remained of the Byzantine empire by 1453. It was defended by less than 7,000 men as opposed to the Ottoman Turkish army of 80,000 which was camped outside the city walls under the command of the twenty-year-old Sultan Mehmet II (r.1451-81). The entire province of Thrace to the west of the city had already been ravaged and a Turkish naval fleet assembled at Gallipoli. Constantinople's ditches had been deepened and the city moat flooded. The final siege of the city began on 2 April 1453. The city gates were closed and a great iron chain was stretched across the entrance to the defensive inlet of the Golden Horn to the north-west. The sultan, however, ordered his fleet of galleys to be dragged overland and into the Golden Horn which, at a stroke, was no longer a Greek harbour.

The Turkish assault started at about half-past one in the morning of Tuesday 29 May. Irregular forces were followed by Anatolians who were succeeded by waves of janissaries – the sultan's own guard – urged on by martial music as they advanced in regular ranks. The sultan led them as far as the fosse and then urged them on up to the stockade. Just before dawn Giovanni Giustiniani Longo, who had been in charge of the defence of the city walls, was injured and a small gate of the inner wall had to be opened so he could be taken off the field of battle. His Genoese contingent of 700 men also retreated through the gate before it could be closed. Retreating Greeks had also left open another gate in the walls and the Turks rushed in. The emperor Constantine XI was last seen advancing on foot towards the fray. Constantinople was sacked in scenes of terrible and indiscriminate slaughter. St Sophia became a mosque. On 21 June the victorious sultan left for his European court of Adrianople. 'What a city we have given over to plunder and devastation,' he murmured as he rode through a desolate scene. For the Greeks, Tuesday is still an unlucky day.

The force which had crushed the last political expression of Greek Christian culture and thereby also extinguished the last flickering flame of the ancient Roman empire was the most effective military machine ever produced in the history of Islam. These Ottoman Turks were descended from the inhabitants of 'Tartary', the Turko-Mongolian steppe land of Inner Asia. Their Turkish language was just one of a large group of languages collectively known as the Turkic group (to which Tatar, Uzbek and Kazakh also belong) which were found in Mongolia and Siberia. The Ottoman arrival at the gates of Constantinople was the last stage in that progressive series of westward movements of the Turkic peoples which had started with the impact upon them of the Huns during the first and second centuries AD. China and its allies on the steppe then pushed the Turks westwards to a point at which there were Turks on the Volga and Black Sea steppes in the fifth century. The early mediaeval period saw the emergence of two Turkish imperial powers, those of the eastern and the western steppe, ruled over by their *qaghans* . These were holy figures whose blood could not be shed. Instead they were deposed and strangled – a custom which would survive into early Ottoman practice. Right from the beginning,with its mixture of Turkic, Monglic and Iranian peoples, of nomads and semi-nomads, the Turkic state in its various forms was multi-lingual and multi-ethnic. The Seljuks, emerging from the collapse of earlier Turkic states and empires, were the first Turks to make a serious impact on the fringes of the European world. Trading and raiding contacts with the Arabs had by now introduced Turkic nomads to Islam. The monotheism of that faith could build on the tradition of worshipping a single sky god which had been an ancient custom among the peoples of the Asiatic steppe.

The rise of the Turks who were loyal to the ruling house of Seljuk is an eleventh century phenomenon and they were the first major Islamic power among the Turkish peoples. Having consolidated their position in Iran and Transcaucasia, they established their power in the old Arab-Islamic heartlands and towards the eastern Mediterranean. Serious and regular confrontation with the clearly ailing Byzantine state to the west now began. The clash between the two empires in 1071 at the battle of Manzikert was the single greatest catastrophe so far in Byzantine history. At a stroke all of Anatolia was lost and a series of principalities (*begliks*) were established in this area by the Seljuk army and tribal commanders. The collapse of the greater empire of the Seljuks (which had included Iran and Iraq as well as Afghanistan and Syria) led to Anatolia becoming a distinct entity separate from the main line and governed by the Seljuks of Rum. These rulers had intermarried with the neighbouring Georgian and Byzantine aristocracy and were full heirs to the tradition mixing culture and religions. Greeks served at the Seljuk court and there were émigré Turks who served the emperor in Constantinople. By the early thirteenth century the Seljuks of Rum were governing a powerful and well-defined state based in Anatolia and comprising much of modern Turkey.

The Mongol invasions in the first half of the thirteenth century destabilized Seljuk power and also pushed the Turkic-Islamic world further west so that it was increasingly in touch with the Byzantine and Christian world. By the late thirteenth century most of Anatolia was Islamic and the most important of the area's principalities was the one ruled by the house of Osman (the state which then grew into the Ottoman empire). Its greatest threat came from Tamburlaine who, although a Turk, aimed at the restoration of Mongol power. His army marched westward from central Asia during the fourteenth century and by the time he died (c.1405) he had brought much of central Eurasia and large parts of the middle east under his rule. He sacked Delhi in 1398 and died while marching towards China. Only his death saved Anatolian Turkey from his sustained attention and, happily for the Ottomans, Timur's son Shahrukh was less driven than his father by a policy of conquest.

The early Ottoman state was an informal organization shaped by the demands of the frontier. Religious divisions within it were not as sharp as they later became and its subjects were essentially plunderers more interested in trade and booty than in pursuing an Islamic campaign. An 'Ottoman' was simply someone who had decided to join the group. Many Byzantine and Balkan Christian warriors therefore became Ottomans purely for commercial reasons although the Christians who joined were soon Islamicized. As the Mongol threat declined during the fourteenth century so the Ottoman state grew in power and so started the long history of confrontation between the Greeks of Byzantium and the Ottoman Turks. In 1261 the Byzantines retook Constantinople after having been driven out of the city by the western European 'Latin' crusaders during the Fourth Crusade in 1204. But the Greeks made a crucial mistake. Their ambition to become once again a major power in the eastern Mediterranean led them to neglect their eastern land defences. A power as relentless as that of the Ottomans found it easy to exploit the internal Greek divisions and they were able to establish themselves in Gallipoli in the 1350s because they had been invited in by one of the warring parties in Constantinople.

From their bases in the Balkans the Ottomans went on to mount their first attempt at capturing Vienna in 1529. During the reign of Selim I (1512-20) they conquered the Mamluks – rulers of Egypt and Syria – whom they also succeeded as guardians of the holy cities of Mecca and Medina. The Ottoman Turks were now incontestable leaders of the Sunni Muslim world, a world power and absolutist state which combined two types of legitimacy: the Turkic with the Islamic. This new status reached its apotheosis in the reign of Suleyman I 'the Magnificent' (1520-66). Suleyman was a counterpart to the Renaissance princes whose bravura signified a new chapter in the history of kingship in western Europe. He was a major military strategist who conducted some thirteen land campaigns, a political reformer who abolished some of his predecessors' arbitrary methods of government, and also an accomplished poet. Yet he also threatened the very basis of Christian Europe. His armies took Belgrade in 1521 and then Rhodes in 1522. His victory at the battle of Mohács in 1526 led to the incorporation of most of Hungary within the Ottoman empire. For a century afterwards the Hapsburgs had a fight on their hands to regain Hungary although the Ottoman failure to take Vienna in 1529 was a major boost for the west. Meanwhile, Suleyman continued to advance against Iran and in 1534 he took Iraq from the Safavids.

The fall of Constantinople was the culmination of the division of fortunes between the Latin Christendom of western Europe and the Greek Orthodox Christendom of the east. Granada fell in 1492 and the last Moors were expelled from Spain. Islam, defeated in the west, concentrated its onslaught on the east. Islamic-Christian confrontation was now on an east-west axis, not a north-south one. A triumphalist western Europe turned towards the Atlantic for new trade routes to replace the traditional eastern ones which crossed the territories dominated by the victorious Ottomans.

By the mid-sixteenth century it was obvious, in retrospect, that the Ottomans were suffering from a classic case of imperial over-stretch and that they could not afford to maintain their borders. In 1552 the Portuguese defeated an Ottoman fleet at Hormuz in the Persian Gulf. During the 1550s the Muscovite army started to press in on the Ottomans from the north and this constitutes the start of the great Russian-Ottoman rivalry which would continue until the collapse of both empires during World War I. The dynamism of Peter the Great (1672-1725) would transform the old Muscovy into Russia and sustain its claim to be the heir to the traditions both of Genghis Khan and of Byzantium. And the Hapsburgs, although caught up in the European trauma of Protestant-Catholic conflict until 1555, nonetheless proved to be a very effective anti-Ottoman bulwark. The problem of dynastic succession was now undermining Ottoman government. Conflict and jealousy had always been endemic within the imperial harem and the weakness of Suleyman's successors aggravated the situation. The custom of imperial fratricide died away but fundamental reforms would elude the waning empire of the Ottomans. In the arts of politics and of war, in administrative practices and social customs, the very word Ottoman was becoming synonymous with inefficiency, ignorance and backwardness.

12 October 1492

Columbus makes Landfall in the Bahamas

The Opening of the Americas

'*I believe that…you will soon convert to our holy faith a multitude of people, acquiring large dominions and great riches for Spain.*'

Columbus, writing to Ferdinand and Isabella, urges the Christianization of 'natives', October 1492

An experienced mariner's knowledge of the winds, the patronage of Queen Isabella of the newly united Spanish kingdom of Aragon and Castile, and a misplaced conviction that he was heading for Asia, brought the forty-one-year-old Genoese explorer Christopher Columbus to the Bahamas on 12 October 1492. He had left the south-western Spanish port of Palos de la Frontera on 3 August with three ships intent on discovering a western maritime route to the eastern coast of Asia. He also sailed as the representative of an aggressive Catholic culture which considered itself 'cleansed' and therefore prepared for expansion. Spain's last Moorish kingdom, Granada, was conquered in January 1492 and Columbus had to delay his departure until after 2 August since that was the deadline for the last Jews to leave Spain following the decree of their expulsion.

Avoiding the strong westerly winds of the north Atlantic he headed at first to the Canary Islands. Then, picking up the north-easterlies, he was carried quickly west along a point parallel with Japan on the north-south latitude. Marco Polo's account of his twenty-four years of travel into Mongolia and China influenced much of Columbus' thinking and Polo had described Japan's islands as lying 1,500 miles off the Chinese coast – which was Columbus' ultimate goal. He was lucky in the late summer weather and deployed a Mediterranean sailor's expertise with the compass. North Sea and Baltic sailors, because their local seas were above the extension of the continental shelf off north-west Europe, could take soundings by casting a lead and line into the waters in order to calculate their direction and movement. But the magnetic compass, ever since its twelfth-century introduction, was a mariner's necessity when travelling along the deep basin of the Mediterranean. Even so, Columbus still had to rely on imprecise and traditional 'dead reckoning' techniques and would measure his speed by calculating the time taken to pass an object observed on the water's surface.

On 28 October the expedition arrived in Cuba where his crew became the first Europeans to see native 'Indians' smoking tobacco. He then set sail in January 1493 from Hispaniola (modern-day Haiti and the Dominican Republic) to return laden, if not with gold, then at least with botanical specimens chosen to confirm his stubborn thesis that he had been to Asia. Three more voyages followed; that of 1493-6, with its seventeen ships and 1,200 men including administrators, settlers and six priests, was a major survey of the Caribbean archipelago including Cuba, Puerto Rico, Antigua and Jamaica. As he cruised along the south coast of Cuba Columbus concluded that the southward direction of the coastline was the start of the Malay peninsula's eastern coast, but a disaffected crew and dwindling supplies forced him back to Spain. During the journey he persuaded the officers and crew to sign a deposition stating that the coastline they had seen was indeed part of the Asian continent. Refusal to sign was to be punished with the offender's tongue being cut out. Mounting scepticism about his claims meant that he could only raise six ships for the expedition which left in May 1498. On 31 July Trinidad was discovered and named. When on 1 August Columbus sailed into the vast gulf of Paria at the delta of the Orinoco river he had arrived in South America but could not accept the implication that he had discovered a new, fourth, continent. He conceded that so vast a freshwater gulf had to be fed by rivers running from the inland of 'a very great continent, until today unknown'. Yet Columbus, the Christian, decided that this was the earthly Paradise described in the Bible; he was attached to the mediaeval Christian view, supported by Ptolemy, that the continents of Europe, Asia and Africa were part of a single land mass – the 'island of earth'– which was surrounded by comparatively small amounts of water. A further separate earthly continent with two vast oceans on either side was inconceivable. The Orinoco river had therefore to be explained away as evidence of another 'island of the ocean'. During his last voyage of 1502 Columbus explored Honduras and Panama but died in the conviction that from 1492 onwards he had been exploring the eastern Asian coast.

By the fifteenth century European palates were used to Indian spices, including pepper which was a necessity as it masked the salt used to preserve meat. Arabian perfumes along with Chinese silks, textiles and porcelain were valued western luxuries. China's advanced technology had also exported cards, paper money, gunpowder and printing techniques. Eastern goods could travel by one of two historic routes towards the eastern Mediterranean. The overland 'silk route' led from eastern China through central Asia. By sea the trade could be carried from the South China Sea along the Indian Ocean and then either up the Persian Gulf to Basra or through the Red Sea to Suez; after this point the goods travelled either across Egypt or through Persia and Syria. Western merchants could travel to the markets of the Levant, and sometimes as far as Aleppo and Damascus, in order to buy goods, but the victorious Turks of the eleventh and twelfth centuries stopped them from going any further and trading directly with producers. The Mongols, victorious over the Chinese, reopened the silk route so that westerners from *c.*1250 to *c.*1350 could travel across the conquered Persian and Chinese territories to India. But China, resurgent after the national rebellion in1368 which established the Ming dynasty, closed down the lines of communication. Expanding western commercial demand, denied a land route to Asia, therefore looked to the sea.

In 1488 the Portuguese Bartholomeu Diaz had achieved the first eastward crossing into the Indian Ocean by navigating around the southernmost tip of Africa but Columbus offered Spain the prospect of her own, possibly shorter, route to the east. This would also break the effective monopoly enjoyed by the Italian and French merchants allowed to trade in the Levant. Marco Polo had already shown the vastness of China's territorial extent towards its east and Columbus' conclusion was that her eastern coast could be reached by sailing from western Europe's Atlantic shores.

The available maps could both inspire and mislead. The second-century AD Greek-Egyptian geographer Ptolemy had been rediscovered during the general renaissance of learning in fifteenth-century Europe. He had developed the grid system to illustrate longitude and latitude on maps which were orientated towards the north at the top. The recovery of Ptolemy was a major advance on mediaeval western maps which, designed to illustrate the theological claim that Jerusalem was the centre of the world, had put Asia and the east at the top, Europe below left, and Africa below right. European mariners' own maps, based on their practical experiences of the seas and therefore unencumbered by dogma about territorial positions, were also becoming more accurate. The Ptolemaic view that the earth was a spherical globe measuring 360° longitude (east-west) at its circumference was also now widely accepted. Explorers had to cope, however, with the fact that cartographers' estimates for the earth's circumference varied between 20,000 and 24,000 miles. The 1/360th length of one degree of longitude at the equator was therefore correspondingly measured by the varying authorities as being anything between 56 and 66 miles rather than the true measurement of 69 miles. At the same time estimates for the number of degrees of longitude measuring the entire Eurasian landmass between Cape St Vincent in Portugal and China's east coast varied hugely between 116° and 234°. Columbus opted for the scale which suited his propagandist purposes as he hawked his 'Enterprise of the Indies' around the courts of western Europe looking for cash and backers. The *Imago Mundi* (c.1410) of the world geographer Pierre d'Ailly, a work much used by him, gave a west-east measurement for Eurasia of 225° as opposed to the correct 131°. It was also a common view that the earth's proportion of land to sea was in the ratio of six to one. With Asia stretching so far towards its east the amount of available sea could surely be navigated by mariners heading west.

The Spanish-Portuguese Treaty of Tordesillas in 1494, under papal authority, was an immediate consequence of Columbus' early discoveries: Portugal gained all the lands east of a north-south meridian line of 46° west longitude which was drawn 370 leagues west of the Cape Verde Islands and Spain got everything to the west. This meant not just a Portuguese Brazil but also Portuguese dominion across any new lands discovered across the Atlantic, Africa and the Indian Ocean to the East Indies. Spain got its western half of the Americas and the lands west of the Pacific extending to the East Indies divided, like America, by the same meridian. The eastward extent of the American Brazilian territory was only discovered, subsequent to the treaty, in 1500 by the Portuguese explorer Pedro Alvarez Cabral and the entire basis of the two overland Iberian empires would be contested later by the British, Dutch and French. The Florentine, Amerigo Vespucci, under a Portuguese flag, sailed down 2,400 miles of the South American east coast in 1501-2 and, equipped with his own near accurate measurements of the length of degree longitude, had to conclude that he was looking at a fourth continent of the earth.

Spanish South America became a crusading opportunity: in 1519-20 Hernando Cortez conquered the Aztec empire of Mexico and in 1532 Francisco Pizarro conquered the Inca empire of Peru. Neither of these empires was more than a century old and the resentments among their subjected peoples helped the Conquistador advance. Spain also dominated the transatlantic trade route and by 1600, 200 ships a year were arriving in Seville from America. In 1591-1600 19 million grams of gold and almost 3 billion grams of silver were imported to Spain. American pepper, coffee, cocoa and sugar stimulated European taste buds. European soil was enriched by the arrival of maize and potatoes which, along with the cultivation of the protein-rich American haricot bean and also the tomato, helped Europeans to reproduce, grow taller and live longer. The population rise also contributed to the sixteenth-century price inflation which paralleled the commercial expansion of an Old World invigorated by the American discoveries. The transatlantic exchange of diseases was unequal: native Americans exported syphilis but were decimated by the importation of European smallpox, pleurisy and typhus. Estimates of Mexico's pre-conquest population vary between 12 and 15 million; by 1568 it was under 3 million. Peru went from 9 (1532) to 1.5 million (1570). Rape and concubinage eventually led to population recovery and the growth of a mixed race society. The consequences of Columbus also included a European division between the west, invigorated by its discoveries, and a stagnating east.

20 September 1519

Magellan Sets Sail for South America

The First Circumnavigation of the Globe

'The gums of both the lower and upper teeth of some of our men swelled, so that they could not eat...and therefore died.'
Antonio Pigafetta (c.1491-c.1534), a survivor

In 1519 the extent of the Pacific Ocean and the precise location of the East Indies' Spice Islands were still unknown. If, as some still thought, the Asian continent stretched far to the east then the western coastline of Spain's South American colonies would be near the East Indies. The Spaniards now needed to discover whether the valuable Spice Islands were on the western side of the meridian line which (under the Treaty of Tordesillas) separated their East Indies' territories from those of the Portuguese to the east of the line. To resolve this issue they turned to Ferdinand Magellan who, having fallen out of favour at the court of his native Portugal, was prepared to sail halfway round the world to assert Spain's claim to its new Asian territories. The five ships that left Spain were poorly equipped and the 250 crew were an international collection of adventurers including Portuguese, Italians, French, Greeks and an Englishman. A risky venture under a foreigner held few attractions for Spanish sailors.

Having reached the coast of Brazil, Magellan guided his ships south along the coast of South America looking for an opening into the newly discovered Pacific. Vasco Nunez de Balboa had become the first European to sight the Pacific (which he named the Mar del Sur or Sea of the South) on 25 September 1513 after he crossed the Panama Isthmus. But Magellan, travelling further south, was advancing into the unknown. By March 1520 the southern winter had arrived and Magellan decided to winter on the Patagonian coast rather than return to the tropics as his crew demanded. Three of his five ships now mutinied but he managed to overcome the mutiny by conciliation and only executed one ringleader. In October 1520 he resumed the southward exploration and on 21 October he sailed into the bay leading to the Straits which bear his name. Far from being, as he had hoped, a narrow but direct seaway leading directly to Japan and the Malay peninsula, the Magellan Straits proved to be a tortuous maze opening out into the world's largest sea. It took Magellan thirty-eight days to sail the Straits' 334 miles. The smallest of his ships, the *San Julian*, had already been wrecked and now the pilot of his biggest ship, the *San Antonio*, mutinied, put his captain in irons and sailed back to Spain.

On 28 November 1520 Magellan's remaining three ships sailed into the Pacific and for the next three months and twenty days they travelled for 12,000 miles in the unusually calm weather which led them to decide that this new ocean should be called 'Pacific'. Deprived of fresh food, Magellan's sailors were reduced to eating sawdust, biscuits that had turned into powder after being eaten first by worms, as many rats as they could find, as well as the oxhides intended as a protective cover for ship equipment and which they tried to make edible by warming them over embers. The intense privations were recorded by one of Magellan's men, Antonio Pigafetta, in his *Primo Viaggio Intorno al Mondo* – a journal which is one of the great accounts of human fortitude. After sailing north, Magellan anchored at Guam in March 1521 to pick up supplies and then headed for the Philippines where he arrived a week later. He was killed on the island of Mactan by tribal warriors on 27 April 1521 while covering his men's retreat to their boats. Just one ship of the original five, the *Victoria*, arrived in Seville in September 1522 with eighteen men having rounded the Cape of Good Hope. The earth had been circumnavigated.

Magellan represented the culmination of the skill and ambition displayed for almost a century before him by his fellow Portuguese on their global explorations. Fifteenth century Portugal, unlike Spain and England, France and Italy, was united and at peace after establishing (with English help) its independence of Castile at the battle of Aljubarrota (August 1385). The naval enterprise, celebrated in the *Lusiads* of the national poet Camoes, reflected a national consensus and an aptitude for long-term planning. Prince Henry the Navigator (1394-1460) conceived of a systematic exploration of the western coast of Africa, after the Portuguese victory in 1415 over the Muslim stronghold of Ceuta on the North African coast revealed the extent of the treasure that had arrived there from Saharan Africa to the south and from the Indies to the east. Sagres, Henry's base on the far southern coast of Portugal, became a centre for intelligence gathering, map-making, navigational skills and ship-building. The *caravel*, a light and easily manoeuvrable ship with its slanting and triangular sails (adapted from the Arab ships seen on the Mediterranean) was a Portuguese invention. Its ability to sail fast and close into the wind made it the most popular ship among European sailors.

From 1434 onwards Henry's sailors advanced by stages along the western coast of Africa. In 1444 the explorer Gil Eanes brought back from Guinea the first genuinely commercial cargo: 200 Africans who were sold in Portugal as slaves. By the mid-seventeenth century, and from Angola alone, the Portuguese had seized 1.3 million slaves. Other imports gave their names to the various parts of the west African coast facing the Gulf of Guinea: the Ivory Coast, the Gold Coast and the Grain Coast, which produced pepper. The explorations of the Portuguese also now benefited from their neighbour's obscurantism since Jewish astronomers and mathematicians fleeing persecution, among them Joseph Vizinho, moved from Spain to Portugal. Vizinho left the University of Salamanca in the 1480s and his southern voyage of 1485 led him to discover how to determine latitude according to the declination of the sun along the coast of Guinea. Previously, mariners could not progress below the equator since from that point on they could no longer see the North Star which was their point of reference for measuring latitude in the northern hemisphere.

New measurements and tables therefore guided the Portuguese explorers ever further south. Bartholomeu Diaz, on a typically well-organized and efficient Portuguese expedition of four ships equipped with three years' supplies, passed the southern tip of Africa at the Cape of Good Hope on his voyage of 1487-8 and entered the Indian Ocean. Ever since the mid-fifteenth century maps, based on rumour, had been produced illustrating Africa as a free-standing peninsula and the Indian Ocean as an open sea. Diaz confirmed the rumours and prepared the way for the achievement of Vasco da Gama who, in his 1497-9 expedition, rounded the Cape and then travelled along the east coast of Africa visiting the Muslim territories of Mozambique, Mombasa and Malindi and encountering their hostile rulers. He then crossed the Arabian Sea and arrived on the south-west coast of India. On his return voyage of 1502 to the Malabar coast of western India, Diaz headed for Calicut where he demanded the expulsion of all Muslims before turning the city into a Portuguese colony and then establishing the first permanent European navy in the Asian seas. The new Portuguese vice-royalty of India oversaw the destruction of the Muslim fleet in 1509. Ormuz, which guarded the entrance to the Persian Gulf, was seized in 1507 and so was Malacca in 1511. In 1510 the west coast town of Goa became the capital of the new colony in India and, as effective controllers of the Indian Ocean, the Portuguese established new maritime routes with Siam, China and the Spice Islands (or Moluccas). Trade was deflected away from the Persian Gulf-Red Sea-Levant route and towards the Cape on its way to western Europe. This also hit Venice and Genoa very hard since their wealth was based on their entrepôt status for eastern goods moving from the Levant towards the west. Egyptian-Venetian trade collapsed almost immediately after da Gama's conquests and by 1503 the price of pepper in Lisbon was a fifth of what it was in Venice.

The Iberian powers were establishing a global dominance over the circumnavigated earth in the first half of the sixteenth century and the Ottoman Turks were their sole significant enemies outside Europe. Arab Muslims, having always been a predominantly land-based power and civilization, failed to mount a naval challenge in a world where power came to those who could dominate the seas. Individual Arabs had navigated the Indian Ocean for centuries and mastered the shifting direction of its monsoon winds in order fill the lateen sails that would be adapted by the Portuguese. Arab mariners had invented the stern rudder and Al-Biruni, a geographer of genius, corrected Ptolemy in the eleventh century and wrote that the Indian Ocean was linked to another sea south of Africa. But the Arabian peninsula could not produce the wood, resin, iron and textiles needed to build ships.The territories the Arabs acquired after their expansion from the peninsula could almost all be reached by land and, content with the riches of their existence, they saw no need to develop the naval capacity which might have pushed them to explore beyond the Indian Ocean.

Further east the explorers were lucky in south-east Asia as well, for they sailed into seas abandoned by the Chinese. In the early fifteenth century the Chinese navy with its main fleet of 400 warships was a powerful arm of the Chinese state and its multi-storied ships were larger than any western equivalents. Between 1405 and 1433 a series of 'Grand Treasure Fleets' sailed from China to the countries bordering the South China Sea and the Indian Ocean as a demonstration of the new Ming dynasty's magnificence and authority. The countries visited became tributary states and, intent on showing their luxuriant self-sufficiency, it was the Chinese who gave the gifts. This pacific and maritime expression of foreign policy was the reverse of western colonial rapacity but the expense led to its abandonment and self-sufficiency turned into isolationism. The 1,000-mile long canal linking Tientsin in the north with Hangchow in the south, a 2,000 year project, was finished and replaced ships for the transportation of goods and foods. A consciously anti-maritime policy led to the disintegration of the navy and by 1500 the crime of building a junk with more than two masts was punishable by death.

The continuing threat of barbarian incursion led China to concentrate on the protection of its northern boundaries, to rebuild and extend its Great Wall (1403-24), and to move its capital northward from Nanking to Peking. But the greater Chinese foe proved to be the European masters of the age of sail who had arrived in the southern seas.

18 April 1521

Luther Defies Charles V at the Diet of Worms

The Spread of Protestantism

On the afternoon of 18 April 1521, in a hall in the city of Worms, the German theologian Martin Luther confronted Charles V, the young Hapsburg prince recently elected Holy Roman Emperor. Early sixteenth-century Germany was a dynamic Christian culture. More churches and religious charities were being established on German soil than ever before and one in every nine German was a priest. But just because it was so Catholic and religious, Germany was ready to be scandalized by the luxury and worldly ambitions of the Renaissance Papacy. Luther's anti-Papal tirades were having an incendiary effect. Now he had been summoned to explain himself.

The Imperial Diet was the central representative institution of the Holy Roman Empire bringing together on a regular, and peripatetic, basis the rulers of the patchwork of territories which comprised that loose federation. In 1521 the Diet was meeting in the city of Worms and, as emperor, Charles was presiding over it. In January of that year the Pope had excommunicated Luther, a monk of the Augustinian order who was also teaching at the University of Wittenberg. For the past four years Luther had been drawing out the implications of his central doctrine of justification by faith: humanity stood alone before God and needed no priests or saints to intervene on its behalf. Only God, not the Church, could save sinners and it was the quality of inner faith which 'justified' human beings in God's sight. In June 1520 the Pope had issued his formal Bull *Exsurge Domine* (Lord, Cast him out) which condemned Luther on forty-one articles of his teaching. His writings were then publicly burned in Rome. The students at Wittenberg retaliated by making a bonfire of some works of Catholic theology while Luther himself consigned a copy of the Papal Bull to the flames. He had raised the most fundamental of all questions: what is the basis of authority and of the laws which enforce obedience?

Luther's rebellion started as a question of theology and church government but it had inevitable political consequences. In his polemic against the Papacy Luther was supported by his local prince, Frederick the Wise, elector of Saxony. Frederick, like many other German princes, thought the issues raised were so important that the reformer should explain his case to the Diet. This enraged the Papacy which thought the Diet should be automatically supportive of its case. But by now the reform movement had become a popular movement stirring powerful, sometimes anti-Italian, nationalism. Having escaped the confines of the university, the court, the church and the monastery, it had now taken to the streets. Which is why, when Luther entered Worms, a troop of German knights accompanied him and the town was filled with his supporters. He appeared before Charles V at the session of the Diet which met on 17 April. When asked to recant he asked for a day to consider. The following afternoon he had a bigger audience before him since the Diet was meeting in a larger hall. Luther now delivered his reply in a prepared speech: he would only recant if he became convinced of his own error either by reason or by scripture. He was guided, he said, by his conscience and every human being's conscience was bound by the word of God. The Diet dissolved in confusion with the Catholic theologian Johann Eck and Luther shouting at each other. Luther probably did not say 'Here I stand, I can do no other.' But the phrase became famous because it really did sum up his position. He is the hero therefore not only of the Protestant Reformation but of the voice of the stubborn individual conscience. With his princely supporters absenting themselves, a rump Diet passed the Edict of Worms which declared Luther an outlaw and proscribed his writings. This limited his movements for the rest of his life. After a pretended abduction, he was smuggled to the castle of Wartburg near Eisenach, where he stayed until 1522. Here he started work on his translation of the New Testament, one of the great classics of German prose and a major element in the consequent spread of German literacy and education.

German anti-Papalism was not new. Its strength in the fifteenth century had resulted in the Roman curia allowing individual princes an increased control over church appointments and land. But the Papacy's monetary demands from all Catholic princes was increasing in the early sixteenth century – partly to pay for its own magnificence but also to finance its military role in the internecine wars between the Italian states. France, England and Spain, countries with a newly revived tradition of vigorous, central royal administration, were able to resist this pressure. But the German territories, where authority was dispersed among so many little states, were more vulnerable to Papal demands and therefore fertile soil for Lutheran protest.

There were other forces at work undermining the Church. Renaisssance learning ('humanism') was recovering the key texts of Greek and Latin antiquity and getting rid of the accumulated errors of the centuries during which monks and other clergy had copied and transmitted those works in manuscript form. This scholarly revival was not of itself anti-Catholic but it did make for a more questioning attitude towards authority. 'Scholasticism', the philosophical method built up by the mediaeval church, emphasized transmitted authority but the freshness and elegance of the new literary humanism made that tradition look stale and derivative. This was why, in February 1517, Luther wrote a series of theses against the Scholastic theologians. But it was the ninety-five theses that he wrote in October of the same year which galvanized first Germany and then Europe. His objection was to the sale of indulgences, papal dispensations from serving time in purgatory. They might require contrition in order to be effective but they were still pieces of paper bought by money which went to the Papacy. This was big business in 1517 since the Papacy needed the money to build its new basilica of St Peter's in Rome and the German sale of indulgences was co-ordinated by the great Augsburg banking family of the Fuggers. Half of the money raised went to Albert, the young archbishop of Mainz who was heavily in debt having paid his way into a series of high ecclesiastical jobs. Indulgences summed up all of Luther's deepest feelings against the edifice of a corrupt Catholic sacramentalism bent on manipulating God's will. Once his questioning started, much else was rejected as well: Papal primacy, the infallibility of the councils of the Church, transubstantiation of the blood and wine into the body and blood of Christ, and clerical celibacy were all dumped unceremoniously. Luther's idea of 'the priesthood of all believers' consciously displaced the spiritual perks of clerical professionals. The seven sacraments were reduced to just three: baptism, the Lord's Supper and penance. This spiritual and inward understanding of Christianity spoke to many Germans and they could also read about it. Printing – still a new trade in 1517 – transformed the prospects for Luther's rebellion and he was a prodigious pamphleteer.

Luther was lucky that, with an election to the throne of the empire imminent in

1518-9, the Papacy needed the support of the elector Frederick and therefore did not stamp on him immediately. Charles V, in deciding what to do about Luther and the German rulers who supported him, also had to consider his own quarrels with the Papacy and with the French crown. And he needed as many allies as possible to build up a coalition against the Turks. This was why the Diet of Speyer (1526) suspended the Edict of Worms and decided that each prince should behave within his own territories according to his own judgement answerable to God. It was the withdrawal of this concession at the second Diet of Speyer which caused the reforming princes to draw up the Protest which gave Protestantism its name. Luther relied on these princes in order to carry out his reforms and believed that secular power should correct spiritual abuses, yet it was a major Reformation paradox that this call for an inward religion resulted in the increased power of state organized churches.

It was a further irony that the man who started this 'Reformation' was soon horrified by popular Protestantism. The Anabaptist movement and associated enthusiasts rejected any secular or church authority and threatened a popular insurrection on iconoclastic lines, attacking religious paintings and sculpture. But Luther went deeper and thought the real power of idolatry lay in men's minds. Once that mental corruption had been corrected by individual repentance then the outward idols would just fall into disuse. This was too subtle a belief for extremists. Some of Luther's greatest fears were realized during the Peasants' War – an insurrection in the Black Forest in the summer of 1524 which defended the peasants' ancient rights as defined in game and forest laws. The rebellion could also be presented as a further implication of Luther's successful defiance of authority. When the Thuringian peasants rose in the spring of 1525 Luther responded with one of his most violent tracts: *'Against the Murdering and Thieving Hordes of Peasants'*.

The Reformation inaugurated a century and a half of European religious wars between equally dogmatic Protestant and Catholic states. It also separated Erasmus, Christendom's most famous scholar, from Luther. In *'Concerning Free Will'*, he rejected Luther's teaching that the human will was totally enslaved. This was a divide between the optimism of the earlier humanists and the harsh new world of dogmatic disputes. In 1531 the Protestant Imperial states of Germany established their own organization with its joint army, the Schmalkaldic League. The Peace of Augsburg (1555) drew the first phase of the Reformation to a close with its decision that the subjects of German rulers had to follow their ruler's faith. This decision was wrested from a reluctant Charles V who looked back to the medieval ideal of Christendom – an ideal which was now dead. The Catholic Church recovered and enjoyed its own reforming revival after it summoned the Council of Trent. In the second half of the century Protestant dynamism moved on from Luther and his legacy to Calvin and his austere theology of an Elect who had been predestined for salvation by God. This represented a further hardening of the dogmatic arteries. But the cultural, social and political consequences of Protestantism were profound and long-lasting. Protestant societies renewed their national institutions, reformed their schools and universities, and responded to the new commercial opportunities of the Atlantic economy. By the end of the seventeenth century, it was a striking fact that most of northern Europe was Protestant and richer than southern, Catholic, Europe.

The Defeat of the Spanish Armada

England retains her Religion, and her Queen

'…it lost us respect and the good reputation among warlike people which we used to have. …Almost the entire country went into mourning.'

Fray Jeronimo de Sepulveda chronicles (1605) the effect of Spain's defeat

The Spanish Armada was first sighted by the English off Lizard Point, Cornwall on 29 July 1588 and beacons signifying a national emergency were lit along the southern English coast that evening. The Armada's aims were to secure the invasion of England by the 30,000 troops commanded by the Spanish regent of the Netherlands, the duke of Parma, to contain the English fleet, and clear the Straits of Dover so that Parma's army could cross from Flanders and land in the south-east of England. Misfortune hit the venture even before it sailed when the marquis of Santa Cruz, its intended commander, died and was replaced by the less experienced duke of Medina Sidonia who was sceptical about the expedition and urged Philip to make peace. The Spanish fleet consisted of some 130 ships and 8,000 sailors, but there were also as many as 19,000 soldiers on board. Some forty of the ships were line-of-battle ships. The rest were transport ships and light craft. Even the best Spanish ships were slower and less heavily armed than their English equivalents. As a result the invaders hoped to force boarding actions onto the English fleet in order to capitalize on their military superiority. Lord Howard of Effingham commanded the English fleet with Sir Francis Drake as his second in command. During most of the fighting in the Channel this fleet consisted of some hundred ships, only forty of which were first class warships. However, the English, unlike the Spanish, did not have to bother with transport ships and their smaller ships were fast and well armed. Artillery was all important. English ships might carry fewer soldiers than the Spanish but they had more, and heavier, guns.

The English fleet gained a strategic initiative by manoeuvring itself to the west of the Armada; it then harassed the Spanish at long range and successfully avoided attempts at engagement in close action. The Spanish formation, however, sustained little damage and arrived in the Straits of Dover on 6 August. It then anchored near Calais with the English navy still to its west. Over in Flanders, Parma (also a sceptic of the Armada strategy) started to embark his troops onto their invasion craft. This took six days during which time the Armada had no safe port and no means of escorting Parma's small craft across the coastal shallows where Dutch and English warships lay in wait. At midnight on 7-8 August the English sent eight fire ships into the Spanish fleet which therefore had to cut their cables and stand out at sea in order to avoid catching fire. As a result the Spanish ships' formation was in disarray. When, at dawn on the eighth, the English attacked the Armada off Gravelines the Spanish ships' heavy guns had not been mounted and the ships were sunk, driven ashore or badly battered. But shortage of ammunition meant that the English had to break off the engagement and follow at a distance. A shift of the prevailing westerly wind enabled the Spaniards to escape to the north, but the wind, as well as the English fleet, stopped them from joining up with Parma's forces. Instead, the fleet had to return to Spain by sailing around northern Scotland. Autumn gales destroyed many of the ships and only about sixty of them returned home. Enemy action killed as many as 15,000 Spaniards and disease killed some thousands of English sailors but hardly any lost their lives in action.

The aim of the invasion was to re-establish Catholicism and to extinguish English Protestantism. Technically it was a crusade and declared as such by Pope Sixtus V in 1587. The religious aim coincided with a political objective: an invaded England would be part of the Spanish Hapsburg empire ruled by Philip II. Spain led the fight against heresy because religious dissent subverted the allegiances owed to Catholic monarchies. Spanish support was crucial to the Papacy which was now running a revived Church. Ignatius Loyola, the soldier who founded the Jesuit Order, was a pre-eminent example of that Spanish mixture of militancy and mysticism which shaped Counter-Reformation Catholicism.

By 1588 Spain had enjoyed a century of brilliant political, military and cultural success. But Protestant England had been a thorn in Philip's side ever since the death of his wife Mary, the last Catholic queen of England. John Foxe's influential *Acts and Monuments*, afterwards known as *Foxe's Book of Martyrs* (1563), vividly described the Marian persecution of Protestants and helped to form the popular English judgement that Catholicism was a cruel and alien force. English piracy against Spanish trade and possessions was also a constant provocation and reached a high point with the raids of Sir Francis Drake on Spanish commerce in the Caribbean. The Treaty of Nonsuch (1585) amounted to an English declaration of war on Spain since it pledged England to support the Protestant Dutch rebels. The Eighty Years War, Spain's true nemesis, had started in 1568 as a protest against the Spanish imposition of orthodox Catholicism in the Netherlands. Spain considered itself and its religion to be threatened by an international, and mutually supportive, band of Protestant heretics who maintained that subjects had rights of conscience against divinely instituted rulers. But Catholic rulers and priests also appealed to a supra-national loyalty in the name of conscience when justifying and encouraging internal Catholic rebellions against established Protestant rulers.

England's Reformation and its established Church of England were still comparative novelties in the 1580s. It was only in 1571 that the Church concluded an attempt at defining its beliefs in the ambiguous hotchpotch of the Thirty-Nine Articles. The year after the accession of Elizabeth I (1558) Parliament had passed the Acts of Supremacy and Uniformity which confirmed Anglicanism as the state religion and the basis of political order. Pope Paul IV responded immediately by issuing the Papal Bull *Cum Ex Apostolatus* which stated that all heretical rulers were to be deposed: the political goals of Hapsburg expansionism therefore received Papal sanction. Elizabeth used diplomacy and evasiveness to negotiate her way around the extremes. The Puritan movement, which stood for a more vigorously Protestant Church of England, was as dogmatic as Catholicism. Both doctrines rejected the right of lay rulers to determine Church policy. Two sets of rival authorities, the Catholic Pope and the Protestant Bible, shared a similar conclusion which contested the new theory of a national sovereignty vested in queen and parliament. In 1571 Pope Pius V issued the Bull *Regnans in Excelsis* which excommunicated Elizabeth and declared that her subjects owed her no allegiance. France meanwhile showed the terrible consequences of using religious belief to justify rebellion. For much of the second half of the sixteenth century the country was consumed by civil war between Protestant Huguenots and Catholic loyalists. This new dissidence was expressed in the argument of the French jurist François Hotman, in his *Franco-Gallia*, that kings could be deposed and should be elected.

The Spanish-led victory over the Turks at the naval battle of Lepanto in 1571 confirmed the country's international authority. In 1580 Spain conquered Portugal and therefore doubled its colonial empire. However, the war in the Netherlands, necessarily conducted at long distance, meant that Spain was not just over-stretched territorially –

as the Armada's failure would demonstrate – but was also financially crippled. In 1575 Philip II had to suspend all payments by the Spanish crown and the country's troops in the Netherlands went unpaid; in 1576 the Spanish army mutinied and sacked Antwerp. By 1579 Spain was impotent to prevent the division of the Netherlands between the Dutch Republic of the seven northern provinces and the Spanish south.

The Armada's defeat was certainly a major humiliation and the subsequent English sacking of Cadiz affected both Philip's prestige and his credit. He tried to repudiate his loans at 45 per cent and refused to pay any more. But England's attempt at invading Portugal in 1589 ended in disaster. Two more Armadas were launched against England in 1596 and 1597 while a fourth was attempted in 1599. Drake and Hawkins would die on their failed 1595 expedition to raid the Spanish colonial territories. Spain revived as a naval power in the 1590s and learnt to build new, English-style galleons. It fortified its bases in the West Indies and developed a new type of fast frigate, the gallezabra, to carry American gold and silver to Spain. The revolt in the Netherlands was the true cause of the breakdown of Spanish authority. Philip had always seen the French wars as an opportunity for Spanish intervention, but he had to make peace after a two year war against the French (1595-7) since his army in the Netherlands could not fight both the French and the Dutch.

Seventeenth-century Spain was a great power grown nostalgic for its past. Its obscurantist clericalism, crabbed bureaucracy and economic decline contrasted sharply with the Dutch state which was lay-run, commercially vigorous and, eventually, tolerant. If Holland was the European future, Spain seemed an unappealing version of the European past. Government finances and the raising of taxes posed chronic difficulties. Inflation hit Spain and its stagnant economy very hard. The country which had led in the discovery of the Atlantic world withdrew to the Mediterranean. Perhaps a *hidalgo* cult of noble honour and disdain for trade contributed to the stagnation. The canvases of Velasquez capture the melancholia of the Spanish court and Cervantes' novel *Don Quixote* is a recognition that modernity made Spanish chivalry look ridiculous. In 1609 Spain was forced to recognize Dutch independence by signing a twelve year truce. Stubbornly, it renewed the war in 1621.

But 1588 was also an English Salamis – a victory which gave a new civilization time to breathe and opportunity to expand. It was a major feat of civilian and military organization on land as well as of naval power, and that experience instilled a national self-confidence. The late sixteenth century is also the time when the European Renaissance, finally, acquires an English dimension. Much of what is regarded as typically Elizabethan, such as the plays of Shakespeare and Marlowe, were produced towards the end of the queen's reign. These years of golden achievement would be idealized during the early seventeenth century when the politically inept Stuart dynasty demonstrated that it lacked the Tudor flair for government. The buccaneering style of the great Elizabethan naval explorers and commanders such as Francis Drake, Walter Raleigh and Richard Grenville, John Hawkins and Martin Frobisher pre-dates the Spanish Armada. In the teeth of Spanish opposition they had established the right of the English to explore the New World. That fact, confirmed by the Armada's defeat, was a crucial stage in the development of an English-speaking, North American, civilization.

21 October 1600

Tokugawa Ieyasu Wins the Battle of Sekigahara

The Age of the Shoguns

'*There are seven emotions: joy, anger, anxiety, love, grief, fear, and hate, and if a man does not give way to these he can be called patient…I have practised patience.*'

Tokugawa Ieyasu (1543-1616)

Japan, after the death of its feudal overlord Toyotomi Hideyoshi (1535-98), was threatened by anarchy. A council of five co-regents had been nominated by Hideyoshi to rule Japan after his death and during the minority of his son Toyotomi Hideyori. Tokugawa Ieyasu (1543-1616), as head of the regency council, emerged as a dominant figure but Ishida Mitsunari (1563-1600), another council member, challenged his authority.

Mitsunari and Ieyasu were supported by the war lords of respectively, western and eastern Japan, and came to do battle at Sekigahara, a narrow pass of strategic importance between Lake Biwa and Nagoya in central Japan on the 21 October 1600. At about 8 a.m, as the mists cleared after a night of driving rain, the first shots of musketry were heard. The contest between the 80,000 strong army of the west and the slightly smaller army of the east was even until midday. But Ieyasu's espionage network, ahead of the battle, had already persuaded elements of the 'army of the west' to defect. A force on the hill above that army's southern line advanced on its own allies and delivered the victory to Ieyasu.

Mitsunari's defeat led to his execution and Ieyasu either banished the nobles who had supported him or deprived them of their lands. He then redistributed the fiefdoms among his own supporters. But since many feudal nobles supported Hideyori's legitimacy the ambitious, but cautious, Ieyasu allowed the seven-year-old boy to keep his father's stronghold, Osaka Castle, and gave him his granddaughter in marriage. The battle was the last major opposition to Tokugawa power. The emperor, whose power was merely nominal, confirmed Ieyasu's authority when, in 1603, he appointed him shogun – supreme military ruler of Japan. When Ieyasu retired in1605 he ensured that the title of shogun was transferred to his son Tokugawa Hidetada. A dynasty had therefore been established but Ieyasu retained effective control until his death.

At the beginning of the sixteenth century Japan had dissolved into a collection of some 400 effectively independent states and the emperor's authority was just a formality. But Japanese attempts at establishing central authority dated back to the country's emergence as a distinctive civilization in the fifth and sixth centuries AD. The constitution of 604 had asserted the emperor's authority over the nobility, the national reforms of 646 established the emperor's title to all Japanese land, and Nara became the country's administrative capital. Buddhism, imported from China through the adjacent Korean peninsula, was used to elevate imperial power. But Japan, unlike Korea, failed to transplant the much-admired Chinese example of a hierarchical and centralized administration. Buddhist monasteries and great families were granted private estates as a reward for crown service and this diminished the imperial patrimony. In 794 the emperors decided to move their court to the new capital of Heian (Kyoto) in order to escape the political influence of Buddhist monks at Nara. However, they then found themselves dominated by the Fujiwara clan whose members intermarried with the imperial family and became the country's predominant power. The absence of a central army meant that the country's provinces were run by the monasteries and by the private armies of nobles. Samurai soldiers roamed the countryside and observed their own chivalric code. By the twelfth century, a time when Fujiwara power was waning, the samurai were influential in court politics.

Shoguns, as supreme military rulers, ruled with the aid of provincial subordinates

– the *shugo*. The flow of power to the peripheries proved to be a chronic feature of Japanese political and military life: the shugo established themselves as regional rulers and the shoguns' power diminished. But the shugo themselves lost their authority in the provinces after the civil war (1467-77) caused by a quarrel about the shogunate succession. The real victors were a new class of feudal warriors and provincial power-brokers known as the *daimyo*. Samurai warriors provided the daimyo with private armies which led to internecine warfare. They in turn, as befitted their vassal status, received their own small estates. In the west such feudalism had led to national legal and political structures but Japanese feudalism militated against any such authority. Daimyo castles dominated their particular areas as centres for trade, urban development and the arts. Within their fortresses some of the daimyo became influential patrons of the ritualized Noh drama, the tea ceremonies, painting and prose romances which gave Japan a national cultural style despite the fragmentation so evident elsewhere.

The man who ended the chaos by establishing a centralized despotism started life as a victim of the age of Japanese anarchy. Tokugawa Ieyasu was born into a struggling warrior family and his father's alliances meant that Ieyasu's mother was separated from the family when her son was two. At the age of seven he became a hostage of the powerful Imagawa clan and two years afterwards Ieyasu's father was killed by one of his vassals. The Imagawa educated Ieyasu as both warrior and administrator and his earliest campaigns were waged on behalf of the clan. But the age's dominant figure was Oda Nobunaga with whom Ieyasu formed an alliance after Nobunaga's defeat of the Imagawa . Nobunaga had captured Kyoto and started an anti-Buddhist campaign, slaughtering monks and destroying temples.The Portuguese had by now introduced firearms into the country: muskets were reproduced and tactics changed. Nobunaga exploited these developments. The castle of Azuchi, built as his base on the shores of Lake Biwa in central Japan, showed the novel quality of his power. Earlier castles were defensive citadels built in remote mountain strongholds but Azuchi, built on the plains, asserted political and administrative order rather than just military control. Ieyasu was able to return to his family's estates near Nagoya on the central east coast where he established a tax regime and a system of civilian administration to run his small army. He replaced the Imagawa during the 1570s as the dominant regional power so that he became the daimyo in charge of a prosperous and well-populated area.

Nobunaga, following an attack by one of his vassals, died in 1582 and Toyotomi Hideyoshi emerged as his successor within the Oda territories. During the 1580s Hideyoshi extended his authority over the daimyo of south-west Japan and his defeat of the Hojo clan enabled him to consolidate control of eastern Japan. Hideyoshi suggested that his ally Ieyasu should surrender his coastal provinces in return for the Hojo lands further east and the Tokugawa vassals and army were therefore transferred to land centred on the fishing village of Edo (Tokyo).

Hideyoshi in his vast domain and Ieyasu in his compact one followed policies designed to sustain their authority. Hideyoshi disarmed the peasantry and insisted that the samurai should now live in castle towns rather than roam the countryside ever ready to lend support to rural rebellions. A land survey yielded new taxes and Hideyoshi moved to suppress the Christian faith established in Japan by the Portuguese in 1572.

Ieyasu placed large tracts of land under the direct administration of his own officials, drew up land surveys, and confiscated villagers' weapons. Artisans and businessmen were encouraged to come and work in his new castle town.

After his victory at Sekigahara Ieyasu issued regulations and established administrative bodies which controlled the activities of the nobility, the Buddhist clergy and the daimyos. His aim was the creation of a stable and self-sufficient state by autocratic means: farming and trade were segregated, private investment banned and different parts of the country were only meant to communicate with each other by travelling along the strictly controlled five Imperial highways which converged on Ieyasu's court. The Japanese were stopped from travelling abroad and, after the ban on the building of large ships (1638), had few means of travel to tempt them. Japanese hostility to trade grew since they saw from the examples of Goa, Malacca and Macau, how missionaries always followed in the traders' footsteps. Francis Xavier, the Jesuit missionary, had first arrived in Japan in 1549 and Christianization had been rapid. By 1615 some half a million of Japan's eighteen million population were Christian. Ieyasu embarked on a systematic anti-Christian policy which later culminated in the slaughter of 37,000 Japanese Christians at Hara castle near Nagasaki after Christian peasants, aided by samurai mercenaries, rose in rebellion. 3,125 officially recognized Catholic martyrdoms occurred during the Tokugawa era. All Japanese now had to register at local Buddhist temples and alien faiths were proscribed.

The need to control the daimyo ensured that both Ieyasu and his son kept them hard at work building, extending and embellishing the castle at Edo. By the time of Ieyasu's death it was the world's largest castle. Surrounding it were the mansions in which the daimyos lived as virtual hostages. The issue of the succession to Hidetada still plagued his father, especially when Toyotomi Hideyori attained his majority in 1614. The seventy-one-year-old warrior therefore led an army to seize Osaka castle and finally crush the Toyotomi clan with the help of Hidetada who raised an army of 90,000 warriors. After a year-long campaign the castle fell and Hideyori, along with his family, committed suicide.

Ieyasu established the isolationism of the Edo period (1603-1867) which was dominated by the Tokugawa shogunate and as a prolonged period of peace, is without parallel in advanced societies. Economically, the experiment was successful for a long time: cities boomed and agriculture expanded. The population grew to some thirty million by the early eighteenth century, but with virtually no foreign trade the state had to be financed almost exclusively from agricultural taxes whose burdens caused many peasants to leave the land. Samurai fell into debt and rural discontent spread. The peace meant that the army was largely redundant and the educated samurai joined the ranks of the bureaucrats who ran the highly centralized administration created by Ieyasu and which remains in place today. This concentration of power also created enormous powers of patronage which proved to be another long-term national legacy. Japan's introspective sense of its cultural uniqueness – and of its distinctiveness among its Asian neighbours – deepened during this period. But keeping the west at bay proved a high-cost policy. Japan could not assimilate western technology on its own terms. And western technology meant western power. A secluded society grew vulnerable to the feared 'barbarian'.

24 May 1607

The Foundation of Jamestown, Virginia

The First Permanent English Settlement in North America

'*Crafty, timorous, quick of apprehension and very ingenious. Some are of disposition fearful, some bold, most cautious, all savage. Generally covetous of copper, beads and such like trash.*'

John Smith describes Virginia's natives (1612)

The London and Plymouth Companies, which were chartered in 1605 in order to establish American colonies, were the result of James I's peace treaty with Spain in 1604. English colonial policy needed a serious approach in place of the easy piracy pursued at Spanish expense in the Caribbean and it was the London Company which established the first English plantation to endure in North America. Of the 144 who left on three small ships, the *Susan Constant*, *Godspeed* and *Discovery* under the command of Captain Christopher Newport, 105 survived the journey. The James River was chosen because it was so wide and deep stretching fifty miles into the interior, and the site of Jamestown, being almost an island, was easy to defend. Here the colonists built their fort. The coast, with its many indentations, was ideal for the naval communications which would sustain the plantation, and the land was well timbered with plenty of game. But by the end of 1607 only thirty-eight survived of those who had landed; malaria bred from the marshes killed off many while bad diet and bad water led to scurvy and dysentry. Captain John Smith quelled a mutiny, forced the settlers to stay and, during his year in 1608-9 as the colony's president, secured a food supply by persuading the natives to supply maize. Livestock started to breed. Even so, the colonists abandoned Jamestown in 1610 and were sailing down river when they encountered the new governor, Lord De La Warr, sailing up-stream with new supplies and extra men. Hundreds of settlers arrived from 1611 onwards – and hundreds died. It took a decade for the population to increase to a thousand. By 1630 there were still only 2,500 Virginians. Smith complained that there were not enough 'good labourers and mechanical men'. Some early settlers deserted to the native tribes and others were just drunken dissidents. In 1622 native Americans, led by Opechancanough, massacred a third of the settlers, but arms sent from England by the London Company enabled the colonists to survive. In earlier years relations had been happier when the natives put on an entertainment in the woods for the settlers, after which their women pursued the embarrassed president Smith.

The English colonization of North America had started as an Elizabethan response to the Spanish conquest in the south although the English claim to Newfoundland with its valuable cod-fisheries dated back to the 1497 expedition of the Italian émigré John Cabot. Walter Ralegh founded (but never himself visited) the colony of 'Virginia' which was named in the queen's honour and stretched along most of the eastern coast to the north of Florida and south of the present New England. The settlers he placed on Roanoke Island in 1589 off the coast of Carolina were carried home the following year by Francis Drake.

North American furs and fish were an attraction but the land would only yield its real riches to those ready to stay and work. South America was easily plundered for gold, silver and slaves but the northern terrain required other colonial qualities. The publication in 1600 of Richard Hakluyt's *Principal Navigations, Voyages, and Discoveries of the English Nation* provided an inspirational programme for English plantations and the ambitions of tenants eager for freehold as opposed to the neo-feudal copyhold tenure drove many across the Atlantic. The concern of Tudor and Stuart governments with social control also embraced the plantation project as a way of reforming criminals.

The companies' investors, having bought shares at a hefty £12. 10s each, looked for a return, but profits were slow in coming. In 1624 the London Company crashed and Virginia became a colony under the English Crown. However, before it fell, the company's head, Edwin Sandys, introduced a new system of land allotment giving each settler fifty acres for himself and as much again for each dependant – family or servants – that he brought to Virginia. The Virginians were realizing the American goal of economic independence. Sandys also established the colony's General Assembly: this parliament of settlers' representatives met from 1619 onwards and by 1635 it was self-confident enough to depose a governor. The English crown had had to concede the principle of government by consent because no other method could bring order to the neo-anarchy of Virginia. All manufacturing experiments having failed, the planters resorted to tobacco which Raleigh, a good entrepreneur, had already popularized by personal example in England. The climate made the plant easy to grow though it exhausted the soil and Virginia therefore moved steadily westwards in search of land. Mass production, at low prices, ensured a world market for the colony. Yeomen planters wanted to expand but cheap and plentiful labour could not be found among independent minded settlers. The solution was African slaves. As the colonists grew richer, and as the price of slaves fell because of their mass export in the seventeenth century, America imported an economic solution, a human tragedy and a long term political trauma.

The European powers now bartered their American possessions just as they bartered their own boundaries. The early seventeenth-century French, liberated by the end of their religious civil war, explored the area of the St Lawrence river, and established French Canada by founding Quebec and Montreal. The English seized Quebec only to return it on the marriage in 1633 of Henrietta Maria to Charles I. The Dutch founded their West India Company, traded up the Hudson river, and established the colony of New Amsterdam in 1625-6 which later became New York. Native Americans were caught up in the European rivalries: the English made the Iroquois tribe their allies and the French opted for the Hurons. New France and New Netherlands were intended to rival New Spain, but it was New England that lasted because its settlers supplemented the commercial ambitions of Virginia with religious vision and the stubbornness of political principle.

The spasmodic persecutions of the 1610s caused a group of English puritans, led by John Robinson and William Brewster, to emigrate to Holland and it was this English community in Leyden which applied to the Virginia Company of London for a patent to settle their own plantation. In 1614 John Smith had been employed by the company to explore the coast up to Cape Cod and his published map named the area New England. Travelling back to England, and led by Brewster, the group managed to raise enough money from London merchants to finance their voyage. The ship they hired, the *Mayflower* , left Plymouth on 16 September 1620. Of the 105 passengers only thirty-five were travelling for conscience's sake; the rest were servants and skilled craftsmen who would be useful in establishing a plantation. The lessons of early Virginia had been learnt. Of the ship's entire complement which, including both sailors and passengers, came to 149, only five died on the voyage. They landed first at Cape Cod in November, tried to get further south into the Hudson but were driven back by winds and the river rocks. The *Mayflower* docked on 16 December in the New World's Plymouth Harbour and the colonists started work on 25 December with a Puritan disregard for a Popish feast.

These pilgrims were people whose covenant with God led them to make a covenant with each other. Congregationalism – the belief that churches should be autonomous, raise their own money and elect their own clergy – was the doctrine that created New England. This demanded a participatory, articulate, church membership and the political consequences were both republican and radical. The doctrine also created its own kind of elite since, as a New England divine expressed it, congregationalism was 'a speaking aristocracy in the face of a silent democracy'. The Mayflower Compact, signed on 11 November, provided for the annual election of the governor by qualified adult males. It also prescribed the legal rules which protected individual rights and property while the governor and his council made the executive decisions. This became the model for subsequent settlements and American states. The influence of the Puritan personality would be equally profound. If the zealousness could topple over into self-righteousness the concern with individual salvation led to introspective seriousness and industrious self-reliance.

Immigration to New England grew as economic depression hit the English cloth trade centred in East Anglia and the south-west, two areas which were also particularly Puritan. During the eleven years of Charles I's incompetent and intolerant rule (1629-40) 20,000 English Puritans went to Massachusetts and most stayed. The foundation of the Massachusetts Bay Company led to the departure from England of the eleven ships carrying the group led by John Winthrop, a Suffolk squire. The company's self-government was legally underpinned by a Royal Charter and its headquarters was in the new state, not in London. The New England government wanted a Puritan religious uniformity and it therefore prosecuted individual cases of heresy. The belief of Roger Williams, who founded Rhode Island in 1636, in a strict separation between church and state was a minority view. Despite the intolerance in religious affairs, colony politics was individualist. Every town elected two deputies who then elected the governor and consulted with him and the other magistrates on taxation. The General Court was the sovereign body of the company and of its colony. In 1634 it was decided that this court would meet four times a year: one meeting would assemble all the colony's freemen to elect magistrates, while the deputies representing the towns would make laws at the other three meetings. An effectively autonomous republic had been created. The Body of Liberties (1641) supplied a written legal code and the cultured commitment to a learned ministry led to the foundation of Harvard College. Massachusetts was still under the rule of the 'Saints' since only church members could be 'freemen' enjoying citizen rights but freemanship would later be extended to all adult males who had sworn an oath of loyalty to the commonwealth. Commitment mattered. The New England township, an extension of the English manorial village, was a local unit of self-government run by town-meetings. But an exploring spirit and land hunger drove many beyond the communities' confines.

'We must consider that we shall be as a City upon a Hill,' said Winthrop, 'the eyes of all people are upon us'. The sense of being an exemplar persisted. New Hampshire, Connecticut and Rhode Island started as offshoots of Massachusetts. Pennsylvania was founded as a Quaker refuge and Maryland as a Catholic one. An English experiment had created a new kind of human society far removed from the aristocratic paternalism, the royal absolutism, and the religious intolerance of early seventeenth-century England.

23 May 1618

The Defenestration of Prague

The Start of the Thirty Years War

'*This business is like to put all Christendom in combustion.*'

Dudley Carleton, England's ambassador in The Hague: 18 September 1619

The armed conflict between the Catholic and Protestant powers of the Holy Roman Empire started when a delegation of local noblemen from the Bohemian representative estates forced their way into Prague's Hradcany Castle. They had arrived to protest against the imposition of Catholic policies on Bohemia (now part of the modern Czech Republic), a country inherited in 1526 by the Hapsburgs as part of their family domain. The rebellion led by the reformer Jan Huss (1369-1415), along with his subsequent martyrdom, had made Bohemia fertile territory for Protestantism. But the Catholic archduke Ferdinand of Styria, cousin and heir to the Holy Roman Emperor Matthias (r. 1612-19), had pursued a policy of intolerant Catholicism since becoming heir presumptive to the kingdom of Bohemia. Jaroslav von Martinitz and Wilhelm von Slavata, the two regents who governed Bohemia in the name of the Hapsburg king and emperor, were now confronted by Bohemian fury. Attacks on Protestant churches had violated the religious toleration enshrined in the charter of 1609 granted to Bohemia by the emperor, Rudolf II. Ferdinand had also assumed the right of succession to Bohemia's throne without prior election by the country's representative estates. The ensuing violence was inspired by a similar defenestration during the Hussite rebellion. The regents were thrown out of a window and fell more than fifty feet into the castle ditch where a dungheap broke their fall.

Count Heinrich von Thurm led the revolt of the Bohemian Protestants and the Protestant Union sent an army commanded by Count Ernst von Mansfeld to support von Thurm's rebels. Wenceslas William von Ruppa formed a provisional government which replaced the Hapsburg administration. The Evangelical Union of German Protestant princes, led by Frederick, the Elector Palatine, prepared to confront the Catholic League of German princes led by Maximilian, elector of Bavaria. The death in March 1619 of the conciliatory emperor Matthias aggravated the crisis since Ferdinand, now reigning as King Ferdinand II of Bohemia, was also elected Matthias' successor as emperor. The Bohemian estates deposed Ferdinand and then elected as king the Elector Frederick V (the Count Palatine) who, in November, was crowned in Prague's St Vitus' cathedral. Radical Calvinists had followed Frederick to Prague and 'purged' the churches of images, pictures and statues. Frederick's queen, Elisabeth, the daughter of James I of England, objected to the Catholic crucifix on Prague's Charles bridge, describing it as a 'naked bather' and had it thrown into the River Vltava. The graphic imagery of printed flysheets spread news of the iconoclasm and defenestration across Europe. Meanwhile, Frederick presented himself as a champion of European Protestantism, and the Spanish branch of the Hapsburgs, drawing on the resources of its possessions in the kingdoms of Naples and Sicily, prepared to intervene as Catholic defenders.

Ever since the Peace of Augsburg (1555) the German states had developed along separate religious lines with the population of each state followed their rulers' confessional allegiances. The arrangement meant peace of a kind but no true religious tolerance (except in the imperial cities) and it applied only to Catholics and Lutherans since the provisions excluded Calvinists. German churches, along with educational and welfare programmes, were administered by the princes and the Christian welfare state acquired its German roots. The emperor Rudolph II, a cultivated and introspective fantasist, was based at the Hradcany palace where he surrounded himself with astronomers and alchemists. Rudolph introduced Counter-

Reformation policies into the empire's Catholic territories but it was his more active brother, and imperial successor, Matthias who attempted the restoration of Austrian Hapsburg authority. Meanwhile, Calvinism became an ever more dynamic presence in the territory of the Electoral Palatinate in the west, which became a centre linking the German, French, Dutch and Bohemian members of an international Calvinist network. Lutheranism, whose chief advocate was Electoral Saxony, aimed at state stability and preached obedience to the ruler's will. Ferdinand, while archduke of Austria, had been responsible for a brutal extermination of Protestantism in Styria, Carinthia and Carniola from 1596 onwards. Maximilian I of Bavaria established a Catholic League in 1609 with Spanish support while Frederick IV of the Palatinate founded an equivalent Protestant Union of German princes in 1608 linked to France, England and the United Provinces. As the religious dispute accelerated the emperor Rudolf was forced to grant religious freedom to the Hungarian estates in 1606 and then to the Bohemian ones. His brother and successor Matthias was elected king within their territories by the Austrian, Hungarian and Moravian estates and Matthias had also given the Bohemian estates the right to elect their king after he became emperor. Ferdinand therefore represented a particularly savage Austrian regression.

The Thirty Years War falls into four phases and shows how, as the Swedish king Gustavus Adolphus said, 'things had come to such a pass that all wars being waged in Europe were mixed up together and became one war.'

During the war's first phase (1618-23) Catholic forces triumphed followng the Protestant defeat at the battle of the White Mountain in 1620 near Prague: Heidelberg in the Palatinate was stormed; Westphalia and Lower Saxony were occupied; Ferdinand was restored to his throne. Bohemia was now governed directly from Vienna: the country was forcibly re-Catholicized and German culture imposed upon it. Christian IV of Denmark emerged as a protagonist during the conflict's second phase (1625-9) and the Bohemian nobleman Albrecht von Wallenstein, a Catholic convert commanding a mercenary army, subjected most of northern Germany to his personal control after the Danish army was pushed back to Jutland. By the Edict of Restitution (1629) the emperor ordered all Protestants to surrender the church lands they had acquired since the peace of Augsburg and when Wallenstein, whose mercenary army contained many non-Catholics, objected he was dismissed.

Gustavus Adolphus of Sweden, the Protestant champion during the conflict's Swedish period (1628-35), was supported by France for tactical anti-Hapsburg reasons. At the battle of Breitenfeld he liberated the Palatinate and then entered Bavaria. With the Swedes threatening Vienna the emperor was forced to recall Wallenstein. At the battle of Lutzen the Swedes were victorious but Gustavus was killed. The League of Heilbronn revived the Protestant cause and Wallenstein decided to start independent peace negotiations with the Swedes and their Saxon allies. He was then placed under the ban of the empire and assassinated. At the battle of Nordlingen Sweden lost its control of southern Germany but a weary emperor concluded the Peace of Prague (1635) with the Lutheran princes.

During the final, Franco-Swedish, phase (1635-48) France protected the League of Heilbronn whose Calvinist members had been excluded from the peace provisions of 1635. France pursued its own state interests by declaring war on Spain, allying itself with Sweden, and invading Alsace. The war now advanced on three fronts: in the Netherlands, on the Rhine, and in Saxony. In 1638 the French gained Breisach on the Rhine and their victory at Rocroi in the Ardennes was a decisive blow to Spanish military might. The death of the emperor Ferdinand and the accession of Ferdinand III (1637-57) led to informal peace negotiations which culminated in the Treaty of Westphalia in 1648.

The treaty confirmed Franco-Swedish dominance and the subordination of the Hapsburgs to the German princes. Calvinists now had the same rights as Catholics and Lutherans. The year 1624 was the point in time which determined church possessions. Individual denominational changes were allowed for, except in the case of the Upper Palatinate and the emperor's hereditary lands where only Catholicism could be tolerated. The treaty gave the German princes the right to sign foreign treaties and all imperial legislation had to be approved by the Diet. Bavaria remained an electorate and the Palatinate returned to its electoral status. Switzerland and the United Provinces were granted independence and left the empire. French power was confirmed: it received the southern part of upper Alsace and acquired sovereignty over Metz, Toul and Verdun. Its border points on the Rhine were secured by bridgeheads at Breisach and Philippsburg. Brandenburg got eastern Pomerania and also therefore a new frontier with Poland. Sweden got western Pomerania including Stettin, as well as Bremen and Verden. The mouths of Germany's three great rivers, the Rhine, Elbe and Oder, were controlled by, respectively, the Dutch, Danes and Swedes. The French held the middle Rhine. German resentment would demand a later restitution. Austria, once an empire, was now just one of the four predominant German states along with Bavaria, Saxony and Brandenburg-Prussia. France and Spain continued their war until 1659.

The ideal of a united Christendom had vanished and was replaced by a European continent whose countries tolerated each other's mutually exclusive sovereignty within internationally agreed boundaries. Witch-hunting persecutions had been a major by-product of the period's paranoia. But the carnage of war confirmed the enlightened view that a secularized state and religious toleration were the only way to gain and keep a European peace. Westphalia established that a subject whose faith was different from the ruler's was not an automatic traitor.

This was Europe's first civil war and would not be repeated until 1914. The German population fell from twenty-one to around thirteen million: urban centres lost thirty per cent, and rural areas some sixty per cent, of their total population. Arable turned to pasture and agrarian serfdom returned as a way of tying down the diminished labour force to a deserted land. Beyond Germany the general crisis of the European 1640s showed the internal problems confronted by central power however 'sovereign' its aspirations. France, victorious abroad, was shaken by the Fronde aristocratic rebellion (1648-53); England's civil war was also an Irish and Scottish conflict; Spain faced rebellions in Catalonia and Portugal; Cossacks revolted in Poland-Lithuania. The foundations of this international order were no more secure than the dead illusion of a united Christendom.

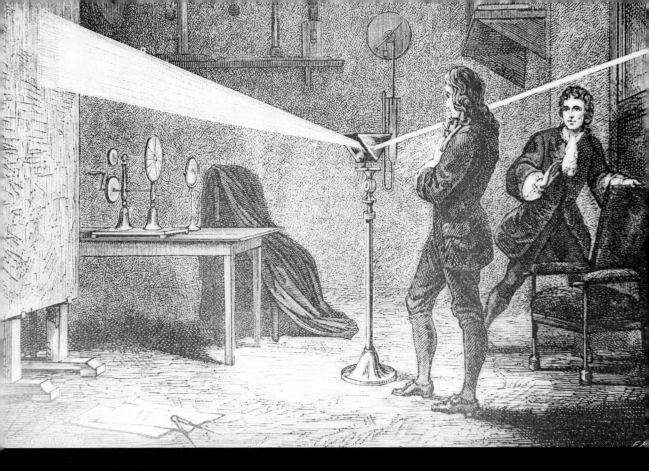

5 June 1661

Isaac Newton Matriculates at Cambridge University

Modern Science Begins

'*Nature is not simply an organized body like a clock...but is a living body which has life and perception...*'

Anne, Lady Conway a self-taught enthusiast, gets Newton's point (1692) orn the poor son of an illiterate Lincolnshire yeoman, Newton arrived at Trinity College, Cambridge as a subsizar – a category of scholar who paid for his education by waiting on other students as a servant. The curriculum of mediaeval scholasticism remained the basis of Cambridge education as was the case in the other great European universities. Education was not a question of discovery or invention; it was based instead on mastering the knowledge of past authorities, especially Aristotle. Science, to the limited extent it appeared at all, was 'natural philosophy' based on the writings of the ancient Greeks. Newton, the first scientist to be knighted for his work, established the authority of a new science and attitude towards knowledge since his discoveries about gravity and motion transformed both the scholarly and popular view of the physical world. Later he also developed the calculus which could measure velocity and rates of change. The notorious invective of his quarrel with the German mathematician von Leibnitz about who first invented the calculus, although an ugly episode, helped to put science in the forefront of public awareness. Newton changed the mental furniture of his time but his age was also ready to receive him since he lived during the initial stages of the Enlightenment, the European movement which excoriated fanaticism and superstition and stood for reason, tolerance and debate. He therefore escaped the accusations of magic and heresy levelled against earlier scientists. 'Rational' and 'irrational' ,however, existed side by side in Newton's own mind. He treated alchemy seriously, took a literalist view of Biblical prophecy, and wrote extensively on both. Newton's sense of an ultimate mystery, a divine unity, was profound and is basic to his idea of an ordered universe.

Newton graduated in 1665 but then had to return home for two years because plague closed the university. During this period he worked out his fundamental ideas about nature according to an 'experimental philosophy'. The French philosopher René Descartes' popular new physical science was an advance on Aristotle who thought that there were qualities, or attributes, within objects which explained why they moved towards or away from each other. Descartes showed a more impersonal universe in which what mattered was the calculation and measurement of rates of movement and change, of attraction and repulsion. For Newton this was a great advance. But he also thought that Descartes was wrong to rely on a mere theory which maintained that all physical objects consisted of invisible particles of matter. Descartes considered the operations of such objects, whether they were trees or stones, animals or humans, were reducible to the motion and interaction of their constituent particles. Newton thought that this theory was just a hypothesis. His science of 'Optics', by contrast, would reveal how a universe constructed on mathematical regularities was a demonstrable truth.

Newton's experiments with glass prisms held against angles of light showed that white light was composed of different colours. He made a further discovery when he directed a single isolated colour from the first prism to the next: some colours were more refractable than others. Any colour could be designated by a number which showed the degree of its refractability. This was a profounder reduction of the qualitative to the quantitative than anything achieved by Descartes. Newton had avoided any hypotheses about the ultimate 'nature' of light – what it might be in itself – and did not seek to demonstrate the means by which colours are made. His scientific rigour was based on humility about what the human mind could, and could not, do. To go beyond the appearances of nature would be a conceited, as well as futile, speculation on ultimate causes and the mystery of the mind of God. The truths of Newton's optics had instead explained what actually happened, and that was more than enough since it involved a major paradox. Common sense had said that colours were modifications of white light. But common sense was wrong. All colours were components of white.

The Copernican intuition that the earth is not fixed and that it is not the centre of the universe had also subverted common sense. The geocentric system of Aristotle and Ptolemy which put the earth at the centre had been accepted because it corresponded to what the naked eye told the human mind. It was perfectly adequate for Columbus and his navigators on their voyages of discovery. The heliocentric theory of Nicolaus Copernicus did not change the ancient Greek description of the universe as a revolution of concentric spheres; he just changed the location of the heavenly bodies within those spheres and his system remained one of circular shapes moving in perfect circularity. Copernicus' work was based on an aesthetic hunch and he had neither made any calculations nor any observations. Neither in intention nor, initially, in effect was this a dissident theory. Copernicus dedicated his *De Revolutionibus* to Pope Paul III at a time when Catholicism was more relaxed about scientific changes than Protestantism with its literalist view of the Bible. Only in the age of Galileo Galilei (1564-1642) did the Catholic Church decide to support Ptolemy's now defunct system since his telescope revealed a multiplicity of stars and suggested a dislocating infinity. The popular acceptance of Copernicanism in the century before Newton's birth was a very gradual and patchy process. Johannes Kepler abandoned the Aristotelian idea of the circular perfection of celestial movements and showed a more subtle symmetry. He also, crucially, showed that the sun actually caused the motion of the planets rather than just illuminating them. This was a major step towards a mechanical explanation of the universe.

Galileo's work on mechanics and the strength of materials helped Newton to develop a science of dynamics as a step towards his account of universal gravitation. He also benefited from Kepler's suggestion that the centripetal force towards the sun would decrease in proportion to the square of the distance of each planet from the sun. Robert Hooke's work on this square of the distance would also be important, but it was Newton who saw how these could be universal principles, who made the calculations that demonstrated them, and who showed that the elliptical orbit of the planets would follow. His new account showed how the centripetal force holding the planets in their given orbits around the sun decreases with the square of the planets' distance from the sun. He could therefore establish the centripetal force necessary to divert a body from its rectilinear path into a given circle. He also demonstrated how a planet moves faster the closer it gets to the sun because the force of gravity increases in order to balance the increased centrifugal force. These discoveries led to Newton's law of universal gravitation which is expressed in three laws of motion: a body remains in a state of rest (the principle of inertia) unless compelled to change that state by a force impressed on it; the change of motion (which is the change of velocity times the mass of body) is proportional to the force impressed; to every action there is an equal and opposite reaction.

It was the generality of Newton's system which was important. He had unified all the physical phenomena on earth with those in the heavens, and the movements

of these phenomena could be both observed and measured. No longer could
the heavenly bodies be seen as determining, causally, the earth. The associated
displacement of astrology into the rubbish bin of exploded beliefs was a momentous
event and one which changed literary as well as scientific culture. Newton's great
work *Philosophiae Naturalis Principia Mathematica* (1687) was a powerful rejection
of hypotheses whether of the occult or the mechanical kind: 'In this philosophy
particular propositions are inferred from the phenomena, and afterwards rendered
general by induction.' The *Principia* was written in Latin at a time when European
scholars were turning to their own languages. But if the abandonment of Latin
meant the break-up of one international tradition the *Principia* also showed how, for
scientists, mathematics could succeed Latin as an universal language.

The Royal Society, given its royal charter in 1662, was a power base for Newton
and Newtonianism – the scientific attitude which saw knowledge as a dynamic and
progressive force rather than a conservative preserver of old systems. Its members
made contributions in the form of letters (the basis of the scientific article) which
were harder to censor than published books. Knowledge was piecemeal, a question
of recording advances in particular areas and advancing provisional conclusions.
The society had evolved out of the meetings of English scientists during the
Commonwealth which had already shown the practical connection between science
and politics. The mathematician John Wallis belonged to this group and helped
the Cromwellian regime to break the royalist ciphers. The belief that a thorough
reformation of knowledge could lead to greater national power had already been
outlined systematically by Francis Bacon in works such as *Novum Organum* (1620).
Whether they had been conforming Cromwellians in the 1650s or equally conforming
royalists in the 1660s, English scientists were continuously Baconian in attitude.
Newton's effect boosted the idea that precision of experiment and the experience of
things should be the reality. The world, therefore, should not be seen through the web
of words, whose fine distinctions of verbal categories and definitions were basic to
scholasticism. This was also part of a wider cultural shift which reacted against the
extravagant and bellicose rhetoric of the Puritan preachers. Keeping the peace meant
sticking to a pared-down language and the simple precision of the new English prose
style of the 1660s marks a profound change in the history of the language.

Newton's revolution, being universal, was a practical one. He invented his own short
telescope which had a magnification power of forty times and used concave mirrors
instead of the lenses used in Galileo's refracting telescope. Astronomical information,
especially about past equinoxes, was the basis of Newton's universal chronology
which applies right across world cultures. He also shared in the contemporary
English zeal for collecting and analyzing social data. The demographer John Graunt
analyzed patterns of mortality in 1660s' London and Sir William Petty's *Treatise
on Taxes and Contributions* showed how productivity was a source of national
wealth. The new understanding of mass, force and motion also stimulated the ability
of advanced western societies to wage war which, in turn, stimulated scientific
discoveries. Newton was a solitary genius and his achievements were based on a
specifically Protestant interest in the individual experience. But Newtonianism as
a system of knowledge helped western European countries to organize themselves
collectively for global expansion and dominance.

12 September 1683

The Ottomans Abandon the Siege of Vienna

The Tide Turns for Turkish Expansion in Europe

'*There are nine kitchens in this Seraglio…feeding 13,400, including more than eight hundred women and about the same number of eunuchs.*'

The Sultan's personal physician describes Topkapi Palace's domestic arrangements (c.1620)

From July to September 1683 Vienna was besieged by an Ottoman army at a time when the German princes also faced a challenge from the armies of Louis XIV on the Rhine. This problem of a war on both western and eastern fronts would recur in German history. Help came from the king of Poland, then a vast country including Lithuania, stretching across central Europe: Jan Sobieski embraced a war with the Turks as a diversion from his domestic conflict with the Polish nobility and, helped by Austrian subsidies, took command of the city's defence in early September.

Sobieski started the day of 12 September by praying in the chapel on the heights of Kahlenberg in the Vienna Woods and then, during the afternoon, rode down the hill to unleash his forces on the Ottoman army which was dissolving in scenes of slaughter and panic. His winged hussars had been especially effective. The following day Sobieski sat down in the tent of the Grand Vizier, Merzifonlu Kara Mustafa Pasa (1634-83) the chief minister, and described, in a letter to his wife, the details of the day. The vizier had escaped with just one horse, leaving behind 'enough powder and ammunition for a million men'. The conquered Turkish encampment was, he thought, as large as the city of Warsaw and the Turks had abandoned their crack corps of janissary soldiers in the trenches while killing as many Austrians as they could before leaving: 'The Vizier had a marvellously beautiful ostrich – but this too he had killed...' The Ottomans had evidently made their quarters comfortable during their siege since the vizier 'had baths; he had gardens and fountains; rabbits and cats, and a parrot which kept flying about so that we could not catch it...' Sobieski later sent the captured green flag of the Ottomans to the Pope with the comment, echoing the remark of Charles V after his victory over German protestant forces at the battle of Muhlberg: *Veni, vidi, Deus Vicit* (I came, I saw, God conquered).

Kara Mustafa was beheaded in Belgrade on the sultan's orders and his head brought back to Istanbul where it was presented to the sultan on a silver dish. The Koprulu, an Albanian family who for thirty years monopolized the office of vizier, adopted a policy of revived Ottoman expansion as a diversionary response to the domestic difficulties created by their attempt at disciplining and controlling the janissaries. A disputed succession in Transylvania brought the Turks into direct conflict with the Austrian Hapsburgs and their assault on central Europe included an attack on the Polish province of Podolia. The Turks also allied themselves officially with the Hungarian Protestants who, under the leadership of Count Imre Tokoly, rebelled against the persecutions of their Hapsburg rulers. Hungary was partitioned after the battle of St Gothard and Austria had to deliver tribute payments to the Ottomans. Declaring Hungary to be their vassal state, the Ottoman force had advanced up the Danube basin towards Vienna.

The immediate result of their defeat was the retreat of the Ottomans under the onslaught of the Holy Alliance which, formed in 1684, consisted of Austria, Poland, Venice and, subsequently, Russia. This Turkish withdrawal continued until 1918. Hungary was liberated from the Turks – the fruition of a long-term Austrian Hapsburg goal. The Imperial Diet meeting at Pressburg transferred the Hungarian crown to the Hapsburgs and led to the creation of the Austro-Hungrian dual monarchy. The Peace of Carlowitz in 1699 confirmed the return of Hungary to Austria, of Podolia to Poland, of Azov to Muscovy and of the Morea to Venice. The

Peace returned Austria to great power status. From now on the Ottomans found that their European provinces were squeezed between Austria in the west and Russian power advancing from the east. Three Russo-Turkish wars in the eighteenth century ended with the whole of the northern Black Sea coast under Russian control. The Russian Tsar became the protector of the Ottomans' Christian Orthodox subjects although much of the Balkans remained under Turkish rule. Europe's 'eastern question' had arrived. Austria conquered Belgrade twice and was supported by many Serbs as an anti-Ottoman force. But it was Russia which emerged as the great pan-Slavic defender of the Serbs. Greece, another Orthodox land, also looked to the Russians as a Hellenic national consciousness developed in the eighteenth century.

The Austria-Hungary which emerged in the eighteenth century was a multinational state with a core of eleven different nationalities held together by the residual Turkish threat, the Hapsburg dynasty and its associated court nobility, Catholicism, and a ramshackle administration. Vienna was reborn as an imperial city and architecturally embellished by Baroque pomp. The slogan 'Austria can accomplish anything she sets her mind to' became both a popular aspiration and an example of self-conscious Viennese irony. Bureaucratic waste, protectionist economics and poor planning of state budgets established a pattern which would last until 1918. The monopolies granted for the production of salt, iron and textiles in areas such as Silesia, Linz and Graz, of silk in St Ploten and of glass in Bohemia, failed to improve the chronic state debt. In 1711, following rebellions of the Hungarian nobility, Austria was forced to grant limited self-administration to Hungary subject to the laws of the Imperial Diet. Hungarian national consciousness, unlike that of the Czechs, was not therefore crushed. This prepared the way for the late eighteenth-century foundation of the University of Buda and a literary revival of the Magyar language.

Much diplomatic energy was spent on gaining diplomatic recognition for the Pragmatic Sanction which would guarantee the Hapsburg succession in the female line since Maria Theresa (1717-80) was the only child of the emperor Charles VI (r. 1711-40). But she only succeeded to the title of archduchess of Austria since the elector of Bavaria seized the imperial throne on her father's death. The title was then transferred to her husband, Francis I and son Joseph II. Her succession also led to the decision of Frederick the Great of Prussia to invade Austrian Silesia, one of the richest Hapsburg possessions and thereby causing the major war of the Austrian Succession. The state of Brandenburg-Prussia, with its army run by an aristocratic officer corps and based on a system of peasant conscriptions, and its formidable education and welfare reforms, had risen from the ashes of mid-seventeenth century Germany. The House of Hohenzollern had deprived the estates of the right to consent to taxation and built up a compliant nobility by granting them exemptions from taxation in return for an unqualified obedience to the royal house. The Prussian government built extensive roads, dykes and canals. The first colonial settlement in west Africa of Gross-Friedrichsburg dates back to 1683. Under Frederick William, the Great Elector (r.1640-88), the army increased from 8,000 to 23,000 and this large fighting force defeated the Swedes, until then northern Europe's greatest army, at the battle of Fehrbellin. Under Frederick William I (r.1713-40) the army increased in size to 83,000 out of a total population of just over two million and Prince Leopold of Anhalt-Dessau introduced the infantry's disciplined, Prussian, drill. Halle became the first Prussian university and the edict of 1717 established a high-quality system of public education. Berlin flowered as distinctively as Vienna. In 1700 Frederick III sold the Prussian electoral vote to the Hapsburgs in return for recognition of the right to Prussian independent kingship. The acquisition of Silesa, recognized at the peace of Aix-la-Chapelle was a major boost to Prussian power and the first partition of Poland between Prussia, Austria and Russia was a policy which could unite three otherwise opposed powers to their mutual advantage.

Russia, under the rule of Peter I and of Catherine II, was the other power that flourished because of the Ottoman withdrawal. During the Great Northern war (1700-21) Peter defeated both Sweden and her ally Poland-Lithuania: the Swedish provinces of Livonia and Ingria were seized and provided the site for the foundation in 1703 of the new city of St Petersburg – the Tsar's 'window on the west' and the symbol of his adoption of western technological means in order to maintain a brutal personal rule. The inefficiencies of the old Muscovite army were replaced by a state adapted to war and a poll-tax supported a permanent army of over 300,000 soldiers. Serfdom and autocracy remained and were even strengthened by the introduction in 1701 of a new political police force. Priests were ordered to break the confessional and nobles were publicly flogged if they evaded state duties. Catherine II presided over a compromise between Peter's autocracy and the rights of the service nobility created by the Romanov dynasty in order to assist their government. But in granting the nobles their new rights the Romanovs had in fact divided their own power base. These contradictions and enfeeblements would become increasingly obvious. For the moment it was Russia's territorial expansion which stunned the rest of Europe: it absorbed the whole of the Ottomans' Black Sea provinces and the Crimea before then moving into the Caucasus and central Asia. The move across Siberia to the Pacific was quite as remarkable: in the 1740s the Russians were exploring Alaska. Ukraine had been a useful buffer state for Russia against the Ottomans and, from the mid-seventeenth century, the Tsarist regime allowed its autonomy and ruled through the local nobility. But, like the Crimea, the political possibilities created by the Ottoman withdrawal led to its complete annexation. Just as in Poland, Russian immigration led to an intolerant Russification bent on extinguishing the local language and culture.

But it was the Poles who were the greatest victims of eighteenth-century Europe. The three partitions of Poland happened because Prussia and Austria would only allow a Russian army into Poland if they received reassurance in the form of Polish territory. The election in 1679 of Friedrich-August, elector of Saxony, as Poland's king Augustus II, after his quick Catholic conversion, led to disaster. Poland-Lithuania was dragged by Saxony into the Great Northern war and was quarrelled over between Russians and Swedes. The king was restored with Russian troops and was therefore seen as a Russian pawn. When the Polish nobles rebelled against Augustus, Peter the Great intervened to turn Poland into, effectively, a Russian dependency – at which point the European balance of power came into play and demanded the appropriate slices of a dismembered Polish body politic. The victory of a Polish king in 1683 had helped to create the international system whose cynical diplomacy ensured the dissolution of his own country.

11 April 1713

The Peace of Utrecht

The End of Louis XIV's Dominance in Europe

'At our age, maréchal, one is not lucky.'

A sixty-eight-year-old Louis XIV commiserates with François Villeroi after his defeat by Marlborough at the battle of Ramillies (1706)

Spain's decline as a great power destabilized the politics and diplomacy of late seventeenth-century Europe and the country's debility was personified in the mental illness of King Charles II ('Carlos the Bewitched'), a genetic victim of the Hapsburg policy of inter-marriage within the dynasty. The fact that Charles' reign (1665-1700) was so long compounded Spain's problems while his childlessness raised the thorny question of legitimate succession. The Peace of the Pyrenees in1660 had confirmed France's displacement of Spain as Europe's greatest power and its provisions included the arrangement of a marriage between the young Louis XIV of France and the Spanish Infanta, Maria Teresa. The Bourbon-Hapsburg dynastic linkage led Charles II to name Philip of Anjou, Louis XIV's grandson, as his successor on the Spanish throne. Charles' death, therefore, realized the threat of a French power block spreading across the Pyrenees as well as into the Spanish American colonies. It was William III of England who had conceived of a Grand Alliance of European powers opposed to French hegemony and by the time the alliance embarked on the War of the Spanish Succession (1701-1713/4), it contained practically every European power of consequence: Britain, Holland, Austria, Prussia, Hanover, Savoy and Portugal. Charles, archduke of Austria, became the coalition's candidate for the Spanish throne.

On the eve of war in 1700, French foreign policy, while still ambitious, lacked the élan of the earlier years of Louis' reign. Europe's most theatrical ruler had tried to establish France's 'natural' eastern boundary along the Rhine. French 'absolutist' government had faced down domestic opposition and the campaign to ensure the country's territorial expansion demonstrated a similar relentlessness. The campaign to extend France's north-eastern boundaries led to war against the Spanish who as a result lost many of their fortresses in the Spanish Netherlands – then known as Flanders. But France failed to achieve her major objectives in the war against the Dutch (1672-9). French aggression had brought out the leadership qualities of prince William of Orange and in 1672 the States General of Holland named the future William III of England as the country's ruler, or stadholder, for life. William would be Louis' implacable foe. The League of Augsburg was formed in 1686 to resist French encroachment on German territory and Louis' invasion of the Palatinate in 1688 led to the war of 1689-97 in which the alliance led by England, Holland and the Austrian Hapsburgs inflicted a major defeat on Louis: the French had to restore the right bank of the Rhine to Austria.

Prince Eugene of Savoy and John Churchill (later created Duke of Marlborough) were the master strategists of the War of the Spanish Succession. A series of brilliantly executed allied victories at Blenheim (1704), Ramillies (1706), and Oudenaarde (1708) forced France on the defensive. Malplaquet (1709) was inconclusive but the battle saved France from invasion. The coalition's objectives changed, however, at the death of the emperor Joseph I since it led to the succession of his brother Charles, the erstwhile archduke of Austria, as Charles III, ruler of the Austrian territories. Charles was also duly elected emperor. The danger to the allies now was not just French hegemony but a restored and reunited Hapsburg axis, uniting Spain with Austria.

The requirements of a balance designed to prevent the European dominance of any single power are therefore illustrated in the Treaty of Utrecht whose provisions resulted from a series of negotiations mostly concentrated between March and April 1713. The Dutch kept their fortresses on the Flanders border and France's ambitions were curtailed but she was allowed to keep Lille, Franche-Comté and Alsace. Philip of Anjou, the first Spanish Bourbon monarch, got his throne and also the Spanish American colonies. But Spain's European empire was partitioned: the Austrians got the Spanish Netherlands, Milan, Naples and Sardinia, while Sicily was handed over to Savoy. This Italian subjection to foreign powers who would impose unjust demands on the peasantry explains the later development of organizations such as the mafia, originally formed to protect the rural poor.

The single greatest victor at Utrecht was the newly created (1707) United Kingdom of Great Britain. It retained Gibraltar which had been seized from the Spanish and gained Newfoundland, Nova Scotia and the Hudson Bay territories from the French. By a separate agreement Spain gave Britain the exclusive right to supply her colonies with African slaves for the next thirty years. This would be a vast source of British riches and Louis XIV's indifference to this major concession reveals both the weakness of a French imperial policy fixated by territorial acquisition and also the economic drive behind emerging British imperial ambition.

Half a century earlier the Anglo-French relationship had been very different. The countries of the British Isles were recovering from a ruinous civil war. The English Commonwealth was a republican regime which became a military dictatorship after Oliver Cromwell became Lord Protector in 1653. The government reasserted order from above but its austerity contributed to its unpopularity and led to a subsequent restoration of the Stuart dynasty in 1660. However, the reign of Charles II also witnessed the return of political and religious tension since Charles, a crypto-Catholic educated at the French court, was an admirer of French absolutism and tried to avoid government through parliaments.

France's recovery from her civil wars in the second half of the sixteenth century had been, by contrast, spectacular. Henri IV, founder of the Bourbon dynasty, had converted from Protestantism to Catholicism for the sake of national unity, and a similar concern with the integrity of the French state shaped his successors' policies. Absolutism, the belief in the elevation of the king's indivisible sovereignty over all other sources of power, was the most dynamic doctrine in seventeenth century politics. And in the persons of the Bourbons kings, as well as in advisers such as Cardinal Richelieu, chief minister to Louis XIII, absolutism acquired its most effective and steely exponents.

The policy was made visible in the elegant regularity of the classical façades which adorned the public buildings, palaces and churches of a country whose elites appeared to agree that the absolutist uniformity of 'one faith, one king, one law' was the only way to keep a country together. The diplomacy of *raison d'état* dictated opportunistic alliances with any foreign power, whether Protestant or Catholic, which served French interests. And the state, through its patronage of the arts and scholarship, by its establishment in 1635 of the Academie Française, discovered the political uses of cultural credibility by demonstrating that France stood in the lineage of every great imperial power which had a self-imposed duty to civilize, as well as subdue, its neighbours. If the sixteenth century had been Spain's golden age, the seventeenth century belonged to France. The classical refinement of the plays of Racine and Corneille, the broader effects of Molière, the harmonious compositions of the painters Claude and Poussin, showed a unique concentration of cultural brilliance allied to political success.

Louis' palace of Versailles, built between 1624 and 1708, showed both the strength and the weakness of this policy of self-confident, and self-conscious, glory. The rebellion of the Fronde (1648-53) was the last major assertion of the independence of the nobility. Subsequently, the king's policy of concentrating the French aristocracy at court bound the nobility to the person of the monarch who was, in absolutist style, the vice-regent of God. Rebellion would therefore be impious as well as treasonable. But Versailles' remote hierarchies also separated the French crown from the French people and, since the glory was founded on fundamental economic weakness, the classicism became sterile. Colbert as minister of finance developed the first national, state-directed, economy of the modern age. This meant state-built roads and canals but also state monopolies which discouraged innovation. And the revocation in 1685 by Louis of the religious tolerance established by the Edict of Nantes (1598) led to the emigration of half a million French Protestants – the class whose business vigour was basic to the economy. From now on the monarchy attracted the mounting criticism of the intelligentsia whose plays and satires, articles, books and pamphlets, teased and condemned this *ancien régime* for its reactionary intolerance and culpable inefficiency. The creativity of the eighteenth-century French Enlightenment was a direct reaction against the rigidity of thought and the political failures bequeathed by Louis XIV. By 1715 the government's net income was 69 million livres, expenditure was 132 million livres, the public debt's figures varied between 830 million and 2,800 million livres, and yet the nobility remained tax-exempt.

Early eighteenth-century England, however, had evolved a constitutional monarchy. The militantly Catholic and pro-French James II (r. 1685-8) had fled to France after the invasion led by his son-in-law, the Dutch prince William of Orange, who was then offered the crown by the English parliament and reigned as William III. The 'Glorious Revolution' (1688-9) confirmed the power of a Protestant landed class and transferred the sovereignty which had been the prerogative of monarchs to a parliament which represented the interests of landowners. The Habeas Corpus Act of 1679 had already established protection against arbitrary arrest. From 1689 onwards English political arrangements, reacting against Stuart attempts at absolutist rule, divided the legislature from the executive and the king's government therefore needed parliament in order to raise taxation. But the English regime, while tolerant of Protestant nonconformity, distrusted Catholicism, and the imposition of the constitutional settlement on Ireland and Scotland led to the persecution of Catholics in both countries. From 1701 Louis XIV officially endorsed the Stuarts' claim to a restoration of their throne and the threat of French-supported domestic insurrection lay behind the Act of Union between England and Scotland. This new Britain, dominated by England and ratified by Church-State Anglicanism, was maintained by the Hanoverian dynasty and the country's parliament developed a two party political system in which Whigs, supporters of the principles of 1688-9 and associated with commercial, City of London interests, confronted squierarchical Tories, some of whom were nostalgic for the divine right of kings. In reality power remained in the hands of a few for the system was lubricated by patronage. The job-hunting nature of the British elite, its devotion to profit, and its indifference to ideology explain the adamantine political stability and the driven commercial vitality of the country whose leaders seized their chance at Utrecht in 1713. Britain's great power status would last exactly 201 years.

26 August 1768

The *Endeavour* Leaves Plymouth

Captain Cook Explores the Pacific and Discovers New South Wales

'Look around…observe the magnificence of our metropolis – the extent of our empire – the immensity of our commerce and the opulence of our people.'

English expansiveness excites Charles James Fox in Parliament (1763)

The *Endeavour* which sailed from Plymouth was a recently renamed Whitby collier ship of a kind that its captain, the forty-year-old James Cook (1728-1779), would have been familiar with while serving his apprenticeship as a commercial seaman in the North Sea. Although not beautiful, it was a sturdy and spacious ship weighing 368 tons and measuring 98 feet in length with a beam of 29 feet. Equipped with eighteen months' supplies, it had been given a sheathing of wood filled with nails as a protection against the tropics' notorious teredos – the molluscs which bored into ships' timbers at sea. Cook, recently and hastily commissioned as an officer in the Royal Navy, had been ordered to sail to Tahiti where, on 3 June 1769, those members of the Royal Society on board would observe the transit of the planet Venus across the Sun. The calculation of more accurate figures for the Sun's distance from the earth would yield better data for celestial navigation at sea. But there was a further objective: Cook's *Endeavour* had been instructed to head south from Tahiti in order to discover whether a southern continent, the speculative *Terra Australis*, existed.

The first, highly professional, scientific expedition to the Pacific included the eminent botanist and zoologist Joseph Banks, Daniel Solander, who was a pupil of Carolus Linnaeus, the Swedish founder of modern botany, two botanist-draughtsmen, two footmen from the Banks'estates and two black servants as well as two large greyhounds. The *Endeavour* was well equipped with scientific instruments provided by the Royal Society as well as chemicals and containers to preserve specimens. The Admiralty had failed to provide a chronometer although John Harrison had only recently been awarded the prize for inventing the sea-going clock to measure longitude. However an astronomer from the Greenwich Observatory was on hand to fix the *Endeavour's* position by making lunar calculations and Cook had a commanding knowledge of the naval charts he had brought with him.

The son of a migrant Scottish farm labourer who had settled in Yorkshire, Cook became a sea apprentice at eighteen, working in a fleet of locally owned coal carrier ships and, studying mathematics in his spare time, became a skilled navigator and a ship's mate. He refused the offer to command a collier and decided to join the Royal Navy as an able seaman and was quickly promoted as a non-commissioned officer. He had a very good Seven Years War (1756-63) since the expertise he showed in surveying and navigating the challenging stretches of the St Lawrence river contributed to the British landing which was the prelude to its successful assault on Quebec – in which Cook took part. During the next five years Cook spent the summers in command of a schooner which surveyed the coast of Newfoundland and returned to England for the winter months, which he spent working on his charts. Having observed an eclipse of the sun in Newfoundland he submitted his calculations to the Royal Society – a confident act for a non-commissioned officer.

In choosing Cook, a clever meritocrat of humble origin, as the expedition leader, the Admiralty showed its priorities. The reforms of Lord Anson had professionalized the navy so that appointments owed more to talent than to birth. The aristocratic Alexander Dalrymple, who had hoped to lead the expedition, was a fine mathematician whose *Account of the Discoveries made in the South Pacifick Ocean, Previous to 1764* had argued for the existence of a vast Southern continent 'to counterpoise the land to the north, and to maintain the equilibrium necessary for the Earth's motion'. This territory was, he thought, probably greater even 'than the whole civilised part of Asia'. And there was also a political dimension to this claim at a time when Britain's North American colonies were becoming restive. Perhaps this southern continent, claimed by Britain, could be a substitute for North America and therefore 'sufficient to maintain the power, dominion and sovereignty of Britain by employing all its manufacturers and ships'. But Dalrymple, despite his connections, was passed over.

The belief in the existence of a vast southern continent was ancient. Ancient Greeks, obsessed by symmetry, argued that a large land mass north of the equator on the surface of the spherical earth needed an equivalent to exist in the south. Fifteenth-century Ptolemaic maps therefore showed a vast Antarctic continent which was attached to the tip of southern Africa. Although subsequent discoveries pushed it ever further south, the speculative continent survived in men's minds. Abraham Ortelius' *Theatrum Orbis Terrarum* (1570), the first modern atlas, still marked the South Polar area as '*Terra Australis nondum Cognita*' (the still unknown southern continent). The Dutchman Abel Tasman had circumnavigated Australia in 1642 and so proved that it was not part of this legendary southern continent. Cook would have to exhaust all the possibilities if he was to conclude that such a continent really was a fantasy.

The *Endeavour* sailed south and southwest of Tahiti down to a point of 40° latitude south. Finding no land there Cook turned west and came across New Zealand whose 2,400 mile coast he chartered in six months and whose two islands, having been circumnavigated, were therefore shown not to be contiguous with some southern continent. It was now March 1770 and the southern summer was ending. A return journey eastward was bound to hit harsh weather. Cook therefore pressed on westward and explored the east coast of Australia (then called New Holland). It was the Dutch explorers of the seventeenth century who had first charted the continent's northern and western coastlines. But there were no European settlements on this 'New Holland' although the ancestors of the Aboriginal inhabitants, who numbered between a quarter and half a million, had first arrived in Australia from Asia at least 60,000 years previously. Cook, on his northward voyage, took the decisive step which led to the emergence of a British Australia. On 22 August 1770 after landing on Possession Island off Cape York, he claimed the whole of the eastern coastline for the Crown and called it New South Wales.

The profusion of Australian nature led the delighted scientists to rename Stingray harbour, on the southeast coast, as Botany Bay. Cook and his men, stranded on land for a month when the *Endeavour* had to be repaired after almost foundering on the coral of the Great Barrier Reef, now learnt how to eat, and enjoy, kangaroo, turtles and clams. The voyage along the northern coast confirmed Cook's view that Australia was separated from New Guinea to the north. Having travelled home past the Cape, he returned to England in 1771, was presented to King George III, fêted by high society, and promoted to commander.

Cook's next expedition, leaving Plymouth in July 1772, would be a full circumnavigation of the earth by the southernmost possible latitude and the commander stuck to his Whitby colliers, choosing this time two such ships: the 462 ton *Resolution* and the 340 ton *Adventure*. Johann Reinhold Forster, a German scholar of international reputation, was the chief naturalist on board. The Board of

Longitude provided an astronomer for each ship and four chronomoters to calculate longitude – including one built to John Harrison's design. This journey would cover some 70,000 miles. After heading south the two ships were within the Antarctic circle at 60° latitude south within two weeks and what they discovered enlarged the human imagination.

The Arctic circle was already known. But the frozen and unpopulated Antarctic with its mountainous icebergs was a weirdly beautiful novelty, especially in the dazzling light of a southern summer in January. Accounts of this sight with its aesthetically thrilling suggestion of a dislocating infinity would feed the burgeoning imagination of European Romanticism in poetry and painting, in the landscapes of Caspar David Friedrich and in the works of S.T.Coleridge, whose 'Rime of the Ancient Mariner' evokes a similar, dangerous, journey. Cook was just seventy-five miles away from the Antarctic coastline when heavy mist forced him back north and then east. Having wintered in New Zealand he returned to the Antarctic circle and, on 30 January 1774, again turned back having reached a point of 71° latitude south and 105° longitude west. 'We could,' he wrote in his journal, 'not proceed one inch further south… the intention of the voyage has in every respect been fully answered, the Southern hemisphere sufficiently explored and a final end put to the searching after a Southern Continent, which has at times ingrossed the attention of some of the Maritime Powers for near two centuries past and the geographers of all ages.'

Cook arrived back in London on 30 July 1775, was promoted to captain and elected a Fellow of the Royal Society having shown conclusively that the fabled *Terra Australis* only existed in the landmasses of Australia, New Zealand and beyond the ice rim of Antarctica. His eastward journey (1776-9) past the cape to America's north-west coast and along the southern borders of the Arctic Ocean established that there was no navigable Northwest Passage, or a northeast one, connecting the Atlantic with the Pacific. He was killed on 14 February 1799 on the beach of Kealakekua, Hawaii on the return leg of his journey, by Polynesian natives who had stolen one of his boats.

The map of the known world had been established by the practical application of a scientific and enquiring mind in answer to an enduring question which had previously been the stuff of myth and legend. Cook is therefore a characteristic, but remarkable, example of the eighteenth-century Enlightenment. The accuracy of his reasoning showed the humanity as well as the efficiency of practical science since he solved the problem of scurvy. The surgeon James Lind had published his findings in 1753 that citrus fruit prevented the disease but Cook, ignorant of that work, drew his own independent and similar conclusions from tests he conducted with his sailors' diets. Because of their commander's experiments with oranges, lemons, sauerkraut, onions, grasses and celery, Cook's men were freed from the curse of scurvy which had habitually decimated crews on long voyages. He also enforced new standards of cleanliness on board by personally inspecting his men's hands and insisting on proper ventilation in their quarters. Cook's achievements are part of the story of British maritime supremacy but, despite his violent death, he achieved his greatest aims peacefully and by the application of a practical science to the advancement of knowledge and the betterment of humanity. That eighteenth-century belief in the possibility of progress inspired intellectual ambition and fired the human imagination.

4 July 1776

The US Declaration of Independence

The American Revolution

'Divided as they are into a thousand forms of policy and religion…they equally detest the pageantry of a king, and the supercilious hypocrisy of a bishop.'

An English pamphleteer describes Americans (19 December 1769)

A month after the British-American war had broken out in 1775, the second Continental Congress of American states was convened in Philadelphia. It was a precarious time to plan for the future as the British army had won the battles both of Lexington and of Concord. Like its pre-war predecessor the Congress was a pan-American institution whose members were learning how to cooperate institutionally within an emergent political union. It was the Virginian Convention a year later which took the bold move of instructing its delegate at the Congress, Richard Henry Lee, to propose the formation of a confederation independent of Britain with each state approving the new constitution. While the delegates debated, the American army started to win and British forces were forced to withdraw from Boston by General George Washington.

The prospect of an independent America raised the question of political authority. What was the basis of the legitimacy which required the obedience of a free people? This question would be answered by Thomas Jefferson – the dominant figure in the committee formed to draft a Declaration. Congress first approved on 2 July 1776 Lee's resolution that: 'That these United Colonies are... free and independent States... absolved from all allegiance to the British Crown.' Jefferson himself thought that 2 July was the real start of American Independence, but 4 July, the day when Congress approved his text (with the exception of its denunciation of slavery), became the date that mattered because the document, in just 1,500 words, crystallized the American cause and the quality of American values. Jefferson reflected the optimism of a successful society when he wrote: 'We hold these truths to be self-evident, that all men are created equal, that they are endowed by their Creator with certain inalienable Rights, that among these are Life, Liberty and the pursuit of Happiness.' The Declaration linked American success with the conviction that governments derived 'their just powers from the consent of the governed'. The people could therefore alter and abolish a government which denied the 'self-evident' truths which were both universally true and basic to American life. Jefferson had explained America to herself.

Church bells rang in Philadelphia where the local militia fired rounds of ammunition into the air in celebration (despite the wartime scarcity of gunpowder). In remote South Carolina a nine-year-old boy who would become America's seventh president, Andrew Jackson, read the Declaration to the illiterate backwoodsmen. George Washington paraded his troops at six in the evening so they might hear the encapsulation of the struggle's aims. Congress could now draw up articles of Confederation confirming that its alliance of states constituted the new government. These rushed to adopt their own radical constitutions which weakened the local executive and forced their legislatures to consult the electorate as often as possible. The confident mood led to the redistribution of lands owned by loyalists who were now accounted traitors.

It was the rigidity of the British government which created the crisis that led to the loss of thirteen colonies. The system was good at running wars but politically inflexible because the abuses of patronage, whereby power rested with a virtual oligarchy, kept governments in office but also insulated them from public opinion. It was therefore possible to persist with a disastrous policy. Mercantilism, the belief that each state should attain self-sufficiency, predominated in the era's economics. Britain's various Navigation Acts therefore stipulated that only British ships should carry goods to and from Britain and her colonies. America's colonists were only to produce goods unavailable in Britain and their profits were meant to be spent buying British goods. Britain's economy thrived as all colonial produce had to go through British ports on their way abroad. But smuggling was the system's chief economic by-product.

Britain was the great victor in the Seven Years War (1756-63). As a result France lost Canada, its Indian possessions, the Floridas and Grenada in the West Indies to Britain. All the glory came at a cost, creating a British national debt of £129,586,789 which carried an annual interest charge of £4,688,177. Britain turned to North America for a solution and Lord Grenville's ministry exploited the Navigation Acts to raise extra money by taxing more articles of trade under the Revenue Act and by introducing a colonial stamp duty which, on becoming law in 1765, started the American revolution. Legal documents in America, just as in Britain, as well as American newspapers and pamphlets, now required a revenue stamp from the British government. Since the colonist were represented in their own assemblies and not in Westminster the measure led to the campaign slogan: 'No taxation without representation.' The Stamp Act Congress, representing nine states, which met in New York to organize opposition, was America's first effective inter-state organization and the Act was repealed. So major a victory required British retaliation. Parliament's Declaratory Act in March 1776 affirmed that it had an absolute right to impose policies on the colonies which were 'subordinate unto, and dependent upon the imperial crown and government of Great Britain'. This was unhelpful. British governmental defensiveness was accentuated by outbreaks of domestic radical agitation, especially that led by John Wilkes.

Pennsylvania and Virginia summed up the difference between eighteenth and seventeenth-century America. The religious toleration of Pennsylvania led to the start of major non-English, and especially German, immigration and Philadelphia became a centre of urban and radical politicization. This was typified in her citizen Benjamin Franklin, businessman, scientist and journalist, whose free-thinking style fused some of the values of European Enlightenment with the established American independence of mind. Pennsylvania was also the home of the abolitionist movement and by 1775 the largest ethnic group after the English were the half million Afro-Americans. Virginia's great planter estates depended on slave labour and the state was in effect an aristocratic republic whose representative figures George Washington and Thomas Jefferson came to reject the English Crown because it interfered with both their economic and their political liberties. Virginia was also on edge as it endured an economic crisis in the mid-eighteenth century because of the collapse in the price of tobacco – a crop which was also exhausting its soil.

Boston, with its tradition of mob populism, lit the spark after Britain's Revenue Act in 1767 imposed new duties on a range of products. Revenue raised would be used to pay the salaries of the colonial governors and customs officers who had previously been paid by, and therefore answerable to, the assemblies. A Boston town-meeting launched a campaign which spread throughout the colony, to boycott imported goods and to buy colonial produce instead. Further Boston rebellions led to its military occupation (September 1768) – an act which angered the normally conservative Virginians. The Boston 'massacre' when British troops shot and killed five locals showed, to the American heirs of the seventeenth-century English rebellion, the intrinsic despotism of standing armies. The duties were repealed but the Tea Act (May 1773) was a further folly. It allowed the East India Company (then in dire economic straits) to import tea cheaply to America, but by selling directly and dumping on the local market the Company would ruin local smugglers as well as the legitimate merchants who had acted as middlemen. On 16 December the Boston mob boarded three tea ships in the harbour and threw their cargo into the water. The government's Coercive Acts (1774) inflamed anti-government factions forcing Thomas Jefferson to the view that there was 'a deliberate and systematical plan of reducing us to slavery'. The members of the Virginia House of Burgesses met in a tavern, having been dissolved by the colony's governor when they declared support for the Boston 'tea-party', and called for an annual inter-state congress.

The battle for colonial consent had long since been lost and British force could not restore it. French intervention, after the American victory at the second battle of Saratoga, was brokered by Benjamin Franklin in Paris. This provided revenge for the 1763 defeat in the Seven Years War but the expense was a crucial element in the French monarchy's final financial crisis. When Spain joined France as an American ally Britain's supply ships on the Atlantic were under pressure. Britain had no European allies in this war and the longer it continued the greater the degree of American solidarity. The end came when General Cornwallis was isolated at Yorktown, Virginia. Admiral de Grasse's French navy sealed off Chesapeake Bay and Cornwallis was therefore separated from his relief ships. Washington's army, along with the French forces under the Comte de Rochambeau, surrounded and besieged Yorktown which fell on 19 October 1781. 'Oh God ! It is all over' said the prime minister Lord North. His government fell and in the second Treaty of Paris in September 1783 the British gave the thirteen colonies their independence and also conceded that the American boundary extended to the Great Lakes in the north and the Mississippi in the west. The Confederation Congress had established, crucially, that the western lands of the frontier were held by Congress on behalf of all Americans rather than being the possessions of individual states. These huge riches led to the historic expansion into the interior of the American West. Spain got back Florida and retained north America west of the Mississippi.

The Confederation Congress's unanimity rule frustrated effective post-war government and had enabled Georgia and South Carolina to reject Virginia and Pennsylvania's desire to renew the wartime ban on slave importation. The Philadelphia Convention (1787) therefore drafted a new constitution under which the populous states conceded that each state (however sparsely populated) would be represented by one vote in the Senate, while the states with low population density agreed that the number of lower house representatives would reflect population numbers. A slave counted as three-fifths of a free man. Election of the new Senate by popular votes rather than through state representatives followed later. The new constitution, ratified by all the states, ensured that the executive and the legislature would have a direct impact on individual citizens. The first ten amendments to the US constitution became the Bill of Rights and their expression of inalienable rights was authentically Jeffersonian. The requirement that persons and properties should not be searched and seized without due legal cause as well as the rejection of cruel and unusual punishment would inform the laws of all future societies that claimed to be civilized.

14 July 1789

The Fall of the Bastille

The Start of the French Revolution

'When the last king is hanged with the bowels of the last priest, the human race can hope for happiness.'

A popular eighteenth-century phrase re-expressed in a Parisian revolutionary journal (11 July 1791).

On the morning of 14 July 1789 some 900 Parisians gathered in front of the Bastille prison; some were soldiers who had deserted from Louis XVI's army and a few were men of property. But most were minor tradesmen whose businesses had long since been concentrated in the area of the faubourg Saint-Antoine which surrounded the Bastille. These people were convinced, correctly, that the king had decided to renege on his earlier promise to reform the government of France. They also knew that the governor of the Bastille, Bernard-René de Launay, was guarding 250 barrels of gunpowder. The crowd's aim was to seize the gunpowder and somehow to neutralize the fifteen cannon which were mounted on the Bastille's eight towers, three of which were in the inner courtyard, and also to disarm the twelve guns on the ramparts. Eighty-two retired soldiers lived in the fortress and they had been reinforced, seven days previously, by thirty-two Swiss soldiers as the threat of a riot increased. Morning negotiations resulted in the removal of the guns but by 2.30, the other demands, made in the name of the citizens' militia representing the people of Paris, had been rejected. The governor's authority, he reminded them, came not from the people below but from the king above.

Louis himself had by now embarked on a day's hunting in the countryside surrounding his palace of Versailles thirty miles and a three hour coach drive away to the west of Paris. The crowd's negotiators, needing further instructions, went to the *Hôtel de Ville*. The sixty Paris districts, formed for the recent elections to the national Estates-General, had produced a college of 470 electors. This assembly met at the *Hôtel de Ville* and was now the effective popular government of Paris. But at about 1.30 p.m. the restless crowd took matters into their own hands and pushed their way across the drawbridge, which had suddenly come crashing down. Shooting now began in the inner courtyard. The drawbridge chains had been cut by some of the crowd themselves but, unaware of that fact, most of the insurgents had assumed that they were being allowed into the Bastille. The shooting therefore seemed further confirmation of a royalist pattern of lying and plotting. By 3.30 p.m. experienced soldiers and officers, armed with guns seized from the barracks of the Invalides, had joined the crowd and were now organizing them for victory. Two cannon were aimed directly at the wooden gate of the Bastille. At 5 p.m. de Launay pushed a note through a chink in the drawbridge wall of the inner courtyard; he wanted an honourable evacuation otherwise he would light the gunpowder and so destroy most of the immediate area. His ploy failed and the request was refused. At which point, with all hope of defence abandoned, the inner drawbridge came down.

The Bastille had surrendered. Inside just seven prisoners were discovered, but eighty-three insurgents had been killed and a further fifteen would die of their wounds. Only one of the defenders had died and just one was wounded. Popular justice demanded a suitable revenge. The governor was marched through the streets of Paris filled now with crowds who abused him. Outside the *Hôtel de Ville* the procession stopped as the excitable crowd debated the governor's fate. De Launay invited his own end. He kicked a pastry cook named Desnot in the groin and fell to the ground under a hail of blows as the swords of his enemies hacked him to death. Desnot then took out his pocket knife and sawed off the former governor's head. It was the French revolution's first political beheading and the beginning of its pursuit of the politics of atrocity.

Early July was always a particularly bad time not just for the French urban poor but also for the not-so-poor. Bread prices, just before the harvest grain became available, were then at their highest and some three-quarters of the average wage-earner's disposable income was invariably spent on bread. It was also the time when the quarterly bills, including rent, were due. The price of a loaf had hit an all-time high in Paris on that morning of the 14th and many of those who attacked the Bastille would have been very hungry. But it was also the capital's political climate which caused them to act.

Money had always been a problem for the cash-strapped French monarchy with its tradition of aggressive, expansionist and expensive foreign wars. Need for money, rather than any genuine desire for reform, was the reason why Louis XVI decided to summon the Estates General for May 1789 – the first time it had met since 1614. Once assembled however, that body proved less ready to grant the king his taxes than to express its own ideas about how France should be run; and its most critical element was determined to assert its own authority. On 6 May the Third Estate, the part which represented the commoners, refused to meet as a body separate from the First Estate representing the nobles and the Second representing the clergy. It went on to call itself the National Assembly and supportive members of the other two estates joined the new body. On 17 June the Assembly members took an oath not to dissolve until France had been given a constitution guaranteeing individual rights and liberties. This was an ambition which had surfaced regularly among those critical of the *ancien régime* – the system of inherited privilege and feudal order. It had been expressed by dissident intellectuals such as Voltaire and Diderot who were instrumental in disseminating the values of the Enlightenment in France. The constitutional agenda was no longer just chatter and pamphleteering; by the summer of 1789 it had become a sustained political challenge to the monarchy.

The Bastille was an appropriate, if not a planned, point of revolutionary departure. Although in 1789 it contained so few actual prisoners, it remained a place of immense symbolic power because it represented the ambition and the ability of the French monarchy to govern secretively and without reference to written law. For over a century and a half, ever since Cardinal Richelieu had first used it as a place of incarceration, the Bastille's prisoners had been detained non-judicially because of a *lettre de cachet* issued by the king. Most of the prisoners were there because their views and writings were considered dangerous. This therefore was one of the most politically charged places in all of France.

It was the king's sudden decision to dismiss his finance minister Necker on 11 July which created the crisis in Parisian public order. Necker's appointment, just a year previously, had carried with it a commitment to the reform of taxation and of governmental corruption, since he had a deserved reputation for personal honesty. The fear of the Parisian streets, shared by a broad body of opinion among the respectable and propertied classes, was of a royalist coup d'état. Louis XVI's own reputation for indecisiveness and double-dealing was another factor. Foreign troops, including the much hated Austrian ones, had been ordered into Paris to maintain order. The French monarchy was losing its grip because it was forfeiting its claim to the affections and loyalty of the people. The decision of Louis XIV to leave Paris and the Louvre for his new court at Versailles had created over a century of disaffection and distance between Paris and the monarchy. In addition by 1789 newly volatile public opinion also thought the Crown was unpatriotic – a judgement vindicated by Louis' Austrian queen, Marie-Antoinette, and her reputation for spendthrift arrogance.

In the days immediately following 14 July the king had to withdraw his forces from Paris, dismiss his reactionary ministry, and then reappoint Necker. On 17 July he travelled to Paris where, on the steps of the *Hôtel de Ville*, he accepted the blue and red cockade which represented the city of Paris and then fixed this rosette to his hat. French kingship was no longer a sacred power and subjects were becoming citizens.

The National Assembly had wanted a peaceful reform process and one which would guarantee liberty, the rights of property and freedom of expression. Those goals were expressed in the Declaration of the Rights of Man and the Citizen which was adopted on 26 August 1789. The document finished the *ancien régime* in France and its influence spread to most of continental Europe. But revolutionary dynamism would have its own inner, uncontrollable and totalitarian logic. New leaders such as Robespierre emerged – men who were ready to use violence to achieve political goals. Divisions between the democratic towns and the more conservative countryside led to civil war in the south and west of France. The extreme revolution also launched a brutal campaign of de-Christianization because its aim was not just a new French government but also a new revolutionary humanity. This bloody process was consumed by its own violence amidst the guillotines and murders of 1793-4, the Year of Terror. In the damp morning fog of 21 January 1793 the deposed king was taken from his prison in the mediaeval keep of the Temple and escorted by 1200 guards to the guillotine. France had been officially a republic since the previous September and Louis XVI was now 'Louis Capet' – one citizen among millions. The newly elected National Convention had been both judge and jury in his trial and, by a majority of 75 among the 721 members who voted, condemned Louis to death on account of his deceitful plotting against the revolution. A twelve-inch blade fell and the executioner took the bleeding head out of the basket to show it to the people. Some dipped their fingers in the flowing blood, others used their handkerchiefs to mop it up. Kingship, as well as a king, had been slaughtered.

Nineteenth-century European politics would be shaped by the fear of the liberal and propertied classes that democracy, though inevitable and even desirable, had to be controlled. Otherwise it would lead to bloodshed followed by a dictatorship whose powers would exceed any of the abuses that had originally led to revolution. Napoleon Bonaparte, the general of genius who was thrown up by the revolution, rose from humble Corsican origins because of the new and meritocratic opportunities that were created in the 1790s. The fact that he established a military despotism which closed down French democracy was the final and sardonic culmination of the events unleashed by those who had stormed the Bastille.

18 June 1815

The Battle of Waterloo

The End of Napoleon's Empire

'*My power proceeds from my reputation, and my reputation from the victories I have won…Conquest has made me what I am; only conquest can maintain me.*'

Napoleon Bonaparte dissects his power base (1802)

On the morning of 18 June 1815, 68,000 British, Dutch, Belgian and German soldiers, a pan-European coalition under the command of Arthur Wellesley, the Duke of Wellington, prepared to do battle with a French force of 72,000 men loyal to Napoleon, at Waterloo just south of Brussels. A separate Prussian force of 45,000 men, under Gebhard von Blücher, had already joined battle. Two days previously Napoleon's marshals, Michel Ney and Emmanuel de Grouchy, defeated the Prussians at Ligny and then, at the battle of Quatre-Bras, halted Wellington's advance. But they had failed to follow through. During the morning of the 18th von Blücher's guard of 17,000 was pinning down the 35,000 French soldiers under de Grouchy's command at Wavre, some seven miles from Waterloo. The main body of the Prussian force had already joined Wellington's army. Napoleon's decision to delay attacking until midday would give the remaining Prussians time to reach Waterloo.

At about 6.00 p.m., after four failed French attempts, Marshal Ney's combined infantry, cavalry and artillery forced their way into the Allied line. Napoleon, absorbed by a Prussian attack on his flank, could not reinforce Ney's infantry for another hour. But by 7.00 p.m. Wellington, helped by the arrival of a corps of Prussians, had re-established his defences. By 8.00 p.m. the French infantry's final assault was crushed by the Allied infantry. Fifteen minutes later the Allies started to advance. Further Prussian attacks to the east meant that this became a two-pronged attack leading to a French retreat. Equivalent losses reflect the even balance between the forces: Napoleon lost 25,000 men killed and wounded, while 9,000 French troops were captured. Wellington's casualties amounted to 15,000 and Blücher lost some 9,000 men. Both the causes and the consequences of Waterloo were global. Napoleon, exiled to the South Atlantic island of St Helena, concluded that the battle had been effectively lost on the plains of Plassey in 1757 when Robert Clive's victory established British dominance in India.

The European conflict began with the French National Assembly's declaration of war against Austria in 1792 and then against Prussia. Britain had been neutral at first. But on 6 November the French routed the Austrians at Jemmapes and occupied Brussels; this aroused the traditional British fears of a great power dominant in the Low Countries. On 16 November the war became ideological when the French Convention decreed 'fraternity and assistance' to all peoples struggling for their freedom. The French declaration of war on Britain and Holland on 1 February 1793 came just eleven days after the guillotining of Louis XVI. British war rhetoric portrayed French government as inherently despotic whether monarchic, republican, or (after Napoleon's *coup d'état* of 1799) Napoleonic.

The French army fought with a novel élan since republican values were now also nationalist ones within an international climate of treason and conspiracy. The English encouraged the royalist rebellion of the Vendée in western France while the French backed the United Irishmen who, in May 1798, organized a nationalist rebellion in Ireland. The French leadership associated its military campaign with superior morality. In 1794 slaves in the French Caribbean colonies were liberated in the strategic hope that rebellions would follow in British territories. Yet Napoleon would re-establish slavery and it was Britain which would ban the trade in slaves in 1807. This, it was hoped, would remove an important French human resource as well as forming part of Britain's moral claim that it was fighting for freedom.

The Wars are dominated by Britain's naval victories and France's territorial ones. That Franco-British balance of offensive capacity reflected the two societies' differing priorities and strengths. The French navy's administration was run by civilian bureaucrats but the British Admiralty was dominated by naval officers and its annual wartime expenditure of £15m meant that the Admiralty was a central institution of government. The British naval officer corps was also much more meritocratic than the socially exclusive traditions of the French navy's upper echelons. The resulting inefficiency meant that the French lost an average of six times as many sailors as the British on naval engagements. But the French army reforms after 1763 included new strategic thinking and an officer corps promoted on ability and proven success, whereas the British army was invariably run down in peacetime because of the profound national suspicion that a standing army would strengthen central power.

Britain and Austria were quickly forced out of the Low Countries but France would lose all its major colonies and overseas bases during the war. The British retained control of the oceans, and therefore of colonial trade. Napoleon's Egyptian campaign tried to find a base for a land attack on India but he was pursued by Nelson who defeated the French at the Battle of the Nile in 1798. Napoleon defeated the Austrians at the Battle of Marengo and the Peace of Amiens in 1802 endorsed the French domination of Europe from the Baltic to the Mediterranean. This was undermined, however, by Napoleon's management of the peace: he imposed new constitutions on Switzerland and Holland which effectively turned these states into French dependencies.

After the resumption of war in 1803 Napoleon's planned invasion of England led to a vast patriotic defence movement. Britain was unique in its reliance on volunteer soldiers and there had never been conscription into the regular army. By 1805 about 800,000 men, twenty per cent of the adult male population, were doing some kind of armed service. But Continental politics also saved Britain. The prospect of Russia and Austria now supporting Britain's war meant that Napoleon's army would be vulnerable on the Continent if an English invasion proved a prolonged commitment. With his invasion fleet delayed in Spain, Napoleon had to shift his army to German territories. At Ulm in 1805 he defeated the Austrian army. The great event for the British was the victory on the following day of Nelson's fleet off Cape Trafalgar near Gibraltar and the Admiral's apotheosis in death as the ideal English hero. But the battle of Austerlitz later that same year and the defeat of the Russo-Austrian army was Napoleon's most complete victory. The war was therefore a stalemate in counterpoint between Britain's navy and France's army.

The Wars boosted the British economy with trade expanding and the City of London booming as a safe haven for foreign capital. By 1814 the government was spending some £100 million a year – six times its pre-war budget – but the strong British economy could pay for the war. Victories at sea led to expanded overseas trade which, in turn, increased the revenue available to run the British navy and expand its manpower. Continental conquest, which meant levying of indemnities, conscription and requisitioning, supplied the French army with men and material, but both the Wars and the Revolution were disastrous for France's domestic economy and her overseas trade. After defeating the Prussians at Jena in 1806, Napoleon therefore tried to turn European continental trade away from the oceans. The Berlin Decree of November

1806 prohibited all trade with Britain and ordered the seizure of all merchandise from Britain and its colonies. The British extended their own, equivalent, blockade as a response to the 'Continental System' whose protected market for French goods was a paradise for smugglers and the black market. British goods found new markets in the Mediterranean, Iberia and the Americas. The French economy slumped. City-traded financial assets also defeated Napoleon: Britain raised cash by liquidating its large overseas credits and it also sold British government bonds abroad. Getting rid of 'Boney' was still expensive with a total bill to Britain of £1,500 million and a consequent national debt of £733 million.

Napoleon's decision to remove the ruling Spanish Bourbons led to a violent national rebellion in 1808, supported by Britain. The outcome of the Peninsular War, which also involved Portugal, was decided by Russia's decision in 1810 to leave the Continental System, for this in turn led to Napoleon's invasion of Russia in July 1812. Austria and Prussia joined Russia's cause. Napoleon had benefited from his enemies' divisions but European states were now co-operating together. Castlereagh's negotiation of the Treaty of Chaumont (1814) would bind the Allies to maintain peace for twenty years. In 1813-14 Wellington's victorious army advanced from northern Spain, crossed the Pyrenees, and began the first and only major British invasion of French territory since the Hundred Years War. Napoleon abdicated on 6 April 1814 and was exiled to the island of Elba whence he sailed in March 1815 with 900 men to reclaim France.

The Franco-British struggle lasted from 1689 to 1815. It started when the Dutch invasion drew Britain into a general European coalition against Louis XIV. Six wars followed of which the last was the Napoleonic in which 1.4 million French and over 200,000 British were killed. Proportionately, the losses are comparable to those of the First World War. The War changed the general view of the two countries. By the mid-eighteenth century Britain was seen as a progressively open, because constitutionally governed, society. But its posture during the Napoleonic Wars encouraged the view that Britain was a conservative and traditional country. France, by contrast, changed from representing the *ancien régime* state *par excellence* and became the model of a republican, secular, state. Britain was now a global power and France a European one. India was mostly British. Spain and Portugal never really recovered as modern countries until the 1970s and their empires were destabilized. Napoleon's rationalist reforms of French administration, together with his legal code, shaped most western European states. Within France his legacy included a tradition of the strong state and a suspicion of quarrelsome political parties.

The essence and novelty of Napoleon's tactics was his aim to obliterate the opposing army rather than just seize territory and strategic positions. His land victories were so crushing that they undermined the European power-politics which had made them possible. The Congress of Vienna was therefore a post-Napoleonic reaction which inaugurated the modern history of negotiated agreements between governments bound together in leagues, pacts and accords. The Congress of Vienna restored the old European dynasties on their thrones but the nationalist feeling aroused among those countries subdued by French nationalism would outlast the Congress's arrangements. This led to a revival of national identity whose political consequences, especially in Germany and Italy, proved profound.

17 December 1819

Simón Bolivar Named President of Gran Colombia

The Liberation of Latin America

'This country will inexorably fall into the hands of uncontrollable multitudes, thereafter to pass under… tyrants of all colours and races.'

The 'country' of Latin America disturbs Simón Bolivar (1830)

In 1819 the High Andes of South America were practically unexplored. Simón Bolivar (1783-1830) therefore took a risk in leading his band of 2,500 soldiers across the mountain peaks separating western Venezuela from Colombia. Spanish forces had re-established their predominance in Venezuela following the outbreak of the Latin-American insurrection and Bolivar's force by 1817 had re-established itself in the country's Orinoco region. Its most reliable component was a band of British mercenaries, 2,000 of whom, mostly veterans of Wellington's Peninsular campaigns, had arrived during the spring of 1819. Wives, mistresses and children were among the camp-followers as Bolivar negotiated the precipitous ravines and led his force across the high plateau's moors and swamps in June and July. The descent having been negotiated, the army had the advantage of surprise when it attacked Spanish-controlled Colombia. Not even Spanish conquistadors had considered the High Andes to be passable. At the battle of Boyaca in August 1819 the colonial army was defeated, the capital Santa Fé (now Bogota) was occupied three days later and the politics of atrocity, tolerated by Bolivar, spread.

In December 1819 Bolivar appeared before the Congress assembled in Angostura on Venezuela's northern coast. He urged, and secured, the creation of a new federal state which would be called the Republic of Gran Colombia. The Congress at Angostura made Bolivar president in title, and dictator in fact, of this new federation. He had already been granted the formal title of 'liberator' during his earlier career training as a dictator in Venezuela (1813-14). Two of the federal components, Ecuador and Venezuela, remained loyalist-controlled but Spanish domestic developments distracted the colonial regime after a liberal revolution in 1820 forced King Ferdinand VII to restore the constitution devised after the ejection of the French. The Spaniards surrendered Venezuela at the battle of Carabobo in 1821 and Ecuador fell to the insurgency after the battle of Pichincha in 1822.

Bolivar had earlier told the Congress, 'We are not Europeans, we are not Indians, but an intermediate species… American by birth, European by right.' This vision of South Americans as a single race now seemed set for realization. And for Bolivar the grandiosity of the vision justified violent means. Francisco de Paula Santander, a Venezuelan crony whom Bolivar had appointed vice-president of Colombia, acted on a whim when he ordered the execution of thirty-eight captured officers before a firing squad in Bogota's Cathedral Square. Taking, he said, a 'special pleasure' in killing Spaniards, he left the scene accompanied by musicians singing a song composed to mark the event. The modern revolutionary combination of liberationist rhetoric with massacres was acquiring its Latin American roots.

The Spanish colonial regime had been lethargic but stable and, having lasted almost 300 years, it presided over a rich civilization in the late eighteenth century. In 1740 the Spanish Bourbons separated the viceroyalty of New Granada (consisting of present-day Colombia, Panama, Ecuador and Venezuela) from the viceroyalty of Peru. However, the American rebellion of the 1770s and the French breakdown of the 1780s, two aspects of a common Atlantic Revolution, destabilized the Spanish colonies by spreading constitutionalist ideas. Bonaparte's assault on the Spanish monarchy in 1808 gave the nationalist rebels a chance to attack the imperial outposts of a shattered European order. But the colonies were already fractured by social divisions since the more prosperous of the Creoles, Latin Americans of white descent, disliked the prospect of independent national states whose rulers might diminish their influence. They also resented the officials who arrived from Spain to run the colonies. Slaves imagined that a rebellion would lead to their liberation whereas the free blacks, the native Indians and many low caste mixed race groups looked to the Spanish crown as a protector against injustice. The war against the Spanish was therefore also a war between different Latin American classes.

In 1810 popular rebellions broke out in the colonial cities as crowds shouted slogans against the French invaders of Spain. But it was the cause of Latin American, not Spanish, self-government which drove many onto the streets. The junta which seized power in Caracas following a coup in 1810 organized Venezuela as an independent state and throughout the two viceroyalties new governments were formed which swore allegiance to the Spanish monarch before then declaring their independence. The viceroyalties simply ceased to exist. The rebellion in Mexico, part of the central American colony of New Spain, was led by Miguel Hidalgoy Costillo – a renegade politicized priest of a type who would recur in Latin America's later history. He led a coup in 1810, raised an army of 25,000, massacred the garrison at Guanajuato and stole three million pesos worth of silver bars and coins which enabled him to raise another army of 80,000 men. The army in Mexico restored order and Hidalgo was arrested and garrotted.

Atrocities were being committed on both sides. In Venezuela, José Tomas Boves, though leader of a pro-Spanish force, massacred the whites in order to colonize the country's central plain with the mestizos of mixed native and European extraction. Francisco de Miranda pushed a 'Declaration of the Rights of the People' through the recently convened Venezuelan Congress. He then ordered the beheading of a dozen loyalists and placed their heads in cages for public display. In the 1810s official armies were becoming indistinguishable from the private armies run by warlords for this was the first great age of the Latin American guerrilla as typified in the rise and fall of Simón Bolivar. His first period as ruler of Venezuela (1813-14) set the tone for an anti-colonial rhetoric which justified slaughter in the name of social and political justice, and his proclamation of June 1813 sentenced to death all Europeans who did not actively help the liberators.

Between 1811 and 1820 Spain sent thirty expeditions across the Atlantic consisting of a total of forty-seven warships carrying almost 50,000 soldiers and over a thousand cannon as it tried to restore its authority. But Spain's instability undermined its colonial campaign. The country went through two constitutionalist periods and Ferdinand VII's absolutist rule of 1814-20 then resumed in 1823. Between 1808 and 1826 Spain had fifty-one ministers of war, forty ministers of finance and forty-six prime ministers. Ferdinand's mismanagement lost him the support of his fellow autocrats among European monarchs. British banking, an important source of monarchs' loans, shunned him as a credit risk while London merchants, speculating on trade possibilities, equipped Bolivar's British mercenaries with arms.

Bolivar's 1819 victory gave power to an oligarchic fusion of white landowners and merchants who ran the new Gran Colombia. US and British self-interest led to international recognition. The US, having already formally annexed Florida following an invasion, feared that European intervention in Latin America would amount to a re-colonization which might then spread north to undermine the US. The Monroe Doctrine of 1823 therefore declared that: '… the American continents…are hence-forth not to be considered as subjects for future colonization by any European power.' Britain endorsed and enforced the doctrine by the threat of naval power. Meanwhile, British banks were backing the new governments by selling their bonds. The claims of liberal nationalism happily coincided with Britain's commercial and strategic interests so that George Canning, the foreign secretary, could claim: 'I called the New World into existence, to redress the balance of the Old.'

The events of 1819 also bore strange fruit in southern Latin America where the Argentinian revolutionary, José de San Martin, had already taken Santiago in 1817 and established Bernardo O'Higgins as Supreme Director of the new state of Chile. Martin had also proclaimed Peru's independence but the Spanish were holding out in the highlands to the east. Bolivar arrived in Lima in 1823 having negotiated, or enforced, San Martin's exile. He then assembled an army which, once again, managed a difficult ascent and defeated the Spaniards at the battle of Junin. This led to a stage-managed Spanish surrender after a mock-battle in the best comic opera traditions of Latin American militarism. Bolivar was now president of both Gran Colombia and Peru. A new country, carved out of the recently conquered eastern Peru, was called Bolivia after its liberator whose power now extended from the Caribbean to the Argentinian-Bolivian border.

In Mexico, following a renewed declaration of independence in 1821, the royalist commander Augustin de Iturbide changed sides and staged Latin America's first military coup which led to his coronation as emperor of Mexico. He then lost power in a counter coup and was shot for conspiring in another. Two more Mexican coups followed in 1828 and 1829 and another president, Vincente Guerrero, was executed in 1831. In June 1826 Bolivar convened a pan-American congress in Panama, excluding Haiti and Brazil, to cement an alliance of Hispanic American states. He thought that such a structure, run imperially by himself, was the only hope for the 'astounding chaos' of the continent – a chaos he had himself created. The talk of a common federation dissolved as did the congress after three weeks.

Venezuela rebelled against its union with Colombia and Bolivar narrowly escaped being killed by rebels. In autumn 1829 Venezuela seceded, and was now also bankrupt, since the global recession of 1825-6 meant that Latin American states found it difficult to raise money in Europe and London. Bolivar fell from power and left Bogota in May 1830 amid scenes of crowds burning effigies of their former president and his mistress Manuela Sáenz. His plan was to leave for Europe but on 17 December 1830 he died of tuberculosis. Near the end of his life he concluded that: 'America is ungovernable. He who sows a revolution ploughs the sea.' Brazil, by contrast, escaped wars of liberation and enjoyed a relatively peaceful transition after gaining independence in 1822 from Portugal. The 1824 constitution of the emperor, Pedro I, son of the Portuguese king, lasted sixty-five years. Nineteenth-century Brazil, a multi-racial and commercially open society, provided a painful contrast with the regimes of colonels and generals ensconced in Latin American presidential palaces. Simón Bolivar had set a tragic example for the anti-colonial insurrections of the future.

15 September 1830

Opening of the Liverpool-Manchester Railway

Dawn of the Railway Age

'I stood up, and with my bonnet off "drank the air before me". When I closed my eyes this sensation of flying was quite delightful and strange...'

Fanny Kemble, actress and novice train traveller (26 August 1830)

In 1830 Liverpool was Britain's fastest growing port and Lancashire textiles had enriched Manchester which was the home of the free trade movement. The thirty-mile railway line laid down by George Stephenson (1781-1848) therefore connected two cities fundamental to Britain's Industrial Revolution. Great viaducts and deep cuttings had been constructed, huge amounts of earth moved, and embankments raised above the levels of the Lancashire plain. It was a spectacular, and expensive, project. The line cost £40,000 a mile to build and the railway company had had to borrow £100,000 from the government. Railway companies could no longer confidently predict that their method of transport would be cheaper than canals. But railways had become the future and their dramatic, noisy, spectacle attracted enthused crowds – especially so for the opening of the Liverpool-Manchester line since this was the first to provide an extensive passenger service.

Stephenson had also won the competition to find the best steam-powered locomotive engine. His *Rocket*, built with his son Robert and equipped with a multiple fire-tube boiler, both weighed less and used less coal than its competitors. During the Rainhill Trials, conducted in October 1829, 10,000 spectators had seen the engine travelling at an average of fourteen miles an hour over sixty miles. Another Stephenson design, the *Planet*, could travel at twenty miles an hour and would be serving the Liverpool-Manchester line by the end of 1830.

Eight trains left Manchester bound for the celebratory dinner in Liverpool. The first, travelling on the south track, carried eighty of the most important guests including the prime minister, the Duke of Wellington, the home secretary, Robert Peel, who was now barely on speaking terms with his boss, and William Huskisson, a Liverpool MP. Pulled by the *Northumbrian* engine, which was driven by Stephenson himself, the train was divided into separate carriages since British railways, unlike American ones, had decided to follow a nostalgic stagecoach design. The other seven followed on the north track. Almost halfway, and after fifty-six minutes, the leading train stopped and Huskisson along with others got out to stretch their legs. The other trains were now meant to pass in procession as a salute to the duke seated in his state carriage. On seeing Huskisson the duke waved at him, opened the carriage door and extended his hand in greeting. Huskisson approached. The *Rocket*, pulling the next train, came puffing along on the north track. Two of the strollers pushed themselves against the duke's carriage but Huskisson, suffering from rheumatism ever since attending King George IV's funeral in chilly weather that summer, stumbled as he tried to get round the open carriage door. He fell on the north track just as the *Rocket* bore down on him. The engine crushed his thigh. 'I have met my death,' he said. Stephenson, ever-practical, uncoupled the first carriage from the others, lifted the dying man into it and drove his engine at a furious thirty-six miles an hour to Eccles where, however, medical assistance failed to save Huskisson's life.

William Huskisson (1770-1830) was a liberal Tory and an advocate of railways as part of Britain's modernization. He had been appointed president of the Board of Trade and then resigned from the cabinet in 1828 because of the government's failure to reform parliament and make it representative of Britain's new population patterns as job-seekers moved from the south-east and towards the newly industrialized Midlands and north. Some ancient parliamentary seats were now almost entirely depopulated.

Viscount Palmerston , who resigned as war secretary at the same time as Huskisson, complained to the House of Commons that it was lamentable that: '... people saw such populous places as Leeds and Manchester unrepresented, whilst a green mound of earth returned two Members...' The Duke of Wellington, prime minister since 1828, resisted these progressive insights and had only reluctantly accepted his own government's Catholic Emancipation Act which had given Roman Catholics the vote. But Wellington in September 1830 had problems. The emancipation, while alienating his natural allies among the die-hard Tories who believed in the alliance of Church and State, had gained him no friends among liberals since Wellington's disposition, while incorruptible, was also openly reactionary. His government had just been re-elected in a general election but Palmerston was emerging as a formidable opposition leader with his talk of how politicians should 'avail themselves of the passion and the interest and the opinions of mankind.' These were un-ducal sentiments but thoughtful Tories were drawing the lesson from the recent revolution in Paris which disposed of the restored Bourbons. A reactionary posture might be self-destructive. Peel, irked by Wellington's dogmatism, was being increasingly distant.

By 1830 the British economy was recovering after a bad crash caused by Huskisson's own policies. As a doctrinaire believer in free markets he had pushed through reductions in taxation and duties which, however, had overheated an already booming economy. Gold and silver flowed out of Britain to pay for imports and this, together with the huge export of capital advanced as loans to foreign governments, led to the banking crisis of 1825-6. In these awkward circumstances Wellington decided that he needed Huskisson's support – and that of his friends among the liberal Tories. The 15th of September, when circumstances would bring the two men together in a location far from London, seemed therefore the ideal opportunity for a discussion – much though Wellington himself disliked these new railways.

Machines producing power from fuels were first used to pump water from coal mines and to wind cables in mine elevators. It was the French engineer, Nicolas-Joseph Cugnot, who in 1769 first used higher-pressure steam to produce a lighter, and therefore mobile, engine which was used to move cannon. James Watt invented (1776) the first modern steam-pumping engine which had proved useful in driving the canal boats. George Stephenson then developed the steam locomotive for railroad travel. Wooden rails designed to carry horse-drawn carriages had been used in British and German pits since the sixteenth century and the Lowther pits near Whitehaven had laid down iron rails as early as 1783. In 1821 a group of northern businessmen got a Bill through Parliament allowing them to build a steam rail route from Darlington to Stockton-on-Tees. Stephenson became the chief engineer on the project and pioneered the steam blast by which exhaust steam was sent up a chimney pulling the air after it and so increasing the draft.

Meanwhile, Thomas Telford (1757-1834) was developing his independent programme for steam locomotion engines to be used on the 920 miles of new roads and the 280 miles of relaid military ones he was building across Britain. He objected to the inherently uneconomic and anti-competitive nature of railways since they required special tracks designed for exclusive use by one company. Goldsworthy Gurney, Telford's colleague, developed instead a steam-powered road vehicle run by a lightweight steam-jet engine which averaged fifteen miles an hour on a return journey from London to Bath in July 1829. But by now Britain's mining and industrial companies had invested heavily in the fixed track system and rail, with its powerful lobby of supporters, benefited from the last years of a parliamentary system open to manipulation by monopolists and special interests. Providers of coach and horse services, frightened of competition, opposed faster forms of transportation on the roads and prohibitive tolls were therefore imposed on a steam-powered road vehicle.

Steam changed the seas as well as the land. Wooden steamboats were a North American invention of the 1800s and their shallow draft proved ideal for the American rivers, but the British stole the march on the US by using iron to supplement steam. Necessity mothered the invention since the Napoleonic Wars had denuded Britain of trees in order to build ships. Britain, however, was rich in the iron ore and coking coal needed to smelt the iron. In 1822 the first true iron steamship travelled across the Channel and up the Seine.

Steam power was part of a general advance in sea communications: the British and French national programme to build lighthouses started in the 1820s and the new steam ships had better maps by which to steer. There were only 109 accurate longitude-latitude positions in about 1800. By 1817 there were over 6,000. The steamships expanded from the rivers to the oceans and in 1830 a mail steamship travelled from Falmouth to the eastern Mediterranean. Steam power cut the cost of ocean-going passenger fares by three quarters and by 1830 a ticket to New York was £5. Cheaper fares met an important demand with the development of mass immigration to the US, a result of Europe's phenomenal population growth from 150 million in 1750 to over 400 million in 1900. Migrations took place overland and within countries as well as across seas. Railways were agents of an urbanization which turned peasants into citizens and a rural proletariat into an urban one; whereas in about 1800 just twenty per cent of the British lived in towns with more than a population of 10,000, by 1851 the figure had almost doubled to thirty-eight per cent.

Quicker communications created suburban conurbations whose villas were homes to a new style of bourgeois politics. They also helped governments to assert order. Telford's London to Holyhead road cost £750,000 and reduced travelling time from forty-one to twenty-eight hours. The British government footed the bill since, following the Union (1801) with Ireland, it needed quicker access to a dissident territory. Prussia and Piedmont led in railway construction across, respectively, Germany and Italy and they subsequently dominated the two countries' unifications. After the American Civil War, the Central Pacific and the Western Pacific became the first transcontinental railroad system when the two lines joined up in Utah in 1869. Railway timetables also became part of military strategy and Spain's suspicion of France ensured that her railway gauge differed from the west European norm.

Wellington's ministry survived for another two months after his return to London and then collapsed after he told the House of Commons that he opposed political reform on principle: Britain's constitution was admirable precisely because it conferred power on the landed aristocracy and gentry. Two years later the Whig government's Reform Act started to nibble away at Wellington's world. Liverpool and Manchester, steam and speed, were winning.

23 August 1833

Parliament Passes the Emancipation Act

The Abolition of Slavery

'*Am I Not a Man and a Brother?*'

Motto of the Committee for the Abolition of the Slave Trade

'*They are not my men and bretheren, these strange people…*'

W.M.Thackeray

Guilt, indifference and hypocrisy marked the British parliamentary debates on the Emancipation Bill and no cabinet minister was present for the backbenchers' speeches during the summer of 1833. The twenty-three-year-old MP William Gladstone, whose family fortune relied on a sugar plantation in Demerara, made his first major parliamentary speech and said his father's estate manager in Jamaica was 'proverbial for humanity'. Still at that time a Tory, he conceded that at some future date slavery had to go and then voted against the Bill. The Emancipation Bill was nonetheless passed (23 August) by the House of Commons and William Wilberforce (1759-1833), the anti-slavery campaign's chief parliamentarian, died on 29 July in the knowledge that his life's work was about to be accomplished. The 776,000 slaves on Britain's plantation colonies were freed from 1 August 1834 – although under a system of bound apprenticeship which lasted until 1837. Slaves who were under six were freed immediately. Slave owners received £120 million in compensation for the human chattels they had lost.

By the late eighteenth century slavery was so ancient an institution that it seemed a natural part of the social hierarchy. Britons might never be slaves but the enslaved Africans in the British colonies had become part of the fabric of a civilization. It helped therefore that William Wilberforce was no revolutionary but part of the English establishment – diplomatic, deferential and humorous – a good 'House of Commons man'. Even his opium addiction was not unusual in the high society of his age. It was his conversion to evangelical Christianity which changed Wilberforce from being yet another amiable and indolent upper class Englishman since it opened his eyes to the iniquity of slavery, and he brought the characteristic emotionalism of evangelical principle, as well as his personal popularity, to the abolitionist campaign. He became a member of the Clapham Sect, a close-knit group of well-connected and prosperous evangelicals who thought that Britain, including its association with slavery, needed energizing national reform.

Britain's abolition (1807) of the slave trade (although not ownership) in the West Indies had been followed by an Enforcement Bill (1811) which prescribed transportation and sentences of hard labour for British subjects who took part in the business. By 1819 all British colonies had established registers so that the rights of those who claimed slaves as their property could be tried in the courts. Britain also ensured that the countries which were a party to the Congress of Vienna agreed in principle to abolish the slave trade. Wilberforce had established the Society for Effecting the Abolition of the Slave Trade and from 1821 onwards he returned to the cause, helping to found the Society for the Mitigation and Gradual Abolition of Slavery throughout the British Dominions. The object now was the abolition of slavery itself as an institution since ownership of slaves continued to be legal throughout the British empire, including the West Indies colonies, and legal protection could not be extended to enslaved individuals. Slavery's abolition would also have to be global, said the abolitionists, since other countries might gain a competitive advantage by retaining slave labour. The economics were important since the West Indies estate owners were a powerful political lobby; out of a total of about 1,800 such planters some 1,200 lived in Britain and by 1798 eighty per cent of all British overseas income came from the West Indies.

Slavery's institutional grip was strengthening from the late eighteenth century because of a global expansion in the businesses that relied on slave labour. Cotton exports from the American south were on a small scale until Eli Whitney invented a cotton gin which could separate the lint from its seeds by mechanical means. A plantation slave could now produce fifty pounds of cotton a day instead of just one. Slavery underpinned the southern states of Alabama, Mississippi, Louisiana and Texas where cotton grew to be a king. Britain's textile industry, increasingly productive and cost-cutting through labour-saving spinning machines, was a huge cotton importer. By 1810 Britain was consuming seventy-nine million pounds of raw cotton, almost half of which came from the US, and by 1860 the total importation was over a billion pounds of which ninety-two per cent came from the southern plantations. At the beginning of 1830 finished cotton constituted more than half of Britain's total exports and cotton itself was America's largest export trade.

The American Congress abolished (1807) the trade in slaves but smuggling and high birthrates meant that the slave supply continued to rise. The slave population of the US increased from 1,119,354 in 1810 to 3,963,760 in 1860 and slave-breeding became an important economic activity in the old south – in Virginia, Georgia and the Carolinas – whose exhausted soil, mostly devoted to tobacco, was unsuited to cotton growing. Physically suitable males were provided to ensure that some female slaves would produce a child a year. Since demand was outstripping supply, the ban on importation had the effect of increasing the value of such 'home-grown' slaves and the slave price shot up in real terms from some $50 in 1800 to between $800 and $900 by 1850.

Central and South America accounted for some seventy-five per cent of the total 11.5 million Africans who were transported as slaves, only 9.5 million of whom arrived alive. This was a good business and British commercial vessels were basic to it. A single east-west voyage carrying 800 slaves would net a profit of some £60,000 in gold during the early nineteenth-century boom years. Half the population of Brazil were slaves in 1800 but numbers fell to fifteen per cent after the 1850s ban on slave importation although the country did not outlaw slavery until the manumission of 1888. In the Caribbean, slaves were the majority of the population, Britain had over 600,000 in her West Indian colonies whose plantations fed the European demand for sugar. Britain's per capita consumption of sugar was the world's highest and in the 1790s Britain was importing 70,000 tons annually.

Abolitionists wished to quicken consciences and to show how slavery degraded the characters of everybody involved, be they slaves, plantation owners, or just consumers at the end of an immoral chain of consequences. English Quakers had first petitioned parliament to abolish slavery in 1783 and their Pennsylvanian brethren had voiced their first formal opposition in 1688. The judgement in 1772 of Chief Justice Mansfield that James Somerset, an escaped slave, could not be forcibly returned from Britain to Virginia, was a landmark decision ending slavery's status in English law: 'I cannot say that this case is allowed or approved by the law of England; and therefore the black must be discharged.' British abolitionism, however, went beyond the occasional insight of individuals and demonstrated for the first time the power of single-issue campaigning. Boycotting sugar became an important gesture among the enlightened and the great parliamentary orator Henry Brougham organized pledges from parliamentary candidates committed to vote against slavery if elected.

Information gathering was key and Thomas Clarkson was the chief activist who interviewed slaves themselves, inspected their living conditions and produced statistics on slave mortality. Just days after the Emancipation Act parliament also passed the Factory Act which restricted child labour for nine- to thirteen-year-olds and abolished it for those under nine. Abolitionism also used the power of well-organized outrage to force governments into action. During the 1820s the government was attempting to stop the worst abuses in the West Indies and a despatch was sent ordering a ban on the flogging of women and forbidding slave drivers from using whips. This was suppressed by the planters in Demerara and the slaves then revolted on the basis of rumours about the despatch's contents. Two hundred slaves were killed and forty-seven formally executed while many others received up to a thousand lashes. The British public reacted with distaste and West Indian incomes, however vast, were now starting to offend that important political and social force – British respectability.

Britain with her naval power was the natural enforcer of the European powers' 1814-15 ban on the slave trade but the European colonies were difficult to deal with – especially after they became independent. Chile, much influenced by British interests, freed its black slaves in 1823. But Brazil evaded the obligations of its treaty with Britain to abolish the slave trade. Most of the former Spanish colonies in Latin America continued with slavery until the 1850s. British pressure was also used to try to stop the trade at source. The navy operated an anti-slave squadron off the west coast of Africa from 1808 and US naval units did the same. But Spain, France, Holland and Portugal did little to stop slave-gathering in their colonies especially since the native economy of Africans themselves, among their chieftains and in their towns, was geared to slavery. The British advance into Africa from 1815 onwards therefore combined humanitarian argument with colonial advantage. Both new strategies and novel ethics were redirecting Britain's empire from its west and the Caribbean, to its east, and India. Imposing enlightened values and rational government from above, British colonialism now wanted to change and improve the customs and beliefs of natives rather than just trade with them. The Indian penal code (1861) therefore outlawed slave ownership.

Other empires abolished slavery among the peoples they subjugated: Russia had turned its agricultural slaves into serfs (1679) and slavery was abolished in the 1860s in the Caucasus after Russian expansion into the region. But the British advance was especially marked by ethical energy and a self-confident Christian morality. This introduced a novel ambiguity into imperial policy, especially in the Middle East. The British navy patrolled the Indian ocean and the east African coastline where black Muslim chiefs co-operated with the Arab merchants and traders whose slave trade, centred on Zanzibar, extended across vast distances. African slaves were sent up the Persian gulf to Persia, Turkey and Mesopotamia. The trade in Christian Abyssinian slaves was particularly offensive to the British and naval officers often had to enter into local deals with rulers prepared to sell their slavery rights for cash. This led to British penetration of the Gulf and to Britain's diplomatic representation in Arabia and the adjacent region. British residences were established in Basra and Baghdad. The moral convictions of the abolitionists had become an element within the calculations of imperial power.

8 July 1853

Commodore Perry Anchors in Tokyo Bay

Japan Opens up to the Modern World

'*The military and warlike strength of the Japanese had long been to Europe like the ghost in a village churchyard, a bugbear and a terror…Our nation has unclothed the ghost…*'
An American sailor (1853)

The officer who steered his two frigates and two sailing ships into the fortified harbour of Uraga near Edo (Tokyo) on 8 July 1853 was well versed in naval diplomacy, the realities of war and the advanced technology of his time. Commodore Matthew C.Perry (1794-1858) had commanded the USS *Fulton*, the American navy's second steam frigate, and organized the US's first corps of naval engineers; he had also seen action during the American-Mexican war which had ended with the annexation of the previously Mexican province of Texas. The victory had realized some of the ambitions of American politics' 'manifest destiny' movement which was convinced that the country had a duty to expand – 'the farther the better' according to Walt Whitman. But Perry was also a careful strategist who had studied Japan's two centuries of isolation and concluded that only a show of naval force along with a 'resolute attitude' would persuade the Japanese to establish diplomatic and trade relations with the US. Appreciating Japanese veneration for rank, Perry called himself an 'admiral' and refused to leave when the representatives of the Tokugawa shogunate, Japan's hereditary military rulers, told him to go to Nagasaki. This, their only port open to foreigners, was where they allowed a limited trade with the Netherlands. Perry threatened a naval bombardment if he wasn't allowed to fulfil his mission of delivering a letter from the US president. The Japanese looked at his vessels and decided to let him in. Ever afterwards 'black ships' would be their phrase for a western threat.

On 14 July, at Kurihama, Commodore Perry handed Fillmore's letter to the shogunate's delegates and told them he would be back for a reply. In February 1854 he returned with four sailing ships and three steamers as well as 1600 men. The Japanese had prepared a draft treaty of acceptance and, after a face-saving diplomatic standoff, Perry was allowed to land and negotiations began. On 31 March Perry signed the Treaty of Kanagawa which promised 'permanent' Japanese-American friendship. Having seen China's defeat by superior western technology in the Opium War, Japan now wanted to win time while developing her defences. The treaty allowed US ships to obtain fuel and other supplies at two minor Japanese ports, enabled a consulate to be established at Shimoda and paved the way for trading rights. The shogunate had proved incapable of maintaining Japanese isolation. In a characteristic postscript Perry anchored off Taiwan on his return journey and spent ten days investigating the island's coal deposits with a view to future American mining. Taiwan, he thought, might be a useful base for the US's future exploration of the region just as Cuba had been for the sixteenth-century Spanish in America. The US government, however, refused his offer to claim American sovereignty. There was, after all, enough Asian adventure to look forward to.

The Japanese response to Perry reflected a power struggle within the Japanese ruling class and the issues raised by his arrival were not new. An unarmed American merchant ship had been fired on in 1837 when it had sailed into Uraga channel; Commander James Biddle commanding two ships – one being a 72 cannon warship – had anchored in Edo Bay in 1846 and been denied trade agreements; Captain James Glynn had sailed into Nagasaki in 1848 and returned to tell Congress that Japan would need a demonstration of force before agreeing to trade negotiations. The Tokugawa shogunate, recognizing that the Perry threat was graver than these earlier forays, received conflicting advice when it consulted the nobility. Many stuck to intransigent isolationism, but Li Naosuke counselled a superficial conciliation which won the day: Japan needed just enough foreign contact to allow her time to build up her strength in order to re-impose isolationism. This approach won and in the next few months Britain, Russia and the Netherlands won their own trade agreements.

This policy divide coincided with a crisis in the succession to the hereditary shogunate since the current holder, Tokugawa Iesada, was childless. Different camps signed up for the competing claims of the shogun's first cousin, Iemochi, who was still a minor, and those of Tokugawa Yoshinobu who, although only distantly related to the clan, was the son of the powerful Tokugawa Nariaki. Li Naosuke was among those who promoted Iemochi as heir apparent, calculating that his youth would allow a noble clique to control the shogunate. Nariaki became the chief representative of imperial loyalism within the shogunate and now tried to involve the imperial court in the shogunate's administration.

By 1858 Naosuke was in a position of real power as *tairo* or chief adviser to the government and his candidate Iemochi had been chosen as shogun on the death of Iesada. However, his decision to sign a further treaty with the Americans proved to be his undoing. Powerful isolationists had hampered the negotiations and Naosuke calculated that a signed treaty with the US would strengthen Japan's negotiating position with the British and the French whose squadrons were on the way and whose negotiators would want even more far-reaching agreements. He therefore instructed the negotiators to sign without gaining imperial permission. This provoked the isolationists who, increasingly, saw the emperor as fundamental both to Japanese honour and to their own standing. Armed followers of Nariaki attacked Naosuke in1860 and beheaded him. In 1862 Yoshinobu, following his father Nariaki's death two years earlier, became the boy shogun's guardian. His own succession (1866) to the shogunate, following young Iemochi's death, proved to be an empty inheritance. The forces of imperial loyalism which had elevated both him and his father – and helped to make him shogun – would turn against the shogunate as an institution, abandon isolationism, and associate the new imperialism with a state-strengthening modernity which took what it needed from western technology.

The Tokugawa shogunate of the 1860s had been destroyed by contradictions. It wanted to strengthen Japan against the foreigners but the only way of doing this was by giving the already rebellious nobility of feudal lords (*daimyo*) the economic means of self-defence. Such a revived force would inevitably be turned against the Tokugawa. At the same time samurai warriors were pushing their lords to more aggressive isolationism while asserting their own authority through sword warfare. The shogunate had become a prevaricating regime which told its domestic critics that it was opposed to further concessions while at the same time trying to conciliate the great powers with trade agreements.

Power, however, was not just drifting away from the shogun and towards the imperial court. It was, once again in Japanese history, flowing to the provinces. The samurai warriors were dominant in the Choshu region following a successful coup and their forces fired on the foreign shipping in the Shimonoseki Strait. They were then bombarded by western powers and a shogun army forced the province to re-submit to the Tokugawa authority. But the Choshu samurai refused to accept the legitimacy of the submission and a further coup brought to power nobles who had originally been isolationists. Choshu became a centre for discontented samurai from all over Japan.

But Japanese power dynamics were shifting in other directions too. Choshu's newly dominant daimyo lords were no longer simple-minded xenophobes; they had studied western military methods in order to reform their military units to dramatic effect. The Shogun army was defeated (1866) when it tried to reassert control in Choshu and in Satsuma – Chosu's neighbouring province and new ally. Now the daimyo saw how western methods applied in Japanese conditions might help them achieve their goal of a renewal. Yoshinobu lasted just one year as shogun. A group of radical samurai seized the palace in Kyoto and declared an imperial restoration. The military units of Satsuma and Choshu were joined by those of Tosa province to become the new imperial army which marched on Edo and forced it to surrender. The emperor Meiji Tenno who had succeeded to the imperial throne the previous year (1867) moved into the Tokugawa castle in Edo which was renamed Tokyo ('eastern capital'); he presided over the Meiji restoration and its experiment in modernity, wore western clothes and liked western food. But as a prolific poet versed in his country's literary traditions he also personified the uneasy dynamism of Japan's experiment in east-west fusion.

A feudal and rural state became an urbanized and bureaucratic one within a generation – a development which had taken centuries in western Europe. The speed of change demonstrated the paradox of embracing emperor worship as a solvent of feudalism, a patriotic duty, a guarantor of unity and a path to modernity. Japan's ancient religion, Shintoism, was reinvented as an ideology at the expense of Buddhism and supplied a pantheon of national deities. The national education system established by the Imperial Rescript on Education (1890) was western in structure and in much of its content. But Shintoism, as well as Confucianism, was an important element in a curriculum which taught Japanese how to be obedient citizens. The adoption of western techniques in technology, government and business was justified and presented as a way of enabling Japan to work towards the eventual revision (1894) of the unequal trade treaties she had been forced to sign. A telegraph and railway network linked cities and towns while Japan's seventy-two administrative prefectures replaced the 250 domains of the daimyo. The samurai who, together with their dependants, numbered some two million, were eventually, after some rebellions, suppressed thereby losing their right to bear swords and sport a distinctive hairstyle. A new power – that of the financial cliques (*zaibatsu*) with close government connections – developed with government selling industrial plants to chosen private investors. Germany, another country yoking modern capitalism to the remnants of feudalism, provided the parliamentary model which tried to balance the claims of representation with those of imperial control. Japan's first bi-cameral Diet met in 1890 with the lower house elected on a franchise of 500,000 males chosen on an annual tax threshold of fifteen yen. European style peerages had been created in 1884 and their holders went into the upper house. The cabinet system, whose members were imperial nominees, was instituted in 1885 and universal conscription strengthened the newly-established national army. Japan experienced the pleasure of defeating its ancient enemy China in the Sino-Japanese war, made an alliance with Britain and savoured the first defeat in modern history of an European power by an Asiatic state when it won the Russian-Japanese war in 1904-05. Commodore Perry, by forcing modernity on Japan, had enabled a new sun to rise in the east.

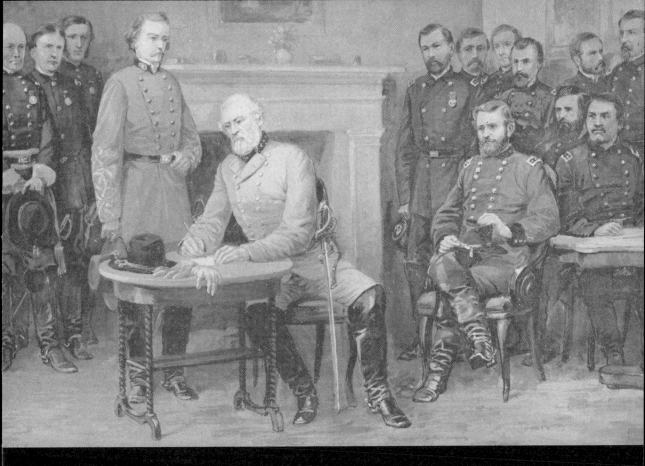

9 April 1865

Robert E. Lee Surrenders at Appomattox

The End of the American Civil War

'*I believe this government cannot endure permanently half slave and half free. I do not expect the Union to be dissolved…It will become all one thing, or all the other.*'

Abraham Lincoln (16 June 1858)

In the spring of 1865 the army of the American southern states, the 'Confederacy', was forced to acknowledge its defeat by the Northern power which had used its might in order to uphold the Union. The Confederate force, which had originally numbered 800,000 men, was now a much diminished band of just 60,000 ill-equipped soldiers, sometimes reduced to their bare feet and often clad in tattered uniforms. General Robert E. Lee (1807-70), commander of the army of northern Virginia, therefore decided he would have to meet with General Ulysses S. Grant (1822-85), the Northern army's overall commander since 1864, in order to discuss the terms of surrender. After an exchange of seven despatches, initiated by Grant at 5 p.m. on 7 April and ending with the delivery of Lee's final reply at 11.50 a.m. on 9 April, the two men agreed to meet in a house in the Virginian village of Appomattox Courthouse, south of Washington DC.

Lee, his ceremonial sword studied with jewels, wore the dress uniform and grey coat of a Confederate officer. He arrived first, followed by Grant whose staff officers had to wait on the lawn before being allowed to enter. The first few moments would be private. Grant's unbuttoned and single-breasted dark-blue blouse was, like his boots, still spattered with the mud of battle. He had a reputation for scruffiness but wished he had prepared better and was suffering from a bad headache. The tanner's son from Ohio told the Virginian aristocrat that there would be no enforced humiliation and that his officers could keep their swords. The Confederacy's cavalry and artillery owned their own horses and, since the spring ploughing was now imminent, Lee asked that his men be allowed to keep them. Grant consented and would also supply the defeated army with rations. The Confederate soldiers were simply to return home. By 4.00 p.m. it was all over and Lee mounted his horse. At fifty-eight, and with seven children to support, he was broke. His father, a former governor of Virginia, had been hopeless with money and Lee depended on the fortune of his heiress wife. But the plantation estates of Mary Anne Randolph Custis, a descendant of George Washington's wife, would now be confiscated.

Trade, partly, had divided the South from the North. Congress raised duties on 19 May 1828 on imported goods, in order to protect the mid-west farmers and the east coast manufacturers. For cotton-exporting Southerners this was a 'Tariff of Abominations', inviting retaliation from the countries they traded with. The Reciprocity Act of 24 May 1828 reduced tariffs for such trading partners but a fundamental economic divergence had emerged within the Union. What really wrecked the States' unity, however, was the interpretation of the written constitution and its relation to slavery.

In 1803, France, needing money for its Continental war, had sold Louisiana – then a vast territory extending to the Rocky mountains – to the US. This area included Missouri which was admitted into the Union in 1820 but the admission was controversial since Missouri was a slave state and northern states had progressively abandoned slavery after the American revolution, New Jersey being the last to abolish it in 1804. Congress's 'Missouri Compromise' of 1820 stated that slavery could not be introduced in any other part of Louisiana. But the terms of a further 'compromise' in 1850 created renewed controversy since this involved the admission of California, a non-slave state, into the Union. This upset the Union's delicate equipoise balancing the number of slave states with non-slave ones. Congress also abolished the slave trade in the District of Columbia, and Southerners, wanting slavery extended, were angered. However, abolitionists and northern liberal opinion were just as outraged when Congress took no action against slavery in Utah and New Mexico which, like California , had been annexed by the US after its war with Mexico. This pro-slavery trend was also evident in the Fugitive Slave Act of 1850, which replaced state penalties for escaped slaves with federal ones. The US constitution had become a hostage in the conflict between contradictory beliefs.

The Kansas-Nebraska Act of 1854 provoked a new crisis by allowing a referendum on slavery in areas which had been part of the Louisiana Purchase. A civil war followed in Kansas before it was admitted into the Union as a non-slave state in 1861. Meanwhile the Supreme Court had inflamed the situation and undermined the Missouri Compromise with its decision that Congress had never had the right to ban slavery in US territories anyway. War was inevitable after the election in 1860 of Abraham Lincoln to the presidency since he was unwavering in his conviction that slavery could not expand – although he also thought present slave states could keep the institution. Naturally, he failed to carry a single Southern state.

Grant and Lee, neither of whom approved of slavery, embodied the North-South cultural difference as well as the tragedy of a conflict which pitted one right, that of human dignity, against another, the rights of individual states. Slavery had never been allowed in Grant's native Ohio or in the other north-western states of Illinois and Indiana. Commercial and industrial development from the mid-century onwards was transforming these areas into powerful centres of the new Northern economy. And the Homestead Act of 1862 inaugurated a new phase of outward-looking pioneering activity by giving American citizens 160 acres of land free of charge on the frontier which was shifting ever-westwards. Grant reflected much of this western and mid-west restlessness. The army bored him and, having resigned his commission, he had an unsuccessful period as a farmer in Missouri and a real estate developer in St Louis. By 1860 he was back in Galena, Illinois, working in his father's leather goods business. War, involving a return to the colours, was the making of him and Grant would be a popular US president after the Civil War.

Lee had been the officer commanded to suppress John Brown's insurrection in October 1859 after the anti-slavery activist had raided the US federal arsenal at Harper's Ferry, Virginia. The consequent slave uprising two days later had been quickly quelled and Brown was hanged in Charleston. But the fact that the revolt was led by a white Northerner caused Lee to worry about the Union's divisions. He had been ordered out of rebellious Texas by the army when, in 1861, the state, along with Mississippi, Florida, Alabama, Georgia and Louisiana, had seceded and thereby joined South Carolina's earlier secession. Back home in Arlington Lee had argued against Virginia following suit but the State Convention resolved not to supply troops to the Union army. Virginia, along with Arkansas, North Carolina and Tennessee, would follow the rebels. Kentucky was neutral. Delaware, Maryland and Missouri were slave states that remained loyal. Lee was summoned to Washington and offered command of a new army but resigned his commission after thirty-six years as an officer because 'he could take no part in an invasion of the Southern states.' The Virginia of Jefferson was in his blood. The four-year conflict began in April 1861 with the Confederate attack on Fort Sumter in Charleston harbour, South Carolina.

Twenty-one million northerners faced nine million southerners (of whom 3.5 million were slaves). Seventy per cent of all America's railroads were in the North which also had 100,000 manufacturing plants as against just 18,000 south of the Potomac. The North also enjoyed a three to one superiority in arms production. Nonetheless, the war started well for the South. General Thomas Jackson had deployed some classically defensive military tactics against the Northerners during the Civil War's first major engagement, the battle of Bull Run, and therefore earned the nickname 'Stonewall'. A second battle at the same site had been won by the South and the Confederate force had followed up these early gains with a successful defence of Fredericksburg in eastern Virginia.

As long as Lee's army was mobile his strategies were usually capable of out-manoeuvring Grant. Even when Grant forced him back to the Virginian port of Richmond, Lee was able to build ingenious fortifications whose engineering originality anticipated trench warfare. The siege lasted from late June 1864 to 1 April 1865 but the defensive lines started to collapse on 2 April. Lee evacuated and withdrew to the west. A running battle was waged over eighty-eight miles before the Confederates were surrounded at Appomattox right on the North-South border. Lee had nowhere left to go. In the south-west Grant's army, having advanced through Mississippi in 1863, had separated the states of Arkansas, Louisiana and Texas from their Confederate allies. Towards the south, beyond the Carolinas, the Union army commanded by General William Tecumseh Sherman had occupied Atlanta, Georgia, a vital industrial centre for the South and the hub of its railway system. Aiming to hit the civilian population hard, Sherman had then stormed through Georgia leaving a trail of destruction fifty miles wide by 250 miles long as he marched towards the coast and the capture of Savannah in December 1864.

Wartime conditions strengthened Northern convictions. This was the first war in which servicemen voted in a national election and the new strength of common purpose culminated in the proclamation of emancipation on 1 January 1863 which freed slaves in the rebel states. On 19 November 1863 Lincoln dedicated a memorial at the sight of the battle of Gettysburg in Pennsylvania where the Confederates had been defeated and he attributed to America's founding fathers his own belief in 'government of the people, by the people, for the people'. Atlanta's fall boosted his campaign to be re-elected in November 1864 as a Republican president and when Lincoln landed in Richmond in 1865 to inspect the city evacuated by Lee he was immediately surrounded by exultant blacks. 'I know I am free,' said one, 'for I have seen father Abraham and felt him.' Ten days later the president was assassinated. But by December, the thirteenth amendment outlawing slavery throughout the reunited States of America had been ratified and become part of the constitution.

Slavery, however, had a tragic and extended postscript when an indifferent North permitted a Southern collapse into political corruption, rural poverty and implacable racism. Institutional slavery was replaced by the institutionalised bigotry of the colour bar in jobs, housing and education. 359,000 Northern soldiers and 258,000 Confederate ones had died in the war which had turned into a crusade but whose ultimate victories were yet to be achieved.

1 September 1870

The Battle of Sedan

Germany becomes Europe's Greatest Power

'…it is not by means of speeches and majority resolutions that the great issues of the day will be decided…but by iron and blood.'

Otto von Bismarck's expression of Prussian diplomacy, 29 September 1862

The battle which destroyed the French Second Empire and led to the proclamation of a Second German Reich was fought at the citadel of Sedan in the Ardennes on France's north-eastern frontier. The town was noted for both its fortress and the chateau which was the birthplace of Louis XIV's marshal Henri de Turenne, the soldier ranked by Napoleon Bonaparte as history's greatest military leader. But after 1 September 1870 'Sedan' became a synonym for French humiliation.

Three Prussian armies totalling 384,000 men were under the command of Helmuth von Moltke, chief of the Prussian general staff and the first soldier to grasp how railways guaranteeing regular reinforcements of men and supplies could change warfare. A battle might now be pursued along an extended front instead of being concentrated on one small battlefield. The strategy had enabled Prussia to humiliate Austria at the battle of Sadowa in 1866 and made her the dominating leader of a 'federation' of north German states. General Patrice MacMahon was, like many French generals, a veteran of the country's North African campaigns waged after the occupation of Algeria. However the Prussian state's war machine was a different proposition compared with Algerian rebels. Many of the 120,000 French soldiers arrived late at the front following Napoleon III's declaration of war on 19 July; the Prussians got there in eighteen days with maps of France showing roads not yet recorded on the ones issued by the French War Ministry.

By late August the French 'army of the Rhine' commanded by Marshal Achille Bazaine was trapped at Metz having been pushed back into Lorraine following an earlier defeat by the Prussians on the same day that they had also defeated MacMahon's separate army on the right French flank in Alsace. MacMahon had retreated west to Châlons-sur-Marne where he attempted a consolidation while the French High Command and the emperor vacillated. Napoleon was in acute pain because of a huge stone in his bladder. Eventually, MacMahon moved north-east to relieve the army at Metz. Word of his intentions reached Moltke on the evening of 24 August in a news report carried in the previous day's edition of *The Times*. It was a calamitous decision since France had no third army left to defend Paris and MacMahon was now moving across the flank of a superior enemy force. Moltke's army of the Meuse intercepted him and three engagements on the River Meuse forced MacMahon northwards to Sedan, sixty miles away from Metz. Bazaine would remain trapped until his eventual surrender in October with 140,000 troops. On the evening of 30 August the French cavalry still felt able to organize a ball at Douzy a few miles south of Sedan but by the morning of 1 September the French had been forced into Sedan and MacMahon was wounded. They would be '*emmerdés*' (shat upon) by the Prussians, said one of the French commanders, General Ducrot. And so it proved.

During the day von Moltke completed the encirclement of Sedan by moving up his third army. There were heroic attempts at a break-out led by the French cavalry. 'Ah! The brave fellows,' said the king of Prussia, Wilhelm I (r. 1861-1888), who had come to watch along with that other great architect of Prussian military might, the war minister Albrecht von Roon. Heavy artillery bombarded the French throughout the day. Napoleon on horseback, trying to encourage his subjects, was rouged up to conceal his pallor. By late afternoon he conceded defeat in a letter which, at 6.30 p.m., was carried to King Wilhelm through the now silent Prussian lines. Since he had not been able to die in the midst of his own troops, he wrote, he would now put his sword in Wilhelm's hands. The French commander de Wimpffen asked later that evening for generous terms of surrender otherwise there might be 'endless war between France and Prussia'. The plea was rejected by the Prussian chancellor Otto von Bismarck who was also at the battle site. France, he said, was 'a nation full of envy and jealousy... we must have territory, fortresses and frontiers which will shelter us from an attack on her part.' Germany's lack of a natural geographical frontier and her consequent vulnerability to encirclement had always dominated his thoughts. The next day Napoleon formally capitulated to Bismarck at a weaver's house in nearby Donchery. Eighty-three thousand French soldiers (including the emperor) became prisoners of war. French losses at Sedan totalled 3,000 killed, 14,000 wounded and 21,000 missing or captured. The German losses at Sedan totalled 9,000 killed and wounded. After the surrender the Prussian army sang together Martin Luther's hymn 'The Old Hundredth' before getting ready to march on Paris.

Earlier that summer France had forced the withdrawal of the Prussian prince Leopold of Hohenzollern-Sigmaringen's acceptance of the Spanish throne which had been vacant since 1868. The French ambassador, meeting the Prussian king at the spa of Ems, had sought an assurance that Leopold's candidature would never again be allowed by Prussia. Bismarck altered the wording of the diplomatic telegram he had received describing the interview and published it as an inflammatory document describing it as a French insult to Prussia. France, having declared war, performed the role of aggressor in a conflict planned by Bismarck as a way of creating a united, Prussian-dominated, Germany.

France entered the war isolated because of the shallow adventurism of her emperor's foreign policy. Ever since his election in 1848 as president of France and the subsequent coup in 1851 which had abolished France's Second Republic and extended his term of office, Napoleon had tried to re-establish France as a great European power following her defeat in 1814. He therefore supported nationalist movements whose agitations unsettled European dynasties. Russia was coldly neutral in 1870 because France had supported the Poles. The US had not forgiven France for intervening in Mexico and supporting archduke Maximilian of Austria with French troops during his brief, doomed, period as emperor of Mexico. Britain was officially neutral but suspicious of France, especially after Bismarck had leaked earlier proposals for a Franco-Prussian division of Belgium. The pro-German queen, Victoria, had, after all, described Paris as 'Sodom and Gomorrah'. Austria would only join if there was an invasion of southern Germany. And Italy hated the sight of French soldiers occupying Rome.

1848 had been a year of liberal revolutions right across Europe. Italy had been especially energetic. Republics were proclaimed in Venice and Rome; Sicily and Naples rebelled against the rule of the Bourbon king Ferdinand II; the king of Piedmont-Sardinia, Charles-Albert, declared war on Austria since he hoped to benefit from the revolt in Milan. Austrian troop bombardments in the north and Bourbon ones in the south crushed the rebellions but the idea of an Italian unification had taken root among Italian liberals, professionals and intellectuals.

Napoleon was central to the subsequent diplomacy which allowed the formation of an Italian state. He declared war on Austria as an ally of Piedmont-Sardinia, the dominant

Italian power in the peninsula's unification. But the consequences of a Piedmontese victory at Palestro and of the subsequent Franco-Piedmontese victories at Magenta in Lombardy and then at Solferino near Verona disturbed Napoleon. His aim had been a loose-knit Italian federation but the wily Count Cavour, prime minister of Piedmont, was creating a unified state whose new democracy might inspire internal opposition to Napoleon's technocratic and authoritarian regime. A prolonged war against Austria in Italy might also expose France to a Prussian attack along the Rhine. A French agreement with the Austrian emperor Franz Josef at Villafranca therefore contemplated an Italian federation presided over by the Pope – perhaps the silliest of this emperor's manoeuvrings. Events were out of his hands after Giuseppe Garibaldi, having landed in Sicily with a thousand red-shirted followers, gave inspired leadership to a rebellion against the king of Naples. Plebiscites all over Italy voted for a union with Piedmont and so in March 1861 a kingdom of Italy was created. Nice and Savoy, generously in the circumstances, were ceded to France in recognition of her earlier, ambiguous, role in the unification. Austria retained Venetia until defeat in the war with Prussia in 1866 forced her to cede the region to Italy. Rome, however, along with what remained of the Papal States, was controlled by French troops. Italian nationalists, deprived of a civic symbol, were angered and the Pope, whom the French were supposed to protect, was unimpressed by his French defenders. The Papacy, after the first Vatican council, was in full flight from modernity and regarded Napoleon as having collaborated with the secularist and anti-clerical tyranny of European state-nationalism. Its views were confirmed when Germany embarked on an official policy of Catholic persecution. Anti-clericalism would also became a force in the late nineteenth century battles of French politics for a secular education system embedded in the values of a revived republican tradition.

Italian troops entered Rome after French troops had to be withdrawn to fight the Prussians. Four days after the collapse of Sedan the French Third Republic was proclaimed. A Parisian crowd, following revolutionary tradition, invaded the Tuileries palace and found empty jewel cases on the floor. The empress Eugenie had fled, seeking refuge in the house of her American dentist who then smuggled her out of Paris and towards an English exile where her husband would eventually join her. Paris capitulated to German troops in January 1871 after a 135-day siege. By the Treaty of Frankfurt France lost Alsace and part of Lorraine to the new Germany which now brought together Prussia, Bavaria, Saxony and Württemberg along with five grand duchies, thirteen duchies and principalities, as well as the free cities of Hamburg, Bremen and Lubeck. France had to pay Germany an indemnity of five billion francs. The Second Reich, proclaimed vaingloriously in the palace of Versailles, was meant to be the successor to the Holy Roman Empire abolished by Napoleon in 1806. Bismarck had taken the liberalism out of 'liberal nationalism' and created a powerhouse which combined political with industrial might: Alfred Krupp's steelworks at Essen produced the guns that killed the French at Sedan. A left-wing central committee, the Commune, emerged out of the shame of Sedan to take charge of Paris and between 20,000 and 30,000 Parisians were killed during the 'bloody week' of its suppression. But the Communards' example meant the birth of an effective European socialism and states sustained by ideological nationalism would now confront this international solidarity.

7 March 1876

Alexander Graham Bell Develops the Telephone

US Patent number 174,465 is issued

'No skilled operator is required; direct conversation may be had by speech without the intervention of a third person. It is unsurpassed for economy and simplicity.'

Salesmanship from the Bell Telephone Company, 1877

Speculation and information about sound, speech and the transmission of the human voice had surrounded Alexander Graham Bell (1847-1922) from infancy. The business of elocution had provided his family with a livelihood for two generations before his birth and Bell, along with his two brothers, was trained to continue that profession in dynastic style. Apart from three years of formal education in the Scotland of his youth, Bell was almost entirely taught within his own family circle and by his own efforts. *Standard Elocutionist*, the volume written by his father Alexander Melville Bell, went through nearly 200 editions and was proof of an immense desire to achieve accurate self-expression in the English-speaking world of the mid to late nineteenth century. Elocution was a good business to be in as literacy became almost universal by the end of the century in Victorian England and new generations of the ambitious sought to better their prospects following the age's classic impulses of self-help and self-improvement. Bell's career and interests themselves illustrated the period's concern with useful knowledge, social progress and career prospects. His first job was as a teacher in Elgin and his practical experience in communicating information about music and elocution influenced his scientific explorations. As with so many go-getting Scots, the Bells headed south and established their business in London where Bell became his father's assistant. But even greater opportunities beckoned when, for the sake of the health of an overworked young Bell, the family transplanted themselves and their business in 1870 to Ontario, Canada. For the rest of his life Bell's career and successes would be part of the history of North America during its great late nineteenth- and early twentieth-century economic expansion.

Teaching speech to the deaf had always been a lucrative part of the Bell business and Alexander Melville Bell's *Visible Speech* had provided a detailed system of phonetic symbols which indicated particular movements and positions for the lips, tongue and soft palate which produce the sound of the human voice. By these means the deaf could imitate the sounds produced by the unimpaired. Using his father's manual, Bell took to the stage with public lectures – whose popularity was another typical feature of this age of cultural ambition. In a series of demonstrations performed in Boston, Massachusetts, he showed how the deaf and previously mute could be taught to speak. The results made Bell a local celebrity and established him in North America. In 1873 he became professor of vocal physiology and elocution at the University of Boston and later in his career Helen Keller would be Bell's star pupil.

Throughout this period of active career development Bell was also engaged in nightly experiments designed to demonstrate how speech and sound might be transmitted by electronic means. In this enterprise he was helped by his assistant Thomas Watson who designed the necessary models and apparatus. On 6 April 1875 Bell was granted a patent for his multiple telegraph by the US Patent Office. And on 7 March 1876 he received what may well be the most valuable patent ever issued – the one for his telephone, described as 'The method of, and apparatus for, transmitting vocal or other sounds telegraphically... by causing electrical undulations, similar in form to the vibrations of the air accompanying the said vocal or other sounds.' Many scientists and inventors had long since grasped the general principles behind the idea of a telephone but what was lacking was a practical instrument demonstrating those principles. Bell had an additional motivation to spur him on towards his invention

– in developing a telephone he was looking for an instrument which would help him to communicate with his deaf wife. Litigation to protect his patent, as a result of its infringement, would plague Bell throughout his life, but his own claim to priority in the discovery and application of the current of undulation was upheld in the US courts and formed the basis of the Bell Telephone Company which, founded in 1877, gave him and his family financial security.

Bell was under thirty when he invented the telephone but his scientific curiosity, along with his zeal to transform scientific discoveries into commercial products, was undimmed by early success. He moved to Washington DC and developed the photophone which transmitted speech on beams of light and would be the precursor of contemporary laser and optical fibre communication systems. The graphophone, developed with his cousin Chichester Bell, was another revolution in the history of sound since its engraving stylus, controllable speeds, wax cylinders and disks enabled sound to be recorded. And another practical motivation, the urgent need to find the bullet in the body of the US president, James Garfield, after he was shot by an assassin in July 1881, led to Bell's hasty invention of the metal detector.

The interlocking pattern of theory and practice, of experiment and application, seen in Bell's life also makes him part of the wider story of American technology which was going through a period of great advance at this time. In 1868 Christopher Latham Sholes invented the typewriter which gave a huge boost to clerical productivity and also provided a large female population with work which took them out of the home. George Westinghouse invented the air-brake in 1869 which raised the safety standards of the US rail network, and American technological flair produced its greatest single figure in Thomas Edison, the inventor of the phonograph in 1878 and of electric light in 1879. American civilization was becoming conscious both of its greatness and of its distinctiveness – qualities which are reflected in the rolling free verse of Walt Whitman and especially in his volume of poetry *Leaves of Grass* which combined the traditional with the experimental in a manner which was now being identified as typically American. Mark Twain's novel *Tom Sawyer*, published in 1876, is in the same tradition of self-exploration and adventure.

The Brooklyn bridge, which was being built throughout the 1870s by the Roebling father and son team, was not only the world's first great suspension bridge; it would also become an icon of the new, post-Civil War, self-confidence of the American spirit. The period also threw up a distinctive American religiosity in the preoccupations of Mary Baker Eddy who founded the Christian Science movement in 1866 and in those of Charles Taze Russell who established the Jehovah's Witnesses in 1877. Bell's own status as a consummate adopted American came when his telephone was the prize exhibit at the Centennial Exhibition held in 1876 to celebrate a hundred years of US independence. However, the vogue for scientific progress had its more sinister side. Eugenics, applying superior knowledge in order to 'improve' humanity for its own good, was one of this period's major interests. Bell was a particular enthusiast for it, advocating sterilization of the deaf and working to outlaw the marriage of deaf people to each other. His interest in the question of hereditary characteristics among the deaf also led to his eugenic experiments in sheep breeding.

Within twenty years of Bell being granted his patent the telephone instrument had acquired its distinctive shape. Used for private purposes, it was a major example of the domestication of science when a major area of technology became so intimate and necessary a part of daily life that it ceased to be seen as remarkable.

Many letters and diaries that might otherwise have existed were never written as a result of the telephone's convenience and availability. The instrument may also have played a part in the standardisation of accents which became increasingly obvious in the world languages from the early twentieth century onwards. Telephones enlarged the opportunities for human gossip, expanded the bureaucratic powers of government and supplied the commanders of armies with a fast method of communicating their strategies on the field of battle. Countries that were both technologically advanced and geographically far flung rushed to use them and in 1912 the US had sixty-seven per cent of the world's telephones. Los Angeles, Chicago, Philadelphia, Boston and New York, together with Stockholm, were the six cities with the greatest number of telephones in the immediate pre-1914 world. The telephone was also part of a much speeded-up world economy in the late nineteenth century as communications criss-crossed the globe establishing faster and closer links between market goods and customer demand. As a result of this process a figure of great social significance emerged in economically advanced societies – that of the clerk or white-collar worker who answered the phones and did the paperwork in offices, businesses and shops. In Britain this workforce in the commercial sector of the economy jumped from 360,000 in 1881 to almost 900,000 in 1911, of whom seventeen per cent were women.

Bell's technological invention had been the midwife to an economic transformation whose consequences widened the range of human experience and provided new horizons for the human imagination. Elected president of the National Geographical Society in 1898 Bell seized the chance to promote the transformation of the society's journal into a magazine with a mass readership intrigued by other cultures and curious about remote areas of the earth's surface. The enterprise typified the skill of an extraordinary genius with an insight into the dreams of the many.

20 June 1900

The Boxer Rebellion

China Turns Against the West

*'In fifty years time there will be millions of Boxers in serried
ranks and war's panoply at the call of the Chinese government.'*

Sir Robert Hart, British colonial administrator, anticipates
Maoist chauvinism, 1901

In the spring of 1900 diplomats based in Beijing had seen the mounting scale of the attacks during the previous two years on foreigners' homes and businesses, on Christian missions and on Chinese Christian converts. Starting in northern China the violence had now gripped the capital. The dowager empress Tzu-hsi (Cixi) had declared that foreign powers were casting upon the Chinese, 'looks of tiger-like voracity, hustling each other to be first to seize our innermost territories'. And her encouragement of the violence was clear: 'If our hundreds of millions of inhabitants… would prove their loyalty to their emperor and love of their country, what is there to fear from any invader?'

On 30 May 1900 the diplomats asked for troops to protect them. Between 31 May and 4 June 430 sailors and marines arrived at the legations within the diplomatic compound just outside the walls of Beijing's Forbidden City and defensive barricades were raised. However a greater force would be needed to repel the insurgents known to the westerners as 'the Boxers'. Sir Claude MacDonald, Britain's ambassador, therefore asked for a larger relief force just before the telegraph lines were cut, stopping any further communication with the governments in London and Washington, Paris, Berlin and Rome, Moscow, Vienna and Tokyo. The diplomats, their families and staff, together with hundreds of Chinese Christians, were isolated within both the compound and the Roman Catholic cathedral. On 18 June the empress ordered that all foreigners in China be killed. Two days afterwards the siege of the compound began as 20,000 Boxers waving swords and stamping feet advanced in a solid mass carrying their banners of red and white cloth and wearing the uniform which defined them: red turbans, sashes and garters worn over blue cloth. 'Their yells,' wrote a survivor, 'were deafening, while the roar of gongs, drums and horns sounded like thunder.' The attackers were just twenty yards from the gate when the compound's small military force opened fire with three volleys and killed some fifty of the Boxers who then dispersed. But, day after day, they returned. By mid-August seventy-six of the besieged had been killed including the German ambassador. There was hardly any ammunition, food or medical supplies left. And then, shortly before dawn on the morning of 14 August, Beijing echoed to the sound of a huge explosion.

The 'Boxer rebellion' anticipated many of the violently anti-western reactions which would recur in the history of the twentieth and early twenty-first centuries. The 'scramble for Africa' was over by 1900 and the continent conveniently carved up to provide colonies for the British and the Belgians, the French and the Germans. China was next on the list and Britain, in particular, seemed poised for its next great Asian expansion after the successful reimposition of colonial order in India following the mutiny of 1857. It had already waged one successful war (1839-42) against China in furtherance of its opium trade with the country and thereby gained the colony of Hong Kong. The Second Opium War, declared in 1856, ended with the Chinese having to legitimize the entire trade – a business with profound and enervating consequences for the morale of the Chinese population and its ruling class. Britain had celebrated its imperial apogee at the diamond jubilee of its Queen-Empress Victoria in 1897 and was ready for a Chinese challenge.

China's defeat in the Sino-Japanese war (1894-5) meant that Austria, France, Germany, Italy, Russia and Britain as well as Japan could press ahead with the establishment of their own 'spheres of influence' giving them exclusive trading rights in certain parts of the country. The US, absorbed in a war with Spain, missed out. However, victory in that war led to the American acquisition from Spain of the Philippines only 400 miles away from China. This reinforced the US view of itself as a power with legitimate Asian interests and the secretary of state John Hay pushed for an 'open door' policy which would give all the powers equal trading opportunities right across China. Other countries accepted in principle but said the policy was unenforceable. They then found that Hay considered them to have provided a 'final and definitive' agreement with his proposal.

'The Fists of Righteous Harmony' was a religious society whose members claimed that their magical spells and ritualized martial arts made them impervious to pain and bullets. Dubbed therefore 'the Boxers' by foreigners, their reactionary anarchism was dedicated to the renewal of China and, initially, to attacks on the imperial regime which had let China down by its failure to defend the country against 'foreign devils' who had to be expelled. Some of the Boxers were disbanded soldiers and others had been boatmen on China's Grand Canal until the arrival of railways made them unemployed. Most, however, were peasants suffering the consequences of recent natural disasters. The first protests of this latest Boxer campaign therefore took place in the northern province of Shan-tung (1898) where a drought was causing mass starvation. At first the Chinese imperial army was ordered to suppress the Boxers but its task was made harder by the dowager empress's declaration in January 1900 that the Boxers were not criminals but an authentic part of Chinese society.

Cixi was right about the Boxers' traditionalism for they were an offshoot of the Eight Trigrams Society which had been organizing insurrections since the late eighteenth century and rebel armies had always been an intermittent feature of the peasantry's 5000-year history. It was also the Boxers' cultural traditionalism which explained the ferocity of their anti-Christian attacks. By May 1900 the imperial government had effectively embraced the Boxer cause but central authority had collapsed and power was increasingly in the hands of regional governors who had different strategies for dealing with the Boxers. In the province of Shensi, for example, the governors incorporated them into the local militia, but those of the south-eastern provinces and of Canton disobeyed Beijing's anti-foreign decrees and agreed with the foreign consuls at Shanghai that they would protect the foreigners under their jurisdiction.

The political career of the dowager empress, Cixi, began humbly enough since she was fairly low down the pecking order of imperial concubines; however, the fact that she was the mother of the Xiangfeng emperor's only son gave her power. Her son, the Tongzhi emperor, was just six years old at the start of his fourteen year reign (1861-75) and an eight-member regency council ruled in his name. After the late emperor's brother, Prince Gong, launched a coup the regency was transferred to Cixi and to the former emperor's chief consort, Ci'an. Prince Gong then ruled through the two female regents and mid-nineteenth-century China experienced its successes: the great Taiping rebellion in the south and the Nian rebellion in the north were both suppressed. China got a new foreign office, an efficient customs regime and arsenals built on the foreign model. After Tongzhi's early death (1875) the two empress dowagers continued as regents since Cixi's nephew, and adopted son, who became the Guangzu emperor (r.1875-1908) was only three at his accession. Cixi was sole regent after Ci'an, in her turn, died suddenly and then became effectively the sole ruler of China after her dismissal of Prince Gong. In 1889 she had, nominally, retired but the post-1895 crisis saw her return to power. Reformers within the imperial circle tried to learn lessons from their victorious Japanese neighbour: schemes to eliminate corruption and to streamline Chinese government were circulated. Cixi's circle mounted a military coup and made her regent again and in 1898 the reform schemes were dropped.

The early morning bombardments on 14 August announced the arrival in Beijing of an international expeditionary force which would rescue the besieged westerners. An earlier allied force had been forced back to its base by both the Boxers and the imperial army. Now a greater allied force of 20,000 left Tientsin and arrived in Beijing having won two major battles. The Forbidden City was ransacked. Cixi, disguised as a peasant, fled the city in a cart. Beijing was looted and then occupied as the allies went on to consolidate their control of the northern Chinese countryside where the Boxers had been numerous and well supported. The Chinese government agreed to abolish the Boxers and then submitted to the humiliating clauses of the Peace Protocol of Peking: European powers were allowed to maintain military forces in Beijing and this meant that the imperial government was effectively under an armed occupation; government officials involved in the rebellion were to be prosecuted; the foreign powers were indemnified for loss of property; forts between Beijing and the sea were dismantled; all arms imports were suspended. America's 'open door' policy prevailed throughout China which escaped partition only because it suited US commercial interests to maintain the country's territorial integrity. China was in fact no longer independent and her enfeeblement meant that she could not intervene in the Russo-Japanese war which led to Japan's far eastern dominance.

Cixi, back in Beijing by 1902, had to implement the reforms so contemptuously abandoned just four years previously. Modernization involved the introduction of female education and the curriculum's bias in favour of classical Confucianism was replaced by one which promoted mathematics, science and engineering. Young Chinese students went to Europe to be educated where some of them were exposed to Marxism which eventually became, after Buddhism from India, China's second most important intellectual import. China's army was also professionalized on western and Japanese lines: the officer corps now provided a structured military career and an integrated command structure. The Provincial assemblies, proposed in the 1890s, arrived in 1909 and a national, democratically elected, Consultative Assembly was established in 1910. Conflict followed between the Assembly and a discredited dynasty. The dowager empress's China had changed but she herself had not. The young emperor died the day before she did in November 1908 and Cixi was suspected of involvement in yet another of the sudden deaths which had punctuated, and made, her career. The Manchu no longer enjoyed popular support and the 'mandate of heaven' – that aura of supremacy and legitimacy conferred by success – had been withdrawn. A major rebellion broke out in 1911 in the western province of Szechwan and this developed into the Chinese national revolution which deposed the dynasty. The paradox of westernization meant that an ancient civilization had been provided with the military, educational and administrative means which would lead to the creation of a new, nationalist, China which, in her turn and in her own way, would return to challenge the West.

30 June 1905

E = mc²: The Special Theory of Relativity

Einstein Revolutionizes Physics

'God is subtle but he is not malicious.'

The world according to Einstein – mysterious but still intelligible

In 1905 Albert Einstein (1879-1955) had been working in the patent office in Berne for four years. The German education system had been an unhappy experience for him and that fact may lie behind Einstein's youthful decision to renounce his German citizenship in 1896. He was born in Ulm, raised in Munich where his father and uncle ran a small electrical and engineering factory, disliked his Catholic primary school and left his secondary school, the gymnasium, early at the age of fifteen without a leaving diploma. Having moved with his parents to Milan – a city he disliked – Einstein then failed at his first attempt to get into the celebrated Federal Polytechnic Academy in Zurich. When he was eventually admitted he avoided lectures and conducted his own experiments on electrodynamics in the academy's laboratories.

One of the series of papers that Einstein published in 1905, his *annus mirabilis*, proposed that light, as well as being a wave phenomenon, consisted of individual particles or quanta (now known as photons). This explained why electrons were emitted from solids when they are struck by light and Einstein was awarded the Nobel Prize (1921) for this elucidation of the photoelectric effect. The most celebrated of his 1905 papers concerned the special theory of relativity which maintained that neither time nor motion are absolute. Instead, they are relative to the observer and only the speed of light, at *c.* 186,300 miles per second, is constant. He also showed the equivalence of mass and energy which are linked by the formula $E=mc^2$ (where E is energy, m is mass and c is the speed of light). In 1916 Einstein, by now working at the Prussian Academy of Sciences in Berlin, published his general theory of relativity which demonstrated that gravitation was not a force, as Newton had supposed. Instead Einstein showed a more subtle and mysterious world in which gravity was a distortion or curved field in the space-time continuum. It was the presence of mass within that continuum which caused the distortion. The authority of Einstein's work had displaced a 200-year-old world view since his insights were utterly at variance with the regular and uniform laws of classical, Newtonian, physics. Experiments carried out during the solar eclipse of 1919 proved the accuracy of his theory and the profundity of its consequences. From that point onwards Einstein was acclaimed globally not just as the foremost scientist of the modern age but also as an intellect unique in the history of humanity.

Einstein's genius transcended his own time but his character, views and influences reflected a particular intellectual and cultural milieu – that of a German-speaking world which created a civilization of unparalleled distinction between the mid-nineteenth and early twentieth centuries. The three ideas whose practical consequences would dominate twentieth-century history all emerged from that culture: the unconscious as explored by Sigmund Freud in Vienna, the quantum theory of the Berlin physicist Max Planck who showed that all energy comes in tiny packets (or quanta), and the theory of genetics which was uncovered by the Viennese-educated monk Gregor Mendel. German literary, humanistic and artistic culture was of an extraordinary brilliance. Johannes Brahms, Alban Berg, Gustav Mahler, Richard Wagner and Richard Strauss among musicians; Paul Klee and Gustav Klimt in painting; the philosophers Martin Heidegger and Ludwig Wittgenstein; the novels of Thomas Mann and Franz Kafka as well as the poetry of Rainer Maria Rilke: these achievements provided European civilization with its profound and transforming themes. The sixteenth century had belonged to Spain, the seventeenth century to France and the nineteenth century to Great Britain. Surely, therefore, the twentieth century would witness Germany's own golden age since, just as in the case of these other civilizations, political unification was providing the matrix of cultural glory. The life and work of Albert Einstein, pacifist, liberal, and non-orthodox Jew, were shaped by the European catastrophe which resulted from the German failure to live up to this promise.

Einstein first became a committed pacifist during the 1914-18 conflict with his view that war was: '... an epidemic delusion which, having caused infinite suffering, will one day vanish and become a monstrous and incomprehensible source of wonderment to later generations.' By the 1920s he was a figure of international celebrity attracting huge audiences on the global lecture circuit but often travelling by choice in third class carriages and invariably carrying with him the violin which was his chief recreation. Einstein had now become the archetypal 'creative genius' and was revered as such right across the world as well as within the European countries whose disputes he viewed with a bewildered, and sometimes naïve, dismay. He had intuited at a deeper level than any of his scientific predecessors the nature of the cosmos and this induced in him a profound serenity in the presence of so great a mystery. Einstein's character combined this contemplative quality with a passionate commitment to human justice and, as a result, he changed the modern view of what it meant to be a genius. Nineteenth-century European Romanticism had celebrated Beethoven as a genius partly because his conduct and temperament – turbulent, solitary and misunderstood – illustrated so perfectly the Romantic idea of how such a character should behave. And there was much of this kind of traditional Romanticism in Einstein the cultural icon as well. He, just like Beethoven, quarried deep truths and was touched by a divine spark of creativity. But the millions who watched him on newsreels, listened to him on the radio and flocked to his public lectures, did so because they detected in him an unaffected goodness. Scientific mastery had taught him humility in the face of a cosmos which could never be completely understood. This touched the hearts and minds of millions in a way that the noisy chatter of self-conscious intellectuals could never do.

The consequences of Einstein's work, however, were anything but serene for they dissolved the old scientific certainties which built self-confident systems of thought based on an objective reason. His dislodgement of previous certainties at a scientific level happened at exactly the same time that nineteenth century Europe's cultural and political confidence about its own evolutionary and progressive ascent came crashing down in the early twentieth century.

The world of Newton was one in which forces operated at a distance: objects were mutually attracted by the force of gravity inversely proportional to the square of the distance between them. But Einstein had replaced this uniform picture with a material world which was pervaded by subtle 'fields of force'. The atom was no longer the ultimate building block of matter, an indestructible solid of impenetrable matter; instead it was a centre of forces and the energy-mass equation stated that a particle of matter could be converted into an enormous quantity of energy. Einstein had therefore made the atomic and the hydrogen bombs a possibility. The relativity principle showed that space and time were no longer part of the structure of the world but were inventions which were relative to where the individual happened to be.

This was comprehensible enough to be psychologically disturbing to non-scientists. *Fin de siècle* had already become a popular 1890s' phrase which described not only the century's end but also evoked a cultivated pessimism about the future along with a suspicion that Europe, perhaps civilization itself, was running out of steam. The writings of Friedrich Nietzsche (1844-1900), including especially *The Will to Power*, were the most celebrated example of a new and neurotic anti-rationalism. Perhaps initially the fears were those of a literate minority with too much time on their hands. But they would be realized in the early twentieth century collapse of European order – a fact which explains the wide readership of the German writer Oswald Spengler and the immense popularity of the thesis he advanced in *The Decline of the West*. Einstein's personal popularity and authority are therefore inseparable from the world crisis which turned into mass tragedy. What he said about the natural world was both exciting and frightening: it was also, in the popular mind, connected with the objective world of political and economic breakdown both before and after 1914-18.

Politically, Einstein became a convinced supporter of the Zionist movement: a nation state in Palestine would be a refuge from the new fury of European nationalism. He was dismayed by the impotence of the League of Nations and established an Einstein War Resisters' International Fund to bring pressure on the World Disarmament Conference in Geneva in 1932. After the failure of the conference, the election (1933) of Adolf Hitler as chancellor, and the refusal of the Collège de France in Paris to give him a job, he settled in the US. By now he had abandoned pacifism and was urging rearmament on Europe's democracies while becoming increasingly pessimistic about humanity's ability to resist self-destruction. His failure to bring order into the political world therefore gave his scientific work a new impetus. Affirming his belief in a 'God who reveals himself in the harmony of what exists', he tried to discover an order within the natural world and the cosmos. Despite the destabilizing truths of relativity, he hoped that the universe as a whole could still be understood as a total system which hung together. Einstein's unified field theory therefore preoccupied him from the 1920s onwards as an attempt at expressing the laws which governed the behaviour of everything in the universe. Building on his relativity theory he struggled to find a mathematical relationship between electromagnetism and gravitation – a single equation which would express and relate the universal properties of matter and energy. But the quantum mechanics of Werner Heisenberg, which had itself evolved out of Einstein's work on relativity, had become the dominant school of thought in modern physics. Heisenberg's 'uncertainty principle' stated that the position and the velocity of an object cannot be measured both exactly and simultaneously. Therefore, the movement of a single particle could not be predicted – a conclusion which convinced most scientists of the impossibility of Einstein's quest.

The scientist whose work had made the atomic age a possibility was also the sage who tried, like Dr Frankenstein, to control the consequence of his own discoveries. Einstein therefore represents the end of a long western tradition which claimed that knowledge is always and intrinsically innocent. After he learnt that the uranium atom had been split in Copenhagen (1939) and also, some months earlier, in Berlin, Einstein wrote to President Franklin D. Roosevelt urging that the US develop its own atomic bomb. Albert Einstein had become, in spite of himself, implicated in the politics of humanity's most destructive epoch.

28 June 1914

The Assassination of Franz Ferdinand at Sarajevo

A Serb Terrorist Triggers the First World War

'*Germany…is a powder magazine. All her neighbours are in terror for fear she will explode, and sooner or later, explode she must.*'

Henry Adams, American historian, writing from St Petersburg, 1901

The decision of Franz Ferdinand, archduke of Austria, to pay an official visit to Sarajevo, capital of the Austro-Hungarian territory of Bosnia, on 28 June 1914 was controversial – like the man himself. The Hapsburgs' multinational empire could only survive, he thought, if no single national grouping felt disadvantaged by any others. Hungary enjoyed complete internal autonomy within the state of Austria-Hungary, newly created in 1867, and Franz Ferdinand had supported minority nationalities within Hungary who objected to Magyar dominance. But the archduke was visiting Bosnia in his official capacity as inspector-general of the imperial army and as the emperor Franz Josef's nephew and heir. Here he was seen as a Hapsburg oppressor.

Under the terms of the Congress of Berlin in 1878 the great powers had allowed the Austrians to occupy Bosnia, previously a province of the Ottoman empire, under an international mandate. Bosnia's large Serb population were Orthodox in religion and ethnically Slavic; their loyalties, therefore, lay with neighbouring Serbia which had been granted autonomy by the Ottomans. In their campaign for inclusion within a greater Serbia the Bosnian Serbs enjoyed the support of Russia – the great patron of an Orthodox, pan-Slavic civilization. Tensions had been particularly acute since the outright annexation of Bosnia by Austria. The archduke had also, foolishly, chosen to visit on Serbia's national day. Serbs everywhere were commemorating the fall of their great mediaeval civilisation in 1389 at the battle of Kosovo when they had been defeated by the Ottomans. The territory of Kosovo had been ceded to Serbia by the Treaty of London which had ended the first Balkan war in 1913, but the treaty, deferring to Austrian wishes, had also created an independent state of Albania in order to deny Serbia overland access to the Adriatic. Serbian pride mingled with Serbian resentment at the country's contemporary condition. A palace coup had replaced the factionalist intrigues of the Obrenovic dynasty with the constitutional, but fragile, Karadjordjevic monarchy. Serbia's government remained unstable, corrupt and incompetent. The Black Hand (also known as the 'Unification or Death' movement) was a secretive Serb nationalist organization led by army officers who despised the civilian government. In 1913 its chief, Colonel Dimitrijevic, had been appointed the Serbian general staff's head of intelligence. Gavrilo Princip, a nineteen-year-old student and Bosnian Serb, had been trained in assassination techniques by the Black Hand and was now among the Sarajevo crowds who lined the route waiting for Franz Ferdinand's car – a 28-horsepower open-topped Graf-und-Stift – to drive past.

Princip was one of six conspirators who were initially frustrated when the archduke's chauffeur took an unexpected route during the morning. Nedjelko Cabrinovic threw a bomb that had bounced off the car and caused no injuries. Lunch at the city hall had gone smoothly enough, with the archduchess Sophie meeting a delegation of Muslim women. But during the afternoon the chauffeur took a wrong turning and, as he was trying to reverse, the car ended directly opposite Princip who fired at point blank range. Within an hour the archduke had died of his wounds; his wife had died instantly. A month later, Austria-Hungary declared war on Serbia which it regarded as responsible for the outrage. Princip was sentenced to twenty years imprisonment – the maximum legal penalty for an under-twenty year old – but died in 1918 in a hospital prison having contracted tuberculosis of the bone. By that date millions of Europeans had died in a war without parallel in European, and world, history.

By the early twentieth century, diplomacy had brought Britain, France and Russia together in a single grouping of powers separate from Germany and its dependent neighbour Austria-Hungary. Bismarck's attempts at protecting the new Germany from French revenge by forging alliances with Russia had unravelled because the western powers, apprehensive of Germany's post-1871 power, had sought a rapprochement with Russia. The Crimean War of 1854-6 had been fought by the British and French in order to assert the Ottoman empire's independence and to frustrate the Russian westward advance after the Tsar had claimed the right of protection over the Ottomans' Christian Orthodox subjects. Russia, under the terms of the Peace of Paris, had been denied the Dardanelles and the Black Sea was neutralized. But in 1893 France, now recovering from the 1871 trauma and investing heavily in the Russian economy, had signed a Dual Entente with the Tsar. This ensured the return of Germany's greatest fear of exposure to military attack from both the east and the west. In 1904 France had signed its own entente cordiale with Britain and in 1907 the Triple Entente was formed between France, Britain and Russia. Bismarck's diplomatic edifice, the Triple Alliance of Germany, Austria and Italy, survived but had been challenged. The first Balkan war, like its successor, confirmed Russia's judgement that Serbia was vital to its own survival since it would ensure that no other country would gain control of the Dardanelles (an eventuality damaging to the rapidly growing Russian economy). The two wars had also confirmed Austria-Hungary's view of Serbia as a threat.

Northern and western European countries were now economically successful industrialized societies whose recessionary cycles were corrected by boom years. Europe's total population grew from 150 million in 1800 to 400 million in 1914 and the continent now had a dozen mega-cities with populations of over a million along with scores of others populated by over half a million. The economic growth created a new plutocratic class, secured high levels of middle-class comfort and also drove the political growth of organized labour and the trades unions. Serfdom had vanished, and the extension of the franchise had created the novel politics of mass democracies with political parties and powerful bureaucracies.

Votes for women was a major issue in advanced societies and, at an elite level, Jews emancipated from previous restrictions and enclosed existences were in the vanguard of European economic success and cultural achievement. Awareness of class identity, class self-interest and also class anxiety (because of the new social mobility) was also shaping European politics. Britain's wave of strikes immediately before 1914 betokened a new crisis in 'industrial relations' and her empire illustrated new problems in European colonial policy. Ireland, absorbed within Britain, was seen by its republicans as a colony and this led to political dissidence. The Second Boer War had seen Britain struggling to assert its sovereignty over the Dutch settlers in its South African colony.

However, the dynamism of an European economy searching for new markets and raw materials ensured trade expansion which produced the world's first globalized economy. Domestic and foreign trade were now interdependent – a fact which also pushed the European search for new colonies. Colonial ambitions also ensured European quarrels. Conflicting territorial ambitions in east Africa, for example, led to Franco-British military confrontation in 1898 at Fashoda in Egyptian Sudan and Germany challenged France's rights in Morocco by sending a gunboat to Agadir in 1911.

Germany was, in every respect, exceptional. State-directed capitalism meant that technically and industrially, it had overtaken Britain but, having unified so late, Germany lacked the colonies seized by more established governments. It therefore embarked on a late nineteenth century naval expansion programme in order to gain German *'lebensraum'* or 'living space'. The failure of the country's liberal revolutions in 1848 continued to have profound political consequences, with the authoritarian forces of the court, army and bureaucracy co-existing with a comparatively weak institutional democracy.

War in the summer of 1914 was not 'inevitable' and Europe had survived the earlier Balkan crises of 1908 and of 1912-13. Generals were not innocents and they knew that a European war would be uniquely destructive because of transformed techno-logical capacity. Germany, in particular, appreciated the near-impossibility of waging a war on two frontiers in the east and west. It also understood the fragility of Italy as an ally: in March 1915 Italy would declare war on Austria-Hungary after the allies promised it Austrian territory in the north of the peninsula. Some diplomatic nego-tiation was still possible in July 1914. Austria after all had not been directly attacked and Serbia, initially, had been conciliatory. None of the western entente powers had a treaty with Serbia and so an Austrian attack on the country would not justify war. Nor was there any such treaty forcing Russia to assist Serbia. Britain's entente deals did not commit her to military action in defence of either France or Russia and her treaty commitment of 1840 to Belgian independence only became a determinant of British policy in August 1914. The lack of inevitability explains why it took over a month for a general war to develop after Princip fired his shots. War resulted from the fears and uncertainties of European politicians, not from the requirements of treaties.

Austria demanded that it be allowed to hunt down anti-Austrian dissidents on Serbian soil. Serbia first hesitated and then ordered only a partial mobilization. Russia decided on 25 July, without consulting Britain or France, to support Serbia. Austria-Hungary, with Germany's implicit encouragement, declared war on Serbia. Russia's consequent mobilization led to a German ultimatum to Russia and also to France. Germany went into war in a panic since it needed to avoid simultaneous east and west invasions. Its Schlieffen plan, relying on a slow Russian mobilization, was meant to ensure a quick German defeat of France before turning towards an eastern front. Germany therefore declared war on Russia first on 1 August and only two days later on France – by which date its troops were already across the Belgian border and approaching French territory. Britain, claiming to defend the rights of small nations, declared war on Germany and then on Austro-Hungary. The principle of nationality, one of the war's causes, was now a war aim and therefore a reason for the conflict's prolonga-tion. Britain's intervention changed everything. Her protection by the encircling seas as well as her naval supremacy made a quick German victory an impossibility. There would either be a rapid German defeat or a prolonged war. Germany thought that Britain's influence should have restrained both France's anti-German sentiments and the pan-Slavist ambitions of Russia. Neither Germany nor Austria had reckoned on war with Britain except as a worst case example of Armageddon. But Britain's global reach meant that this European war would also be the first world war.

1 July 1916

The First Day on
the Somme

The Carnage of Trench Warfare

*'No Man's Land under snow is…chaotic, crater-ridden,
uninhabitable, awful, the abode of madness.'*

The poet Wilfred Owen describes the terrain created by the
battle of the Somme, 19 January 1917

The Somme offensive on the western Front, planned by Marshal Joseph Joffre and Field Marshal Douglas Haig, was intended to break the German military stranglehold on northern France. Franco-British forces launched an attack along a twenty-one mile front north of the River Somme. After a week-long artillery bombardment the British infantry tried to advance but found that the well-entrenched German forces enjoyed a strategic superiority. As a result 1 July became the worst day in British military history with 57,470 casualties, including 19,240 killed, 35,493 wounded, 2,152 missing and 585 taken prisoner. The Germans sustained some 8,000 casualties on the same day.

In September the British, still attempting a breakthrough, deployed the innovation of tank warfare but the heavy rainfall of that October turned the battlefield into a sea of mud. By the end of the 140-day offensive on 18 November the Germans had been driven only seven miles back from their initial position, the British and French between them had suffered a total of 794,000 casualties, and there were 538,888 German casualties. The Somme offensive had helped to relieve the French at the battle of Verdun (21 February-18 December) where the German army was pursuing a relentless policy of attrition aimed at the fortress of Verdun and the surrounding fortifications along the River Meuse which constituted the heart of France's defensive system. General Erich von Falkenhayn, chief of the Imperial German general staff, was convinced that the war would be won in France and he therefore concentrated his forces on the western front at the expense of Germany's eastern offensive against the Russians. Fourteen railway lines supplied German reserves of men and material along the 130-mile arc of a military pincer movement which bore down on the Verdun area. After four days' advance the Germans took the fortress of Douaumont which was then regained by the French under General Pétain and the Germans eventually had to concede defeat. Almost 800,000 men, consisting of some 400,000 French and an almost equal number of Germans, died at Verdun. In the course of just two years Europe had collapsed in the futility and squalor of a military stalemate which reflected a civilization's loss of self-confidence. The scale of the losses at the Somme and Verdun wiped out a generation of the young and the barbarism which had been unleashed haunted all future European generations. In August 1914 there had been talk of being home in time for Christmas.

Britain had started the war without a large standing army and it took her two years to develop her full strength in land warfare. France did have such an army but by the beginning of September 1914 it was facing outright defeat after a strong early German advance. However, a Franco-British recovery forced the Germans back after the battle of the Marne in September and during the battle of Aisne later that month the first trenches were dug. By October the western front was a line of trenches running from Switzerland to the Channel: this remained unaltered for three years as leaders on both sides stuck to the use of massed artillery deploying high explosive shells in offensive actions against enemy positions on the battlefield. The fact that elements of that same strategy were working in some circumstances on the eastern front was one reason for sticking with the plan in the west following the German failure to break the Allied line at the first battle of Ypres.

Italy's entry into the war on the Allied side was also significant and the heroic battle of Caporetto in 1917 fought on the alpine passes inflicted a major defeat on the Austrians' southern flank (with half a million total loss of life). The Central Powers (Germany and Austria-Hungary) gained a surprisingly tenacious ally in the Ottoman empire which entered the war in November to defend itself against Russia. The ambitious war aims of the different nations also explain the length of the conflict. Germany wanted eastern Belgium and the expansion of its overseas colonies while also seeking dominion over Poland and an Austrian-controlled Serbia in order to establish its economic and political hegemony in central Europe. France wanted Alsace-Lorraine back. The British – while having no Continental territorial ambitions – sought to strengthen and extend their overseas empire. Italy wanted to finish off its unification process in the north of the country. Russia was secretly promised control of the Dardanelles by its allies and foresaw a post-war resumption of its push into eastern Europe. If Germany had an historic *'drang nach ost'* ('striving towards the east'), Russia had its own *'drang nach west'*: the collision between these two thrusts provided the geo-political theme which would shape all of twentieth century European history. This Russian-German confrontation was the real key to 1914-18 and its political consequences overshadow the tragedy of the western front. Poles, wanting a restoration of pre-partition Poland, fought with the Austrians and against the Russians. The Ottomans just wanted to survive. Spain, Holland, Switzerland and the Scandinavian countries remained neutral – and prospered accordingly. Both China and the US joined the war on the Allied side in 1917.

Russia mobilized faster than expected, entering east Prussia in the north and Galicia in the south during the war's first month but the battle of Tannenberg ended in a humiliating defeat. The battle of the Masurian Lakes was a further substantial German victory under the command of Field Marshal von Hindenburg and General Ludendorff. The Russian advance in the north had been stopped. Meanwhile, their southern advance was being contained by Austria-Hungary near Cracow – albeit with heavy, Russian-inflicted, losses. The Germans broke the eastern line in May 1915 in Galicia and then occupied Warsaw in August. By September the Russians had lost most of their Polish territories and by October the Germans had entered Lithuania and Rumania. Tsarist Russia now faced an invasion along an extended thousand-mile front. 1916, the year of catastrophic stalemate on the western front, saw the Russians mounting a remarkable counter-offensive in the east. Between June and August, General Brusilov pushed back the Austria-Hungarian army towards the Carpathians on the Hungarian border and took 375,000 Austrian prisoners in all – 200,000 of them in the first three days of the offensive. This had a crucial consequence on the western front since German forces were diverted from Verdun to support the Austrians and that withdrawal helped the French to defend their fortresses. Brusilov's campaign convinced Rumania that it should enter the war on the side of the Allies and it also ensured that the Austrians were deflected from their north Italian campaigns. But the Russian success came at immense cost and by 1917 the armies of the Central Powers were reasserting their dominance by advancing into the Baltic provinces and the Ukraine after the Germans had already occupied Bucharest in December 1916. The Tsar's army was now collapsing: for every 100 Russian soldiers killed there were 300 who had surrendered. Authority was draining away from the Romanov dynasty as soldiers voted with their feet.

Seeking to escape the western stalemate the British launched an attack on the Turks by landing in Gallipoli in the Dardanelles. It was calculated that a Turkish defeat would enable the British, supported by Australian and New Zealand troops, to link up with Russian forces and so open up a new frontal attack on the Central Powers. This strategy, however, ended in the slaughter of the expeditionary force. Meanwhile the British forces based in Egypt remained militarily active and encouraged Arab nationalists who were working for the overthrow of their Ottoman rulers. At the same time France was consolidating her position in the Lebanon. British forces occupied Baghdad in Mesopotamia in 1917 and Jerusalem in Palestine by the end of the year. The nature of the alliances of 1914-18 shaped the future politics of the Middle East since Arab leaders and pro-Zionist Jews expected the victorious allies to support both an Arab national state and a Palestinian homeland for the Jews.

For most of 1916-18 peace seemed a distant prospect and the strains were evident in the domestic politics of the Allied powers. Britain had to use armed force to suppress the Easter Uprising in Ireland in 1916. French war-weariness was profound after Verdun until Georges Clemenceau formed a new ministry which re-enthused his countrymen with the prospect of victory. Russia's revolution knocked her out of the war and, following an armistice with Germany, Russia signed the Treaty of Brest-Litovsk in March 1918 which handed over the Baltic states and other Russian territories to Germany and also created independent states in Finland and the Ukraine. This disaster for the Allies was only partly counterbalanced by US entry into the war on their side. As Russia's resistance weakened throughout that year the Central Powers could transfer their resources from the east to the west and by the beginning of 1918 they were ready for a major spring offensive commanded by Ludendorff. The attack launched on 21 March saw the German army pushing forward to a point just thirty-five miles south of Amiens but it was unable to maintain this early momentum. The Allied lines held and by July the counter-offensive began. The German advance was held at the second battle of the Marne and then came 8 August – dubbed by Ludendorff 'the black day of the German army' when, at the battle of Amiens, a massive British offensive, led by tanks, broke through the German lines, inflicting 20,000 German casualties and taking 30,000 prisoners. The advance was maintained and the Hindenburg line was attacked. In just six days the British broke through the line which had been previously been deemed the strongest defensive system in Europe.

At 11.00 a.m. on 11 November an armistice was signed in a railway carriage at Compiègne, near Paris, between the defeated Central Powers and the victorious Allies. The first global war had ended in the deaths of 1.8 million Germans, 1.7 million Russians, 1.4 million French, 1.2 million Austrians and Hungarians, 900,000 British imperial subjects, 460,000 Italians, 325,000 Turks and 115,000 US citizens. Another 20 million had been wounded. European politics in the next twenty years would show that not one of these deaths and injuries had contributed to a resolution of the problems which had consumed the continent in a new and terrible darkness. This unresolved tragedy would continue.

7 November 1917

The Storming of the Winter Palace

The Bolshevik Revolution

'*Seizure of power is the point of the uprising; its political task will be clarified after the seizure.*'

V.I. Lenin shows that power comes first and ideology later, 6 November 1917

On the evening of 7 November 1917 (25 October by the Julian calendar which was still in use in Russia) the ministers of the Russian provisional government had sought refuge inside the Winter Palace in Petrograd. During the previous twenty-four hours Vladimir Ilyich Lenin (1870-1924) and Lev Bronstein Trotsky (1879-1940), leaders of the faction of socialists who called themselves the Bolsheviks ('the majority'), had been implementing the details of their planned coup. 'Red Guards', a workers' militia led by Konstantin Yurenev, now surrounded the main government buildings and offices.

By 7 November Lenin had emerged from hiding to take charge of a revolution which was encountering little resistance. The government had collapsed and the imperial army had disappeared. The assault on the Winter Palace started with the firing of a blank shot directed from the cruiser *Aurora* at 9.45 p.m. on the evening of the seventh. Some thirty shells were then fired from the city's Peter and Paul fortress. Two of these hit their target at about 11.00 p.m. The palace, previously guarded by Cossacks and a corps of military cadets, was defenceless when it was taken at 2.00 a.m on the morning of 8 November. The ministers surrendered at 2.30 a.m. Lenin's press release on the morning of the eighth was addressed 'To the citizens of Russia' who were informed that their provisional government had been deposed and that authority now lay with the military-revolutionary committee of the 2,500 strong Petrograd Soviet or 'Council of Workers' and Soldiers' Deputies'.

The German Chancellor von Bethmann-Hollweg said on the eve of war in 1914 that: 'The future belongs to Russia, which grows and grows, looming above us as an increasingly terrifying nightmare.' More well-disposed observers agreed that early twentieth century Russia was the world's next economic superpower with its vast energy reserves, agricultural riches and sources of manpower. It also had the world's largest army. External investment poured into the country in order to exploit huge mineral deposits. Russian music, ballet and literature had suddenly and unexpect-edly flowered in the nineteenth century thereby resolving the debate about whether Russia should be a predominantly Slavic and eastern civilization or one open to western European influences. Its strength lay in its evident ability to be both. But the landless ex-serfs of an overwhelmingly peasant-based society dominated Russia's economic and political problems. P.A.Stolypin, prime minister from 1906 to 1911, introduced a reformist programme designed to turn a rebellious peasantry into obedient, conservative-minded, subjects. Peasants could now elect their own repre-sentatives to the *zemstvo* (councils of local government). They had new legal rights – including land-ownership – and could also leave the communes to which they had previously been restricted. These innovations had followed the 1905 revolution which led to the creation of the first *Duma* or parliament. Russian liberalism seemed to be winning over Russian autocracy. But Stolypin dismissed the first Duma in 1906 after it tried to influence his agrarian reforms and his programme had to be imposed by executive decree. A second Duma was again dissolved when it refused to ratify the reforms. Stolypin also introduced a network of courts martial which executed thousands accused of terrorism. These measures alienated the political centre as well as the left. By 1910-11 the third Duma had agreed to approve the 1906 reforms with the support of the centre right Octobrist party. But persistent objections to Stolypin's executive high-handedness led to the parliament's temporary suspension and his assassination in September 1911 merely confirmed yet another Russian political tradition. Russia's intrinsically despotic nature seemed tempered only by her anarchic predisposition. With parliament ignored and the bureaucracy decomposing, power centred on the St Petersburg court but Tsar Nicholas II, keen on uniforms but hopeless at military strategy, was away at the Eastern Front. His tsarina Alexandra, a German princess of Hesse-Darmstadt, chose a debauched flagellant and sham-monk, Grigory Rasputin, as her confidant until he was poisoned by aristocratic conspirators on 30 December 1916 and thrown into the Neva river in a scene grimly reminiscent of the excesses of Russia's mediaeval boyar nobility.

1917 was a year of two Russian revolutions. The first in March had started with two days of food riots and strikes in Petrograd followed by the mutiny of 160,000 peasants conscripted as soldiers in the city's garrison. After the Duma appointed a provisional government without consulting him, the tsar had abdicated on 15 March. But the Duma's authority was rivalled by that of the Petrograd Soviet which had ordered every military unit to elect its own soviet council and thereby ensured the collapse of the Tsarist army's command structure. However the Soviet itself was divided. Those dubbed 'Mensheviks' (the minority) – along with similarly moderate socialist groupings within the Soviet – agreed with the Duma's constitutional liberals that a Constituent Assembly should be elected on the basis of national democratic elections. The Menshevik and orthodox Marxist view of revolutionary progression was that a liberal and bourgeois revolution had to take place before there could be a proletarian one. This was too boringly gradualist for Lenin whose Bolsheviks were a revolutionary vanguard designed to rev up the motor of history without having to wait for later stages of historically determined socio-economics to kick in. Acting in the name of the proletariat, the Bolsheviks therefore sought immediate control of the Russian soviets as a prelude to grabbing hold of government.

The decision of the parliamentary liberals, with some Menshevik support, to continue with the war was unpopular and the Bolshevik advocacy of an armistice correspondingly popular. Bolshevik significance had been implicitly demonstrated during the 'July Days' when 20,000 armed sailors, acting spontaneously, had marched into Petrograd and demanded that the Soviet take power. The uprising had shown that Petrograd's seizure was an achievable aim. It had also followed the collapse within three days of the catastrophic military offensive launched in Galicia by the Russian army on the orders of Alexander Kerensky, minister of war in the first coalition provisional government formed in May. After the 'July Days', Kerensky, by now prime minister, had appointed General Lavr Kornilov as commander-in-chief. Lenin, blamed by the government for the insurrection, fled to Finland. Trotsky, who had been recruited by Lenin from the Mensheviks after the July Days, was in jail. But at the end of August Kornilov, in a move interpreted by Kerensky as a *coup d'état*, had ordered his troops to move towards Petrograd. Railway workers prevented the arrival of Kornilov's troops and the general himself was forced to surrender. But the Red Guards had offered to defend the city during the crisis and Kerensky had even armed them to that end: the idea that the Bolsheviks were the city's true defenders had therefore taken root.

Lenin had slipped back into the city by 20 October. The Petrograd Soviet remained divided but the Bolsheviks controlled its key Military-Revolutionary Committee which supplied the soldiers, sailors and armed workers necessary for the revolutionary takeover. Meanwhile a 'Second All-Russian Congress of Soviets of Workers' and Soldiers' Deputies' (following the first such congress of 3 June) was summoned to meet in Petrograd on 7 November and would sideline the Petrograd Soviet. Its 649 delegates consisted of 390 provincial Bolsheviks supported by some 100 delegates who belonged to the left-wing element within the Socialist Revolutionaries (SRs). At the announcement of the fall of the Winter Palace, the Congress passed a decree transferring power from the provisional government to itself. Some of the SRs and Mensheviks regarded this as illegal and walked out. As they did so they were taunted by Trotsky who told them that they now belonged to 'the dustbin of history'. The mantle of historical inevitability had, it seemed, enfolded victorious Leninists to the exclusion of all others.

On the evening of 8 November Lenin submitted three decrees to the Congress of Soviets: he proposed a three month armistice and a 'democratic peace'; a decree on land transferred private property to village communes; and a decree on government created a Council of People's Commissars (*Sovnarkom*) chaired by Lenin and subject to approval by a future Constituent Assembly. These, unsurprisingly, were swiftly accepted. But the peace abroad was a prelude to civil war at home as Bolsheviks hunted down their opponents. The communes and their peasants would be subjected to the murderous Bolshevik campaign which imposed a state monopoly over prices and food production. Elections to an assembly did go ahead in November but after the body's first meeting on 5 January 1918 Lenin closed it down. *Sovnarkom* was Russia's government. The autocratic Russia of icons, mystics and monks was overwhelmed by a peculiarly murderous form of modernity in which a neo-scientific faith in 'central planning' produced its own form of tyranny. Repression's earliest opportunities came during the Russian 'civil war' (1918-21) which was not only a fight between the Tsarist 'white' army and the Communist 'red' army but also an assertion of autonomy by Russia's colonized nationalities. Communist Russia's successful reconquest of the Ukraine and the Caucasus amounted to a restoration of the Tsarist empire.

Russian Communism killed, of course, Tsar Nicholas and his family in January 1918 but totalitarianism *à la Russe* also consumed its own supporters in a wave of paranoia which was initially part of the revolutionary cycle and then settled down to being part of the bureaucratic apparatus of state terror as administered by Joseph Stalin (1879-1953), secretary-general of the Russian Communist Party from 1922 until his death. Grotesque show trials were designed to 'purge' the state of 'class enemies' and 'counter-revolutionaries'. By these and other means, Leninists and Marxists, priests and nuns, peasants and nobles, generals and bureaucrats, *littérateurs* and liberals were slaughtered with equal indifference and an implacable subversion of legality. Stalin first exiled Trotsky and then had him killed in 1940. Lenin, in the last year of his life, considered Stalin an anti-socialist and wanted him removed from power. But Stalin, whose organized robberies had helped to provide the pre-1917 Bolsheviks with money, understood the precise calculations of the politics of fear. A former seminarian, he promoted a semi-religious national cult of Lenin as Russian redeemer while devoting himself to the detailed mastery of the interlocking system of committees which ran Russia. The German prophecy of Karl Marx's *Das Kapital* with its vision of the end of the state and the socialist recovery of human dignity – as interpreted by Lenin the lawyer – had spawned Stalin: a systems man who liked to kill.

22 June 1941

Operation Barbarossa

Hitler Invades Russia

'We have only to kick in the door and the whole rotten structure will come crashing down.'
Adolf Hitler, summer 1941

The military campaign which would claim seventy-five per cent of all German casualties in World War II started when history's largest invasion force consisting of three million men advanced along a 1,800 mile front in a surprise attack on Germany's ally, the USSR. 156 German divisions, nineteen of which were Panzers, were supplemented by thirty Finnish and Rumanian ones. Operation Barbarossa, supported by 2,500 aircraft, was equipped with 3,000 tanks and 7,000 pieces of artillery. The Soviets had almost three times the number of German tanks and aircraft but their airforce collapsed within days – a victim of its own obsolete equipment as well as of German attack. The initial offensive was three-pronged: the northern force moved from east Prussia into the Baltic states and towards Leningrad; the divisions in the south headed from southern Poland into the Ukraine, then towards Kiev and the ultimate goal of the Black Sea; the forces in the centre, including the armoured group led by Heinz Guderian – a major architect of the German policy of lightning war (*blitzkrieg*) – advanced northeast towards Smolensk and Moscow. Initial success was remarkable. Panzer divisions raced forward over the line which divided Poland into its German and Soviet occupied areas; 300,000 Russian soldiers were taken prisoner during the first onslaught. Guderian's tanks covered fifty miles on the invasion's first day and a further 200 miles by the time they got to Minsk on 27 June. In some of the USSR's colonies, such as the Baltic states, the Germans were seen as liberators from Russian imperialism. By September the German army had started its 872 day siege of Leningrad.

The German high command had calculated that the Red Army was fatally weakened because of Stalin's purges of the officer class and that the USSR would collapse internally within about three months because of internal opposition to Stalin's dictatorship. But Russian troops fought with nationalist fervour. German intelligence had correctly estimated that there were 150 Soviet divisions in the western regions of the USSR and they also thought that their enemy only had some fifty reserve divisions; by mid-August the Red Army had summoned up more than 200. Large numbers of Soviet soldiers also escaped to the east as happened after Guderian's tanks had reach Smolensk despite the capture there of 200,000 Soviet troops.

German progress was impeded as the unexpected rains of mid-July turned the Russian roads into mud. The advance was also frustrated by the Soviets' scorched earth policy: crops were burnt, bridges destroyed, steel and munition plants dismantled and taken to the east where they were rebuilt. The Soviet army also destroyed or removed most of their rolling stock and, since the Russian gauge differed from the German one, the invaders could not use the railway network. Despite these obstacles the German army had advanced more than 400 miles by mid-July and the central force was 200 miles from Moscow. The offensive force in the south, having reached the shores of the Black Sea, moved north to join up with Guderian who had now directed his forces southwards. By the end of September this gigantic pincer movement encircled the Soviet forces behind Kiev and led to the capture of 520,000 Soviet soldiers. August was a month of time-consuming debate on military strategy in Berlin. Hitler wanted the major effort to be directed southeast towards the Ukraine and the Caucasus with a lesser thrust towards Leningrad. His generals thought that Moscow should be the main objective. That autumn Hitler made three decisions: the northward drive had to concentrate on the siege of Leningrad; it was imperative to press on from the river Dnepr and towards the Caucasus with its rich agricultural land and its industrial plants (which by now, however, had been mostly dismantled); the advance on Moscow could resume. Meanwhile, the worst Russian winter in decades was approaching.

Adolf Hitler's frequent self-contradictions were often intended to confuse observers and conceal his intentions. As he once said: 'I shall always have three levels of motive – one for the public, one for my intimates and one for myself.' The contradictions in his domestic politics were the result of the Nazi readiness to cultivate anyone who might be useful. Despite its initial socialism therefore the Nazi party promised freedom to 'productive' capital – that is to say party donors. Hitler, however, did have three consistent goals to be achieved in three stages: the totalitarian supremacy of a Nazi state in domestic politics, followed by German domination over central Europe, would culminate in world power status. The absorption of the Soviet Union's European territories within a continental German empire was represented as the Nazi resumption of the eastward destiny of the German *volk*. That eastern movement was also an intrinsic part of Hitler's further goal of abolishing the 'Jewish question' by killing every Jew – as actions in German-occupied Poland were already demonstrating in 1941. The elimination of first the French empire and then the Soviet one was intended to leave Britain, Japan, the US and the Third Reich as the only remaining world powers. Germany would then have, at last, its African colonies and its own Atlantic naval bases. Hitler's strategies both assumed and required endless conflict. He therefore envisaged a future war between Germany, its envisaged ally Britain, and the US. He could be flexible about the means adopted to secure his aims. The Nazi-Soviet Mutual Non-aggression Pact of 1939, despite Hitler's intense anti-Bolshevism, had been a coup. The two powers had carved up eastern Europe into mutual zones of influence; secret protocols provided for the Russo-German partition of Poland while Hitler had Stalin's blessing for an invasion of France and Britain.

The Versailles peace treaty created Hitler's opportunities. The reparation clauses, insisted on by the French, had tried to force Germany to pay the bill for the 1914-18 war. This created German resentment and aroused western liberal sympathy for the country. By stages the international arrangements restricting Germany had been set aside and the 'national question' of pre-1914 Europe re-emerged as Hitler exploited the discontent of Germans forced to live outside Germany's boundaries in the new states established at Versailles. Germany was allowed to re-arm and then to occupy Austria (March 1938). In the Munich Agreement (September 1938) Britain, France and Italy handed over Czechoslovakia's German-speaking Sudetenland region to Germany. But the agreement, although demonstrating the spinelessness of western democracy's leaders, also showed Hitler's limits. He had expected Czechoslovakia's other enemies – Poland and Hungary – to support the country's dismemberment. But they only did so after the Munich agreement and so Hitler only got the Sudetenland. Subsequently, Hitler intrigued to ensure Slovakia's declaration of independence (March 1939) by threatening to hand the country over to Hungary (Slovakia's ruler until 1919) if it did not secede. This gave him the opportunity to establish a German protectorate of the Czech lands.

The German ambition to link East Prussia, separated since 1919 from the rest of Germany by a corridor of Polish territory, caused the ultimate pre-war crisis. In the summer of 1939 Hitler laid claim to the mostly German inhabited Free City of

Gdansk (Danzig) which was located within the Polish corridor. The Poles objected and got a British guarantee against any German attack. Hitler, and many others, thought the commitment was impractical since Britain, after the Nazi-Soviet pact, no longer had a Russian ally to help it honour the 'Polish guarantee'. But the decision to stick to the agreement meant that Hitler faced war with Britain – a contingency he was unprepared for. A scheme was therefore presented to the British ambassador in Berlin on the morning of 29 August. A 'corridor through the corridor' would give Germany railway access to East Prussia and internationally supervised plebiscites would take place within the corridor's disputed areas. Most observers thought these proposals hypocritical. In any event, Britain was ready for war in September 1939 since its radar system giving advance warning of aerial attack was now in place.

The political feebleness of European democracy, further undermined by the economic recessions of the early 1930s, was confirmed in 1940 as France, Belgium, Denmark, Norway and Holland came under German occupation. Hitler had initially planned to invade Russia in 1943-4 once the short localized campaigns in the west had secured Germany's rear. The scale of German military success meant that he could contemplate an invasion in mid-May 1941, but by that spring he had yet to complete western Europe's subjugation. It was his suspicion of Stalin's intentions which led him to plan Barbarossa which relieved the German pressure on an embattled Britain. The unforeseen need to invade Yugoslavia and Greece then pushed the invasion date back to late June. Balkan victories came quickly but the five week delay was serious since in 1941 the Russian winter arrived early.

The major early consequence of Barbarossa was that the Third Reich gained its *lebensraum* – a vast area of the former USSR was now under a military govern-ment which ruled with a racist anti-Slav ferocity. German detachments got to the Moscow suburbs by early December 1941. But the campaign ground to a halt in the sub-zero winter temperatures of 1941-2 for which German troops were ill prepared. The Red Army's Siberian troops now came into their own. The Soviet communist government, having killed untold millions of its citizens, acquired a new rationale as the patriotic defender of sacred Russian earth. General Zhukov launched the Red Army's offensive in defence of Moscow and then advanced towards Smolensk. By March 1942 the Soviet army had covered 150 miles in some areas. German troops were not allowed to retreat and the Luftwaffe was strained to its limits as it tried to deliver supplies. Hitler, who had now appointed himself commander in chief, overruled his general staff and instructed Field Marshal von Paulus to persist with the campaign to take Stalingrad – the furthest point of German penetration. The command exemplified the cult of strenuousness, suffering and death which was basic to Nazism. When von Paulus finally surrendered in February 1943 the siege had claimed almost a million German lives and just over a million Soviet ones. After Stalingrad the resistance movements of Nazi-occupied western Europe could think about a post-war world. But those of occupied eastern Europe realized the danger of one totalitarian system replacing another as the Soviet army advanced towards their national borders. The Anglo-Soviet agreement of July 1941 committed the two powers to mutual assistance and British and Soviet forces jointly invaded Iran in order to stop German bases being established there. A cynical west had decided to tolerate a Soviet tyranny in order to help it defeat a Nazi one.

7 December 1941

The Japanese Attack Pearl Harbor

World War II in the Pacific

'*We must be the great arsenal of democracy.*'

F. D. Roosevelt, 29 December 1940: the re-elected president
prepares America for war

It was an early Sunday morning and the ships of the American Pacific fleet anchored at its naval base of Pearl Harbor on the Hawaiian island of Oahu were therefore unmanned. A US army private had detected on his radar screen a large number of planes heading for Hawaii but was told by his superior officer not to worry since a contingent of American B-17s was expected to arrive later in the day. But at 7.55 a.m. the first Japanese dive bomber appeared over the harbour followed swiftly by almost 200 aircraft including torpedo planes, bombers and fighters. This was just the first wave of a total of some 360 planes which were launched from a Japanese fleet consisting of six aircraft carriers, two battleships, three cruisers and eleven destroyers which had sailed from Japan on 26 November and was now anchored 275 miles north of Hawaii. Very few of the military aircraft at the US Naval Air Station located nearby on Ford Island could get airborne in time to repel the Japanese.

By 8.30 a.m. the eight American battleships had suffered a devastating attack: the *Arizona* was destroyed, the *Oklahoma* had capsized, and the *California*, *Nevada* and *West Virginia* were sunk in shallow waters. Three other battleships, three cruisers and three destroyers were among the many other damaged American ships. The US lost some 200 aircraft and the Japanese less than half that number. Total US casualties were over 3,400 including 2,300 killed but fewer than a hundred Japanese were killed in action. Three of the Pacific fleet's aircraft carriers, however, had left Pearl Harbor for exercises at sea and so avoided any damage. The six surviving battleships were repaired and Oahu Island's oil storage facilities – an important Japanese objective – survived the onslaught. But the damage to the American naval and air command in the Pacific was substantial, so also was the blow to American prestige. Information restrictions meant that the US public were told that just one battleship had been sunk and one capsized.

'Pearl Harbor' persuaded a previously hesitant American public opinion to abandon US neutrality. Roosevelt's private conviction that America would have to enter the war had been increasingly obvious ever since his re-election for a third-term presidency in November 1940. Washington officialdom had known for many months that a Japanese attack on the US was highly probable without knowing exactly where and when it would take place. Japanese assets in the US had already been frozen after Japan's occupation of French Indochina in July 1941 and the US navy had effectively been at war ever since Roosevelt's command in September that German and Italian submarines were to be sunk. In August the president had agreed the principles of an Atlantic Charter with Winston Churchill and since the charter outlined a programme of war aims, including national self-determination, the Axis Powers regarded the US as an enemy. Now that the US had been attacked without any Japanese declaration of war Roosevelt, an arch rhetorician, could describe 7 December as 'a date which will live in infamy'. And since Japan had formed an alliance with the Axis Powers of Germany and Italy, Asian militarism and European fascism could be seen as two aspects of a common, anti-American, foe.

On 8 December the US Congress voted to declare war on Japan. Three days afterwards Germany and Italy declared war on the US. Rumania and Hungary were emboldened to imitate with their declarations on, respectively, 12 and 13 December. The American response to Japan's attack linked up the Asian, Pacific and European theatres of a world war. By 22 December Winston Churchill, a prime minister intensely committed to the survival of Britain and her empire, had arrived in Washington DC to discuss future war strategy with Franklin Delano Roosevelt, a New England patrician who took a dim view of all empires – including Britain's.

The causes of political conflict and military tensions, unresolved by the 1914-18 war, resumed both their bitterness and their global reach during the post-war era. The general European war of 1939-45 started eight years after Asia had witnessed the period's first eruption into armed conflict. In 1931 an authoritarian faction within the Japanese military had ignored the civilian government and ensured the occupation of the vast Chinese territory of Manchuria – a region where Japan had been steadily extending its influence ever since inflicting defeat on Russia in 1905. Manchuria's rich natural assets also attracted a Japanese economy badly hit by the global 1929 crash. In February 1932 Japan proclaimed Manchuria as the puppet state of Manchuko and, in the following year, left the League of Nations which had protested with characteristic futility against its actions.

Japan was in the vanguard of military dictatorships and the country's last democratic election, before its post-1945 settlement, was held in 1929. The internal Chinese collapse presented Japanese expansionism with its opportunities. By 1930 large areas of communist controlled China were rejecting the authority of the Nationalist government led by Chiang-Kai-shek. For almost two decades, a series of intermittent civil wars consumed the country and the Communists' eventual victory in 1949 owed much to their self-presentation as the true party of Chinese patriotism in the face of Japanese aggression. Bombing of civilian populations, which would be a feature of the Spanish civil war and of the later European phase of global war, was first deployed in January 1932 when the Japanese attacked Shanghai. A major Japanese invasion of north-east China started in July 1937 and the subsequent 'rape of Nanjing', when the occupying Japanese killed some 250,000 Chinese civilians, was a further anticipation of European atrocity. Japan, traditionally anti-Russian, signed an anti-Comintern pact with Germany (and then Italy) in November 1936 and the subsequent Tripartite Act (1940) between the Axis Powers and Japan was implicitly anti-American. The three powers pledged to assist each other in the event of attack by another power not yet at war with any of them. Since Russia at the time was Germany's ally the envisaged power could only be the US. Distance and rival claims of racial superiority separated Germany from Japan: the Germans, for example, were not told about the Pearl Harbor plan. But Japan, a military dictatorship already at war in the 1930s, set the standard for European fascism's war conduct.

The US declaration of war led to a huge increase in the federal budget and in the scale of federal powers. In September 1941 Roosevelt, preparing for war, introduced the largest tax rise in US history. But unemployment in 1940 stood at almost fifteen per cent of the total workforce despite seven years of New Deal programmes and the country's GNP was less than it was in 1929. Government spending during the same period had increased from ten to eighteen per cent of GNP. By 1942 government investment in an economy geared to war production brought the unemployment figures down by almost two-thirds. But inflation, already rising to ten per cent by the end of 1941, showed the consequences of the government boost in spending – just as it would in the politics of western European democracy.

America's Pacific war started in the Philippines following the capture of Manila by the Japanese in January 1942. Some 36,000 US troops stationed on the Bataan peninsula surrendered in April and within a month the remaining American soldiers stationed in the Philippines had also surrendered. But in early June, after US intelligence had broken the Japanese naval code, the balance started to shift and US forces won the naval-air battle of Midway in the central Pacific ocean. Britain's Asian war, however, was going badly despite the support of its Australian and New Zealand allies. The only significant British naval force in the Far East was destroyed by Japanese bombers in December 1941 and on 25 December the British had to surrender Hong Kong. Following the Japanese invasion of Burma in January 1942, British forces retreated to Singapore which was also lost to the enemy a month later. And in August 1942 the Indian National Congress passed the 'Quit India' resolution calling for the sub-continent's immediate independence. Under pressure from both the US and his Labour Party coalition partners Churchill promised a negotiated settlement to take effect after the war. But the Congress movement refused to wait and the British imprisoned its leadership. The British imperial capacity was stretched to breaking point in Asia – the scene of its first expansion two centuries earlier. After Pearl Harbor, Australia and New Zealand were directly threatened by Japan and their troops were therefore recalled from the European, North African and Middle Eastern campaigns in order to serve with US forces in the Pacific. Both countries drew ever closer to their US defender and ever further from Britain.

In January 1943 US, Australian and New Zealand troops landed in south-eastern New Guinea thereby increasing Australian security against Japanese attack. Revenge for Pearl Harbor came the following August in the Solomon Islands when US planes, acting on intercepted Japanese intelligence, shot down the plane carrying Admiral Yamamato Isoroku and thereby killed the chief architect of the attack on the US. 1944 was a year of consistent US advance in the Pacific. The Japanese were defeated in the June battle of the Philippine Sea and the battle for the island of Saipan in the Mariana Islands of the western Pacific marked a new supremacy for the US-led alliance. The Japanese lost 400 planes and their airpower never recovered. The Japanese government fell but its successor could not retrieve the situation. In October 1944 the Allied invasion of the Philippines began and, after a gruelling campaign, forces led by General Douglas MacArthur entered the capital, Manila, in February 1945. The subsequent capture of the western Pacific Japanese island of Iwo Jima was crucial since this would provide the US with a base for the fighter aircraft needed to escort bomber planes to Japan.

American forces had to operate both in the Pacific and in Europe. The fall of France in May 1940 deprived Britain of a valuable ally in the Battle of the Atlantic fought to protect the sea routes against attack by German U-boats. Despite heavy losses the Anglo-American alliance was able to keep open the sea-borne lines of communication which carried American troops and materiel to Europe. After December 1941 a previously reluctant US accepted its role in a war which would demonstrate both to others and to itself its true stature as a mid-twentieth-century colossus. Pearl Harbor, an attack planned in Asia, meant that American power would be the decisive liberator of the European continent.

6 August 1945

The Bombing of Hiroshima

Weapons of Mass Destruction

Piloted by Paul Tibbets Jr, the US B-29 bomber *Enola Gay* approached the south-western Japanese city of Hiroshima. Six hours had passed since the plane's take-off from the western Pacific island of Tinian – a base taken from the Japanese by US forces in the previous year and whose runways at the time were the world's longest. On board was the bomb dubbed 'Little Boy' by the US military. The explosion occurred at 8.15 a.m. A flash of light, a wave of heat and then a profound roar preceded the rise of a ball of fire followed by a mushroom-shaped cloud. Explosive energy and heat released through nuclear fission reduced an entire city to dust and ashes. Fires spread over 4.4 square miles. 100,000 were killed immediately and more than 70,000 others were injured. Three days after Hiroshima's destruction, *Bock's Car*, another B-29 bomber, dropped 'Fat Man', another atomic bomb, on the city of Nagasaki, devastating an area of 1.8 square miles and causing an equivalent number of deaths and injuries. Women, children and elderly men comprised the overwhelming majority of the 200,000 killed at Hiroshima and Nagasaki: the survivors suffered from varying degrees of burns and the effects of radiation sickness. Cancers and tumours would develop among the two cities' inhabitants in the next fifty years. The *New York Times* on 7 August reported the new US president Harry S. Truman as saying: 'We have spent 2 billion dollars on the greatest scientific gamble in history – and won.'

US atomic bomb research started in February 1940 on a government budget of $6,000 allocated to a committee of scientists. But by 1942 the scale of the work required the direct involvement of the War Department and research was carried out in centres right across the US. The physicist J.Robert Oppenheimer, of the University of California at Berkeley, had been committed to the democratic left ever since the Spanish Civil War. As soon as Germany invaded Poland in September 1939 he started work on separating uranium-235, the fissionable component of an atomic bomb, from natural uranium. Once given security clearance, Oppenheimer established a laboratory near Santa Fe, New Mexico where he led a team working on nuclear fission and the manufacture of an atomic bomb consisting of fissionable material. He demonstrated the results before a small number of observers at 5.30 a.m. on 16 July 1945 at Alamogordo air base, New Mexico, when the world's first atomic bomb exploded and generated power equivalent to more than 15,000 tons of TNT. The surface of the desert surrounding the point of the bomb's detonation was fused to glass for a radius of 800 yards.

On 17 July seventy scientists working on the atomic bomb's development, alarmed by its power, petitioned Truman not to use the bomb on Japan unless the terms of surrender had been both published and refused. These were now crucial points in relation to the morality of atomic warfare. Japan, under the weight of intensive aerial bombardment and suffering the effects of naval blockade, was on the point of collapse. On 30 July Japan refused to surrender unconditionally after the Allied leaders meeting at Potsdam had called on it to do so. The US government and its allies justified the detonations on the basis that so unsurpassed a horror would enforce a surrender and prevent a long and costly territorial invasion. It was fundamental to the Japanese that any surrender would not upset the constitutional status of their emperor whom they considered divine. Even after Hiroshima and Nagasaki the Japanese government, when suing for peace on 10 August, still sought a guarantee that the emperor's sovereign position would be maintained. The surrender went ahead (14 August) after the Allies had given that assurance.

Both generals Eisenhower and MacArthur thought the bombings unjustified and harmful to the US's moral standing. President Truman in his broadcast of 9 August described Hiroshima as 'a military base' and no more. This was false. His diary entry for 25 July recorded his view that atomic bombs should be used only on military targets, but the written order for the bombing, approved by him on the same day, made no such provision and specified the cities of Hiroshima and of Nagasaki as targets.

6 August 1945 was in fact the planned culmination of a sustained US aerial bombardment. Some 124,000 civilians had been killed in Tokyo during the air attack of 9 March and from July the bombing of Japanese towns and cities intensified. The Allied bombing of Germany illustrated the same strategy of terror: Dresden was destroyed in one night and 135,000 civilians killed.

The main air attacks on Japan accompanied the progress of US land forces after the fall of Okinawa in June in a battle which claimed 50,000 American lives and 100,000 Japanese ones. The US military advances of the late winter and early spring in the Pacific also ran in parallel with the Allies' thrust through both western and eastern Europe as they converged on a shattered Germany whose besieged army fought tenaciously throughout the last campaigns of 1944-45. Although the US won the race to develop an atomic bomb, Germany was ahead in the development of jet engines and rockets. A jet-powered Messerschmitt 262 first flew in 1942 and the *Vergeltung* or revenge rockets, the V1 and V2, were targeted on London from 1944 onwards.

By March troops of the US 5th division had crossed the Rhine at Oppenheim and established a bridgehead on the river's east bank. The Soviet army entered Austria at the beginning of April and occupied Vienna on 14 April. Nuremberg was taken by the US 7th Army on 21 April but by now the Soviets were on the outskirts of Berlin with many of their units running wild. The two invaders met on the River Elbe at a point just south of the German capital on 25 April and the final siege of Berlin was left to the Soviet army. Germany surrendered on 7-8 May. The true nature of Nazism also began to emerge in early 1945: in January the Soviets liberated Auschwitz concentration camp in Poland where a million Jews had been killed in the gas chambers; General George Patton's 3rd Army liberated Buchenwald north of Weimar on 11 April; Dachau in Bavaria was liberated on 24 April by the Allies. By the spring of 1945 the German regime had killed some 14 million 'racial inferiors', about six million of whom were Jews. Other victims included Slavs and Gypsies. By November the Allies had started their trials of war criminals at Nuremberg but confined the indictments to crimes committed by German officers, politicians and other civilians.

At Yalta in the Crimea between 4 and 11 February 1945, Roosevelt, who would be dead in two months, and Churchill, who would be voted out of office within six months, negotiated with Stalin – who promised that the post-war nations of eastern Europe would be allowed to be democratic. It was agreed that Germany would be divided into four separate zones of Allied occupation and the USSR was allowed to enter the Pacific war at a date soon after the end of European hostilities. Stalin's declaration of war on Japan came two days after the bombing of Hiroshima when he sent his troops into Manchuria – the Chinese province invaded by Japan in 1931. The defeat of Japan meant that the USSR was denied a pretext for Asian expansion through war, but it still got a good deal in the terms of Japanese surrender signed aboard the battleship USS *Missouri* in Tokyo Bay on 2 September. Outer Mongolia, the Kuril Islands and south Sakhalin were ceded to the USSR; Inner Mongolia, Manchuria, Taiwan and Hainan were ceded to China. The US and USSR would occupy Korea pending the creation of democratic structures for the country; a US army of occupation under General Douglas MacArthur ruled Japan. The separate Japanese surrender to China at Nanking on 9 September ended a fourteen-year period of Sino-Japanese conflict. 585,000 Japanese troops in south-east Asia surrendered to the British at Singapore on 12 September. This was the last formal surrender of a power involved in the global struggle and it therefore marked the end of World War II.

Among the military personnel who served during the war, the USSR lost 7.5 million, Germany nearly 2.9 million, China 2.2 million, Japan 1.5 million, the UK 398,000, Italy 300,000, the USA 290,000, France 211,000, Canada 39,139, India 36,092, Australia 29,395, New Zealand 12,262, South Africa 8,681 and the remaining territories of the British empire 30,776. For the first time in armed warfare the combatant countries' civilian populations had been attacked on a major scale and, although it proved impossible to produce a precise figure for civilian deaths, the total is unlikely to be less than 40 million.

1914-18 and 1939-45 were two phases of armed hostilities separated by a twenty-one-year armed truce during a thirty-one-year period of conflict whose origins were Asian as well as European and whose ramifications were global. Europe had annihilated itself. Britain, the only European country not to be invaded , was broke and war loans had turned it into the US's debtor state. Across the corpse of old Europe two superpowers glowered at each other. Ideological communism met its match in an equally ideological anti-communism. Robert Oppenheimer became a victim of the new paranoia when, in 1954, he was accused of past associations with communists and had his security clearance revoked. In Poland, Hungary and Czechoslovakia, Bulgaria and Romania, the USSR had acquired client states run by puppet regimes answerable to the Soviet politburo. The USSR had also re-absorbed the Baltic states and reasserted its control over the Caucasus.

The build-up of military alliances in defence of democratic powers together with the expense of modern weaponry led to the consolidation of Washington DC's military bureaucracy. On 24 July, while the leaders were at Potsdam, Truman told Stalin that the US had 'a new weapon of unusual destructive force'. That evening back at Stalin's quarters he and his foreign minister Molotov resolved that work on the Soviet equivalent had to be speeded up. After Hiroshima, international relations were plagued by the dilemma of 'mutually assured destruction': the nuclear power which deployed an atomic bomb against another such power was ensuring its own destruction through retaliation. This abolished traditional warfare between major states. In its place came surveillance and calculation – a time to test the nerves of the great powers. The armed truce had returned. Meanwhile, on 1 January 1946, emperor Hirohito made a gesture which, in the circumstances, proved helpful. He renounced his divinity.

25 March 1957

The Treaties of Rome

It was the age of the acronym. Leaders on their feet did their best to declaim them while men in suits at their desks interpreted them. The leaders of France and West Germany, of Belgium and the Netherlands, of Italy and Luxembourg sat down soberly at a long table. Rome with its history of imperial intrigue and papal pomp surrounded them. However, these leaders arrived with neither crowns nor tiaras to demonstrate their power. And the new kind of authority they wished to create would arrive with the stroke of a pen. By their signatures these democratically elected governors together created an EEC (European Economic Community) which would then become an EC (thereby dropping the 'economic') before eventually growing up into an EU (European Union). An ambiguous treaty preamble did after all commit them and their successors to the establishment of 'the foundations of an ever closer union among the peoples of Europe'.

It had all started with the ECSC (European Coal and Steel Community) and the plan had grown to fruition while COMENCON (Council for Mutual Economic Assistance) glowered communistically behind a metaphorical iron curtain part of which, in Berlin, would soon become a real and physical wall. The new Euratom (European Atomic Energy Community) authorized by the treaties regulated a purely civilian industry. But, reassuringly, the leaders had NATO (North Atlantic Treaty Organization) to protect them, EDC (European Defence Community) being an idea that had come and then gone away leaving in its wake an only faintly military and very consultative WEU (Western European Union). OECD (Organization for Economic Co-operation and Development) had put these countries back on their feet as it administered the 'Marshall Plan' made possible by US dollars. But many thought that USE (United States of Europe) should be the goal. Ahead lay many an IGC (Intergovernmental Conference). EFTA (European Free Trade Area) contained seven western European countries on the outside who wouldn't join the new club. But the six, who enjoyed railway metaphors as well as acronyms, often presented themselves as passengers on a train bound for alluring destinations such as CAP (Common Agricultural Policy). Stragglers should hop on board before it was too late. Many did. Then they were six but soon they would be twelve. There would be more.

Perhaps western Europe had earned the right to be boring by 1957. Immediately after the war waves of refugees flowed across the continent: eight million Germans were expelled from Czechoslovakia and Poland while over two million Poles travelled west. Berlin, like Germany herself, was divided into four zones. Communists, who had often been active in the resistance movements, enjoyed success in Italian and French elections. For a while it seemed possible that both countries might become communist and authority was precarious.

Three developments shaped the recovery of western Europe. First, the three western zones of Germany were united by the Allied powers to form a single economic area in 1946-7 while the eastern zone refused to join. A western German economic recovery started. Secondly, the US decided to contain the spread of communism. Britain, being bankrupt, asked the US for money to help the Greek government fight a communist insurgency. The response was the Truman Doctrine announced in March 1947 when the president asked Congress for $400 million in economic aid for Greece and Turkey: the US would 'help free peoples who are resisting subjugation by armed minorities or outside pressure'. This doctrine would have profound consequences in Asia and South America later in the twentieth century. Thirdly, the US government decided that Europe needed to recover quickly and was prepared to spend $12.5 billion between 1948 and 1951 to that end. The plan, named after the secretary of state, George Marshall, recognized that the US's isolationism in the interwar years had harmed its own interests as well as Europe's. One quarter of the money went to Britain, a fifth to France and the rest made available to other European countries who applied for it. Moscow scorned the plan as a capitalist ploy and ordered its satellite states to refuse the offer. Sixteen western European countries benefited accordingly.

The western German economic zone introduced the Deutschmark on 18 June 1948 and on the 28th Soviet troops sealed off the whole of Berlin to save its sector from contamination by the new currency. From this point onwards Soviet policy attempted not just the political and military control of eastern Europe but also its economic isolation from the capitalist west. The attempt drained the Soviets' own economy of resources and impoverished that of its dependent states. The cost to the USSR, however, was not obvious at the time. For this was the age of the man with a plan. Central planning by 'scientific' means was all the rage in all European countries. A great war had been won by the co-ordination of communication, by newly extended powers which controlled and supplied equipment, resources and manpower. Since it had worked for armies it would surely work for economies too? And nobody had bigger and better plans, at least on paper, than the Soviets.

Western Europe, and especially West Germany, surged ahead in the 1950s and at the level of the administrative, cultural and political elites there was a Franco-German rapprochement. The period of the Fourth Republic (1946-58) was one of French political history's intermittent periods of chronic instability deepened by the futile attempt to hang onto its colony in Algeria. Nationalism, a European invention, was a potent export which, ironically enough, had helped to dissolve colonial power everywhere. Eventually, European empires decided with varying degrees of reluctance that the game was up. The need to enforce order had turned colonies, once a source of glory and wealth, into an expensive burden and western Europe's countries could now concentrate on solving their own problems. France opted for a burst of executive centralism (another national tradition) and Charles de Gaulle, president from 1958 to 1969, abandoned the Algerian war. The need to develop and maintain Franco-German amity was fundamental to the reasoning behind the Treaties of Rome. In 1957 West Germany was booming economically but needed a political anchor. The reconciliation deepened when de Gaulle and Konrad Adenauer, chancellor of West Germany, signed the Elysée Treaty in 1963 which committed their countries to joint programmes in foreign affairs, defence and education. Those who signed and supported the Treaties of Rome held the franchise on political respectability and the movement claimed, rather unhistorically, patron saints such as Charlemagne and Erasmus. European unification's greatest appeal on an individual basis was to high-minded politicians and administrators who thought that democracy, having thrown up totalitarianism, needed a guiding hand from above to stop it from degenerating. Jean Monnet, whose famous Monnet Note (1950) inspired the ECSC's establishment and much of the rest of the project (including Monetary Union), was an inspirational but also characteristic figure. He had worked for the League of Nations, been a banker and then ran the French government's post-1945 programme of economic modernization. He was a very clever, and very good, man who never held elective office. The Messina Conference (1955) of the original six EEC member states had concluded that political union, while desirable, was too ambitious and too early a goal for them. They therefore decided to pursue that aim by economic means. As a result the EEC was initially a 'common market' seeking, with some success, to abolish individual countries' tariffs, to promote a free flow of goods, and also to establish a common external trade policy. In time accusations of 'protectionism' would be made against a prosperous western Europe which developed its own common trade barriers in order to protect itself against the world's new economies – especially in Asia. But an agenda for political unification persisted without being formally acknowledged. This led to accusations of calculated ambiguity and dishonesty.

In the 1950s the countries who had most to gain from unification were those who were most frightened of a renewed German militarism: France and Germany itself. Other motivations emerged as more countries signed the Treaties of Rome. Countries going through an economically rough patch, such as Britain in the 1970s and ex-Communist ones in the 1990s, found that an external authority helped them to impose financial discipline internally. Unstable countries such as Greece were keen on a regulator to keep them on track. Small ones such as Ireland benefited from regional funds and recently ex-fascist Portugal and Spain benefited from being seen as 'good Europeans'. The post-war world was obsessed by the need for strong international bodies whose members, tightly regulated by treaty clauses, would stop the two World Wars recurring. Post-militarist trauma, exhaustion and an American nuclear threat were the real forces that stopped Europeans from killing each other again. But enlightened members of the west European governing class could still point to the three pillars of a new order established by the treaties: a Council of Ministers, drawn from the national governments, formulated policies, a European Commission administered them, and a European Parliament debated them – usually toothlessly. But the fundamental innovation was Community Law which enjoyed supremacy over the laws passed by member states' parliaments and was interpreted by a European Court of Justice: this was a new element in modern European politics.

France under de Gaulle had been through a phase of being a European rogue state when it resisted integration. In the 1990s it was Conservative-ruled Britain's turn to be odd man out as debates raged on the Maastricht Treaty which created a stronger European union and Britain refused to join a single European currency. Its 1980s' economic success with free market capitalism had strengthened Britain's US links. The British Left, having been hostile to a 'capitalist club', warmed to EU-style social consensus. European state-regulated capitalism, underpinned by subsidies, had created prosperity but was now facing competition from deregulated economies and developing ones. Britain also started to be noisy about keeping 'parliamentary sovereignty'- something its own parliament had signed away on joining the Community in 1973. Britain's EU partners thought many of their fathers' and grandfathers' generation had died precisely because selfish states had been so obsessed with their sovereign rights. On both sides emotion mingled with reason and the interpretations of treaties were once again caught up in the deep currents of history which divided as well as united Europe.

28 October 1962

Krushchev Agrees to Remove Missiles from Cuba

The Superpowers Step Back from Armageddon

'We're eyeball to eyeball, and I think the other fellow just blinked.'

Dean Rusk, US Secretary of State

In October 1962 an American president and a Soviet premier balanced their own political reputations and their countries' security against the likely consequences of nuclear war. Cuba produced the first and also the gravest crisis of the Atomic age with the reports and rumours of diplomatic calculation and armed threat dominating daily lives and anxious speculation in homes across the world. Radio and television communicated the reality of danger and the possibility of imminent annihilation to the millions who waited for the latest bulletin. News meant war or peace.

Early on 16 October McGeorge Bundy, national security assistant to the president, brought to J.F. Kennedy's White House bedroom the results of a recent aerial reconnaissance of Cuba. High-altitude photographs taken from U-2 planes showed Soviet soldiers setting up nuclear-armed missiles. The Soviet activity contradicted Khrushchev's assurances that he would not send offensive weapons to Cuba – just ninety miles away from the US coast. The crisis culminated on 26-8 October. Khrushchev's cable to Kennedy on the 26th proposed dismantling the installations if the US promised not to invade Cuba. The US government had already agreed not to do so. But on the 27th the Russian premier added another condition – the US should withdraw its nuclear weapons from Turkey. Kennedy bought time by accepting the terms of the 26th and not responding to the demand of the 27th. His small group of advisers urged him to reject the new demand. Kennedy disagreed, pointing out that: '...most people would regard this as not an unreasonable proposal... '. News then arrived that a U-2 plane had been shot down over Cuba killing the pilot. This action, inviting retaliation, weakened the Soviet bargaining position and may have led Khrushchev to abandon his second demand. However escalation was in neither party's interests and Kennedy refused to bomb Cuba despite his earlier assurance to the military that he would do so in the event of aggression. He turned to covert diplomacy. Kennedy's brother Robert visited the Soviet ambassador Anatoly Dobrynin and told him that the US missiles in Turkey were obsolete and were going to be withdrawn in six months' time anyway. But this would have to be a secret between Moscow and Washington. If the USSR claimed that a deal had been struck then the president would deny the claim and the missiles would stay. But on the 28th, and before any Soviet response to Kennedy's message, Khrushchev acknowledged the president's reply to his message of the 26th and the deal was struck on that earlier basis.

John Fitzgerald Kennedy (1917-63) had been elected president of the US in November 1960 on a cold war agenda and the aggressive liberalism of his inaugural speech had committed him to 'oppose any foe to assure the survival and success of liberty'. The Republican presidency of Dwight D. Eisenhower, he maintained, had allowed the Soviets to acquire a presumed superiority in nuclear-armed missiles. The former general, understanding conflict's costs, certainly thought that 1950s' America should make money and not war following the Soviet explosion of a nuclear device in 1949. 'Ike' had ended the war in Korea against the Soviet and the Chinese, stopped the Franco-British invasion of Suez (1956), controlled his militaristic secretary of state John Foster Dulles, and warned against the development of a 'military-industrial complex' of US big business. Now Kennedy, in his flat Bostonian accent, said there was a 'missile gap' and the US had to catch up. By October 1962 the US had more than 25,000 nuclear weapons while the USSR had less than half that number. Moreover, the Soviet missiles were still only partially developed – a fact known to the US from the information given it between 1961 and 1962 by the double agent Oleg Penkovsky. The imbalance worried Nikita Khrushchev (1894-1971), first secretary of his country's Communist Party since 1953 and premier since 1958.

While Kennedy was educated in the liberal conformities of Harvard , Khrushchev was trained by the bloodier ones of the Red Army in which he had served as a junior political commissar during the Russian Civil War. Both men were the products of political machines. Kennedy's political base was the Democratic party in Massachusetts where he had served as congressman and senator. He had run for office ever since a childhood of enforced athletic and intellectual competitiveness.

Khrushchev's political base was in the Ukraine and in the city of Moscow where, in the 1930s, he had been first secretary of the local Communist Party organizations. He had supervised the details of Stalin's purges in the Ukraine and overseen the completion of Moscow's metro system. Both achievements had won him plaudits. After Stalin's death, and in the best traditions of Russian autocracy, he had ousted his rivals in the collective leadership. He ensured the execution of Lavrenty Beria, the head of the secret police, but chose not to kill his defeated opponents. This made him, in Russian politics, rather progressive. Khrushchev's denunciation of Stalin's crimes against the Communist Party (rather than against the country itself) at the twentieth party congress in 1956 was clever and selective. The party's authority was maintained.

Both leaders were showmen. Kennedy had the looks, the tightly fitted suits, and the elevated oratory. Khrushchev had a wily peasant charm, an opportunist's survival instinct and a populist flair. Both were keen on 'gesture politics'. Kennedy talked about the 'new frontier' which, vaguely, beckoned American democracy forward. Khrushchev talked of 'peaceful coexistence' with capitalism, an assertion which reflected his conviction that capitalism, collapsing internally, was bound to be 'overtaken' by an intrinsically superior communism. Since the USSR had put the first dog, the first man, and the first woman in space many agreed. In the intelligence and security contest between the two systems Kennedy had the CIA (consolidated in 1947) while Khrushchev had the KGB (established in 1954).

Kennedy's foreign policy was financed by US prosperity during the first great age of mass consumerism which came with the steady 1950s' advance of American business. Khrushchev had diverted money from Stalin's investment in heavy industry to agriculture. Following a visit to Iowa in 1959 the premier became a corn enthusiast and a huge expansion into seventy million acres of Siberia had followed. But the harvests, in an unsuitable climate, had failed – repeatedly. The reduction of expenditure on conventional armaments in favour of nuclear missiles was also unpopular with Soviet military chiefs. As 1961 turned into 1962 Khrushchev had much to prove. But so had Kennedy. For some time the Soviets had been openly sending weapons, including surface-to-air anti-aircraft missiles (SAMs) to Cuba, a communist ally since Fidel Castro's rebellion of 1959. The Cuban coup formed part of a 1950s' pattern as communism spread through decolonized states in a potent fusion of nationalism with Marxism. Mid-term congressional elections would be held in November 1962 and Kennedy could not afford to be seen as 'soft' on communism. He had already warned the Soviets that if they introduced offensive weapons into Cuba 'the gravest issues would arise'. On 16 October they did.

The attempted invasion of Cuba by 1,500 US-backed Cuban exiles had ended in the debacle of the Bay of Pigs in April 1961 and Kennedy blamed the defeat on the bad advice of narrow-minded soldiers. He turned instead to a hand-picked group of the clever whose experience was wider. Robert McNamara, the defence secretary and former head of the Ford motor company, proposed the creation of the Executive Committee of the National Security Council (ExComm). This group of twelve applied the skills of corporate management brainstorming to questions of war. At first everyone on ExComm wanted to bomb Cuba. Some just wanted surgical strikes against the missiles while the chiefs of staff wanted to attack air defence sites. But by 18 October secretary of state Dean Rusk thought such a surprise attack on Cuba would be wrong. The US's moral stature mattered. Another strategy emerged. The president's televised speech of 22 October announced the presence of Soviet nuclear missiles in Cuba, declared a blockade of the island to stop any further deliveries and insisted on a withdrawal of the missiles already there. Some on ExComm wanted military action followed by an invasion if this ultimatum did not work. On 24 October the president was told that Soviet ships had stopped just before getting to the US ships blockading Cuba.

Cuba really meant Berlin. The Soviet attempt at a takeover of the city by blockading it in 1948-9 had been frustrated by an Anglo-American airlift. But the threat returned. In 1961 the Soviets and East Germans had built a wall round West Berlin to stop the exodus of those leaving the Soviet-controlled parts of the city. Kennedy in October 1962 expected a Soviet takeover of Berlin without being able to forestall it through US troop deployment. Threatening the Soviet Union with attack over Cuba was a way of protecting Berlin. Khrushchev had in fact started the de-Stalinization of the USSR and the satellite governments of eastern Europe enjoyed greater autonomy than previously during his period in office. But he also often tried to control the consequences of his own actions. When therefore the Hungarian government threatened to withdraw from the Warsaw Pact – eastern Europe's military counterpart to NATO – he sent the troops in and at least 2,000 rebels were shot in the Hungarian uprising of 1956.

The agreement of 28 October was implemented and three months after the Cuban crisis US nuclear missiles were secretively moved from Turkey and from Italy. The Test Ban Treaty of August 1963 prohibited the testing of nuclear weapons in the atmosphere. But the USSR, having been shamed, was determined to acquire an equivalent nuclear capability to the US and achieved parity by 1972. The expense wrecked the Soviet economy. The US, having called Khrushchev's bluff, was now convinced that the USSR would not go to war to protect another communist power. This encouraged American anti-communist activity in Asia and Latin America. Cuba also aggravated a Sino-Soviet communist split caused by the USSR's refusal to help China develop its nuclear capacity. From 1959 onwards the Chinese leadership had already been accusing Khrushchev of 'revisionism'. It therefore presented the Soviet climbdown as a consequence of mental feebleness brought on by inattention to Marxist-Leninist orthodoxy. Khrushchev survived until 14 October 1964 when he was replaced by Leonid Brezhnev – a consummate *apparatchik* who knew that any reform of a system suffering sclerosis would simply wreck it. The ten million members of the USSR's *nomenklatura* of office holders breathed more easily. The Democrats did well in the November elections of 1962. A year afterwards J.F. Kennedy was assassinated in Dallas, Texas. Some blamed Cubans.

28 August 1963

'I Have a Dream'

Martin Luther King Speaks at the Lincoln Memorial

'…his violent end…reflects the hostility of mankind to those who annoy it by trying hard to pull it one more painful step up the ladder from ape to angel.'

I. F. Stone, 1968

The voice which filled the air by the banks of the Potomac river was that of a young Baptist minister – eloquent and handsome, intellectual and black. 1963 marked the centenary of the Emancipation Declaration, the edict which had freed the slaves of the Confederate states during the rebellion against the Union. Over 200,000 had gathered in the damp savannah heat of a Washington summer to hear Dr Martin Luther King speak of the conquest of prejudice and of the fulfilment of prophecy. He stood before the Lincoln Memorial whose columns were designed to evoke the Parthenon and thereby to link the democratic claims of fifth century BC Athenians with those of mid-twentieth century AD Americans. And the words, though so simple, were woven into a pattern of soaring oratory and moral exaltation. A century after legal emancipation 'we must face the tragic fact that the Negro is still not free'. Subjected to 'the chains of discrimination', condemned to exist 'on a lonely island of poverty in the midst of a vast ocean of material prosperity', the black American was 'an exile in his own land'. Now was the time 'to rise from the dark and desolate valley of segregation to the sunlit path of racial justice'. Black Americans would not rest 'until justice rolls down like waters and righteousness like a mighty stream'. His audience, said King, included ' veterans of creative suffering', those whose pursuit of civil rights had led to their persecution, beating and imprisonment. But 'unearned suffering is redemptive' and there was no need to 'wallow in the valley of despair... I say to you today, my friends, that in spite of the difficulties and frustrations of the moment, I still have a dream. It is a dream deeply rooted in the American dream.' The union of states would one day live out the true meaning of its creed that 'all men are created equal' and his own four children would then be able to 'live in a nation where they will not be judged by the colour of their skin but by the content of their character... When we let freedom ring... we will be able to speed up that day when all of God's children, black men and white men, Jews and Gentiles, Protestants and Catholics, will be able to join hands and sing in the words of the old Negro spiritual, "Free at last! Free at last! Thank God Almighty, we are free at last!"' King had reminded America of her own best self.

Born in Atlanta, Georgia, Martin Luther King (1929-68) was a son of the educated black middle class who had followed his father and father-in-law into the Baptist ministry and in 1954 he was ordained a minister in Montgomery, Alabama. Protestant theology was going through a post-war period of creative renewal and King's intellect responded powerfully to its strongly ethical interpretation of the gospels. From the beginning of his career he was acknowledged as an inspirational preacher whose intelligence and oratory touched the sublime. King was also a good organizer and led the successful campaign to desegregate the public buses in Montgomery following the refusal of Rosa Parks, a local activist, to give up her seat to a white passenger. The Southern Christian Leadership Conference provided King with an organizational base for campaigns which spread right across the south. A visit to India in 1959 confirmed his view that Mahatma Gandhi's path of non-violence had been an effective way of 'meeting physical force with soul force'. By 1960 he was co-minister with his father of the Ebenezer Baptist Church in Atlanta, Georgia and a full-time civil rights activist running a mass movement.

The Supreme Court's 1896 ruling in favour of 'separate but equal' provision had allowed southern state legislatures to support black-white segregation in parks, cemeteries and theatres as well as in schools and restaurants. Sit-ins and protest marches now pinpointed this iniquity by creating a mood of crisis while televised scenes of dramatic confrontation with brutal local police forces provoked the consciences of white liberals. By 1963 the civil rights movement had broadened out into a campaign against black poverty and unemployment which is why the crowds addressed by King in the capital had been part of a 'March on Washington for Jobs and Freedom'. He remained committed to an inter-racial coalition. Black Americans could not, he said, walk alone and 'our white brothers… have come to realize that… their freedom is inextricably bound to our freedom.' The truths of the first century gospel and of the 1776 Declaration of Independence were universal. But the equality of the right to 'life, liberty and the pursuit of happiness' awaited fulfilment in America – the land of its original imagining.

After 1918 many southern blacks migrated to the north whose factories were expanding to meet the post-war economic demand. The move gave blacks new opportunities both culturally and commercially: Chicago became the world's jazz capital in the 1920s with the arrival of King Oliver and Louis Armstrong from New Orleans. The same migration brought Berry Gordy Jr's family from Georgia to Detroit – the city where, in 1959, he founded the Motown recording company and so introduced the whole world to black soul music. By the 1950s those black inventions – the sound of swing, the crooning of the blues, and the thrust of rock and roll – were all integrated into American popular culture – a fact which made southern segregation appear anachronistic as well as wrong.

The south was hard hit by the 1930s' depression but the region's politicians, then a dominant force in the Democratic Party, ensured that New Deal projects had an energizing local impact. Economic change and diversification meant unionized labour and higher wages which led to the greater economic and political independence of southern workers, including the region's blacks. The experience of serving in the segregated, and very racist, US army of 1917-18 also heightened black awareness although black political rights remained largely stagnant during the inter-war years despite the work of the National Association for the Advancement of Colored People (NAACP). In 1935 the Supreme Court had upheld the rights of states to ballot presidential primaries on a white-only basis. Roosevelt told the NAACP that, despite his personal anti-racism, he could not introduce an anti-lynching bill because of the seniority of southern Democrats in Congress. But his New Deal did save southern blacks from starvation and this ensured that the south en masse favoured the Democratic party.

War once again boosted both the southern economy and black awareness. Northern blacks especially resented the army's segregation and institutions which included separate black units. The position was untenable, especially given the commitment shown by black soldiers fighting totalitarianism, and the US army was totally integrated by the early 1950s. Businesses awarded government defence contracts were forced by Roosevelt's Executive Order of 1941 to accept a clause forbidding racial discrimination in their employment practices. The workplaces of the industrialized north became fairer if not entirely just and black passivity in the face of intolerance diminished. In the summer of 1941 race riots spread in Detroit where a southern workforce of both races had migrated to work on the city's automobile lines. The violence showed a new black readiness to retaliate against white aggression in the north, while in the south a white community keen on its prosperity confronted a black one readier to assert its dignity. The Supreme Court, liberalised by Roosevelt's appointments, ruled in favour of greater educational provision for blacks and in 1944 it judged white-only primary elections to be unconstitutional. In 1954 the real revolution started when the Court decreed that school segregation – the central pillar of an entire edifice of white supremacy – violated the constitution. 'Separate but equal' was, judicially, abandoned.

Legal eminences might adjudicate but southern state governments, supported by local 'Citizens' Councils', resisted. Federal legislation failed to stop the continued intimidation, by means both physical and administrative, of southern blacks who tried to register as voters. The 'Freedom Rides' campaign of 1961 saw groups of the young defying segregation on public transport systems all over the south: this raised local tensions without changing the power structures. Birmingham, Alabama was forced to desegregate after a notable campaign of street marches led by King in the spring of 1963. But by now it was obvious that such partial local victories would never solve the wider problem. Kennedy, previously a president of warm words against prejudice but few anti-racist deeds, introduced a comprehensive Civil Rights bill which, after becoming law in July 1964, outlawed segregation in public places and forbade racial discrimination in any enterprise which used federal money.

A raft of new federal bodies now existed to ensure the executive enforcement of the congressional legislation on race relations. For President Johnson this was part of an immense expansion of federal activity which aimed to correct historic social injustices and to advance opportunities for all sectors of American society. His Voting Rights Act (1965) was highly effective in outlawing discriminatory procedures in voter registration. But as the south started to adapt, the north exploded. On 12 August 1965 the Watts area of Los Angeles, a ghetto of 80,000 blacks, erupted in six days of race riots. The summer of 1966 saw similar violence in other urban centres of the north. America's race problem was now merged with the social crisis of inner city decay. Poor housing, inadequate education and unemployment had created a black proletariat which, not being heard, decided to riot. King could see that the Gandhian sit-ins of bourgeois pacifists were irrelevant in these circumstances and said that the US defence budget would be better spent renewing the inner city. But his coalition was now breaking up with the emergence of a new class of black activists whose urban rage preached anti-white 'black power'. Malcolm X (1925-65) scorned integration and urged black self-dependence. He was shot dead by a rival group of black Muslims and on 4 April 1968 King himself was assassinated by a sniper's bullet in Memphis, Tennessee. Over a hundred cities rose in rebellious and grief-struck rage. On the evening of 3 April King had addressed a local church congregation and told them that he had '... seen the promised land. I may not get there with you. But I want you to know tonight that we, as a people, will get to the promised land.' Bereft of its leader, black America lived with the memory of his prophecy and the grace of his witness in a time of trial. The pilgrimage went on.

21 July 1969

'The Eagle has Landed'

The First Men on the Moon

'Human knowledge and human power meet in one.'

Francis Bacon (1561-1626) in his *Novum Organum* (1620) argued that a planned scientific programme would benefit mankind: justifications of space-exploration followed the same line

The *Apollo 11* spacecraft had been fired into orbit by the world's most effective rocket, the *Saturn V*, when it left its launchpad near Cape Canaveral in Florida on 16 July 1969. On board were three astronauts: Neil Armstrong, Michael Collins and 'Buzz' Aldrin. The complexity and expense of twentieth-century space projects meant that governments had to run them and this venture was the latest demonstration of American cold war superiority over Soviet Russia. The three men, like all the first humans in space, were travelling in modules or capsules. *Apollo 11* comprised a command module containing the crew, a service module housing the rocket engine, and a lunar module designed to carry two astronauts from the moon's orbit to its surface and then back to the spacecraft. Armstrong piloted the lunar module (nicknamed 'Eagle') and avoided the boulders on the moon's surface before landing on a flat lava plane named the Sea of Tranquillity at 4.18 p.m. US eastern time on 20 July. He then reported back to the command centre of the National Aeronautic and Space Administration (NASA): 'Houston. Tranquillity base here. The eagle has landed.'

Six and a half hours later Armstrong, followed by Aldrin , stepped on to the moon and enunciated a pre-arranged sound bite: 'That's one small step for man. One giant leap for mankind.' The two astronauts spent two and a half hours on a desolate surface and then returned to their module with rock samples. Twelve hours later they blasted off to return to the command module. A retro-rocket slowed down their speed as the craft re-entered the earth's heavy gravitational pull on the return journey, enabling it to survive intact. On 24 July the crew splashed down in the Pacific Ocean.

The history of the rocket science which made *Apollo 11* possible started with the experiments in aerodynamics of the mathematician Konstantin Tsiolkovsky in the Tsarist Russia of the 1890s. Robert Hutchings Goddard was carrying out rocket experiments in Worcester, Massachusetts in the years before the First World War and, as early as 1915, the US Congress had established a National Advisory Committee for Aeronautics. Hermann Oberth in early 1920s' Heidelberg showed mathematically how a liquid-propelled rocket could defy the force of gravity and his work led to the launch of a rocket near Berlin on 7 May 1931. Rocket clubs were popular in 1930s' Germany and the young Wernher von Braun joined one of them – the Society for Spaceship Travel. As the civilian head of a research team he developed the V-2 rocket, the basis of both American and Soviet Russian space technology. In 1945, having surrendered, along with many of his team, to American forces advancing into Germany, von Braun joined the US space programme.

Von Braun's Soviet counterpart was Sergey Korolyov whose group of scientists launched the first Soviet liquid-propellant rocket in 1933. Arrested and detained during the Second World War for conventionally paranoid Stalinist reasons, Korolyov modified details of the V-2 missile system after his release and was the genius behind the Soviet launch on 4 October 1957 of *Sputnik 1* – the first satellite to go into space. *Sputnik* was powered by the same engine developed by Korolyov for the Soviets' intercontinental ballistic missile.

Explorer 1, prepared by von Braun for the US army, was the first US satellite and it was launched in January 1958. Its scientific instruments provided one of the first great discoveries of aeronautics: the fact that the earth was surrounded by two zones of radiation both of which contained particles of energy trapped by the earth's magnetic field. On a more secretive basis the US was now also developing reconnaissance satellites which gave it detailed pictures of Soviet missile sites and air bases.

Yury Gagarin became the first human in space when he completed his one orbit journey around the earth in the Soviets' *Vostok 1* satellite launched in April 1961. *Project Mercury* represented NASA's first effort to launch humans into space after its establishment in 1958 and the project's first manned space flight, that of Alan B. Shepard Jr, was launched in May 1961. The US achieved two other manned flights later that year and John Glenn became the first American astronaut to orbit the earth when he accomplished a three orbit journey launched in February 1962. In March 1965 the Soviets could claim priority again. They had modified their spacecraft to carry three persons and Aleksey Leonov became the first human to leave an orbiting spacecraft when he stepped outside the redesigned *Voskhod* spacecraft in March 1965. This achievement was seconded by Edward H. White II on a mission of the US's *Gemini* programme which was now powered by two-person spacecraft in June 1965. *Gemini* had also shown that human beings could live and work in space for as long as fourteen days. Korolyov was still aiming further however, and had started work on the second generation of Soviet spacecraft. *Soyuz* was designed for a lunar landing as well as for orbital flights around the earth and the moon. But the first sign of a real Soviet failure came when *Soyuz 1* crashed after its launch on 23 April 1967.

Meanwhile, the US had been working on achieving a manned lunar landing before 1970 – a goal to which President Kennedy had committed it on 25 May 1961. NASA's budget was increased five-fold within three years so that at its height the agency employed 34,000 people with some 375,000 working on various industrial and research contracts.

The USSR hoped to achieve a flight around the moon before the fiftieth anniversary of the Soviet revolution in 1967 and developed a new rocket, the *Proton*, to that end while also producing the giant *N1* rocket designed to land a man on the moon. Korolyov's death in 1966 was a severe blow to the Soviet programmes which were, in any event, plagued by personal rivalries and scientific disagreements as well as by inadequate budgets. After four failed attempts at a launch between 1969 and 1972 the *N1* programme was cancelled in May 1974 and ended the Soviet hope of a manned lunar landing. The Soviets also failed to achieve a manned orbital flight of the moon although they succeeded with unmanned flights.

In January 1967 *Apollo 1* caught fire during a ground test and killed three astronauts but in December 1968 *Apollo 8* was launched, achieving a close orbit of the lunar surface and producing pictures of the planet earth. *Apollo 12* launched in November 1969 was another success but *Apollo 13*, launched in April 1970, only returned to earth with great difficulty after a fire broke out in the oxygen tank of its service module. On the final three *Apollo* missions the crew used a small space cart to travel around the area of their landing. But after the launch of *Apollo 17* in December 1972 the US, having made its political and anti-Soviet point, abandoned for over thirty years the idea of a manned lunar landing. Sending humans to Mars or other distant planets also dropped off the agenda although robotic spacecraft did land on Venus and Mars as well as on the Moon.

Interest in both the US and the USSR space programmes now concentrated on developing earth orbiting stations with manned space platforms. The US from 1972 onwards was also preoccupied with its space shuttles: rocket-launched transport vehicles carrying people and cargo around the earth at a low orbit before then gliding back to earth on a runway landing. These shuttles would also eventually carry people and supplies to space stations. The US *Skylab* launched in May 1973 orbited for eight and a half months and its final crew worked on board for eighty-four days. The Soviets' *Salyut* space stations were succeeded by the *Mir* space station, launched in February 1986 and which accommodated human explorers until mid-2000. By then space co-operation was in vogue between established states and an international space station co-ordinated the ventures of the US, its partners and those of the newly established Russian Republic.

Forecasts of weather patterns and crop yields became more accurate because of space technology. Environmental changes were mapped more closely at a time when humanity became more concerned about the earth's fragility: the arrival of photographs of a beautiful planet as seen from outer space had prompted something of a leap of the imagination. Communications were transformed. Satellites allowing the instantaneous transfer of voice, images and data became a hugely profitable business from the end of the twentieth century onwards. Some satellite exploration of the universe, galaxies and stars produced evidence supporting the hypothesis that the universe was created in a primordial explosion or 'Big Bang'.

By the middle of the first decade of the twenty-first century some 500 people from thirty different countries had travelled in space. Eighteen had died and only twenty-seven had travelled beyond earth's orbit. Twelve Americans set foot on the moon as a result of the six *Apollo* missions launched between July 1969 and December 1972. But no humans since then had left earth's orbit travelling on their way to other planets. The desolation revealed on the moon and the failure to find conclusive evidence of organic life on any other planet suggested that the earth was humanity's sole possible home. China became only the third country to achieve human space flight when it launched an airforce pilot into orbit on its *Shenzou* spacecraft in October 2003. In a surprising reassertion of US commitment President George W. Bush announced in January 2004 a programme to establish a permanent manned base on the moon by 2020 and a staging post for expeditions to Mars by 2030.

By the beginning of the twenty-first century Israel, Canada, China, Japan, India and Brazil were making their own advances in space exploration and thereby raising their standing within their own geopolitical regions. The European space agency tried to co-ordinate the efforts of a continent. Space exploration therefore continued to enlarge the human horizon while also reflecting the patterns of power politics among states on earth. The 1967 Outer Space Treaty prepared by the UN had established that no country could claim sovereignty over the Moon or other celestial bodies. A further provision of the treaty prevented any country from placing nuclear arms or other weapons of mass destruction in orbit. But the arrangements reflected a super-power duopoly which had already ceased. The proliferation and easy availability of sophisticated weaponry and the emergence of a mosaic of states, some of them both unstable and aggressive, raised the possibility of new dangers descending from the explored firmament above and endangering a fragile earth.

29 March 1973

The Last US Troops Leave Vietnam

America Suffers a Rare Defeat

'*The conventional army loses if it does not win. The guerrilla wins if he does not lose.*'

Dr Henry Kissinger, national security adviser to the president, explains America's military dilemma, January 1969

The peace accords agreed between the US and North Vietnam on 28 January 1973 anticipated the end of a decade of destructive warfare. From the summer of 1972 onwards US and South Vietnamese land forces were in retreat in the face of a major North Vietnamese offensive. Seeking to show a residual US resilience, President Nixon had ordered a resumption of bombing in the north in April 1972 but by the end of that year both the North and South Vietnamese were still rejecting US peace terms and negotiations had been dragging on for four years in Paris. In December 1972 the North was subjected to another bombing campaign but US military commitment to the South was already much reduced and the North knew that its victory was near. By the terms of the peace accords the US agreed to withdraw its troops from Vietnam within sixty days and a political process was established to end the conflict in South Vietnam. This still left 100,000 North Vietnamese and Vietcong troops in the south and the struggle resumed in late 1974. On 30 April 1975 Saigon fell. Vietnam was reunited with the official declaration on 2 July 1976 of the Socialist Republic of Vietnam. 56,000 American soldiers had been killed and 270,000 wounded to no purpose whatsoever.

The US became involved in Vietnam because its government had decided to contain and oppose 'worldwide communism'. The vogue theory of policymakers in Washington DC was the 'domino effect' which maintained that communist governments, once in place, ensured the ideological contamination of their neighbours. If all Vietnam went communist then the whole of South-East Asia would suffer a knock-on effect and this, in turn, would impact on Japan and the Philippines – areas of the eastern Pacific where American interests were at stake. Europe's governing class had decided that colonialism was no longer practical because of the rise of nationalism in the Third World. In Vietnam the US government would be forced to a similar conclusion. The troops that it sent in to fight communism were, in fact, defeated by nationalism.

Vietnam had formed, along with Cambodia and Laos, part of the French Indochinese empire. Japan's conquest of Indochina during the Second World War effectively ended French power in the region, and American power at that time supported Vietnamese nationalism. France tried, and failed, to resuscitate her empire after the war. President Truman was persuaded by the French that it was holding the line against an international communist threat and the US involvement of the 1950s meant money and military equipment. In May 1954 the siege of Dien Bien Phu by the Vietnamese resistance force ended in a humiliating defeat for the French. A very rapid process of French decolonization in Morocco and Tunisia as well as in Indochina was now under way. Cambodia was already independent by the end of 1953 and, within a year, so was Laos. But the US insisted on the partition of Vietnam along the line of the 17th parallel. The North would be allowed to be communist under its leader, Ho Chi Minh, while the South was built up as an independent power with further US military and financial support. But the South Vietnamese regime run by President Ngo Dinh Diem, while anti-communist, was unpopular and its refusal to countenance land reform measures cost it the support of a hard-pressed peasantry. And Mao's China had already shown how a discontented peasantry could be attracted by a fusion of Leninist-Marxism with nationalism.

The Kennedy administration conceded that a left-right coalition was the only way to stop the civil war which had broken out in Laos in 1959. But it committed itself to the cause of an independent South Vietnam and increased the number of military 'advisers' in the country to 17,000. This foreshadowed the more doctrinaire conviction of President Johnson that the country's defence constituted an anti-communist crusade. By the end of 1964 the communist Vietcong, an underground guerrilla army, seemed poised for victory. The fact that both the Russians and the Chinese were backing the Vietcong confirmed the American administration's view that there was a globally united communist conspiracy despite the evident hostility between Moscow and Beijing. Needing to justify its intervention in what was really a Vietnamese civil war, the US argued, implausibly, that history and culture meant that the North and South Vietnamese were two different peoples who, therefore, needed different governments. Defence of South Vietnam's sovereignty, however, led the US to support the unlovely series of military dictators who ruled the country after a 1963 coup toppled the government and assassinated President Diem. This seemed a quixotic way to defend 'democratic values' against communist tyranny.

In August 1964 a North Vietnamese naval force fired torpedoes at the US destroyer *Maddox* off the Vietnamese coast in the Gulf of Tonkin. The American navy had been involved in covert actions for many months but the US government presented the incident as an unprovoked attack. Five days later Congress passed the Tonkin Gulf Resolution authorizing the president to 'take all necessary measures to repel any armed attack against forces of the US and to prevent further aggression'. In December Johnson announced a huge increase in 'aid' to South Vietnam. Overt military hostilities started on 7-8 February 1965 when US bombers went into action over North Vietnam in order to stop the infiltration of arms and troops into the south. Some 3,500 marines landed in the southern port of Da Nang near the border. By July there were 75,000 American troops in Vietnam – a figure that rose to more than half a million in 1968 and was supplemented by Australia and New Zealand's own troops.

The rural economy of South Vietnam proved a major war casualty as the peasantry fled the war-ravaged countryside and sought safety in the cities, thereby creating major social problems. Vietnam changed from a rice-exporting country to a rice-importing one. The country's underdeveloped economy suffered further when the inflow of dollars led to major inflation as well as a flourishing black market. The advantages of the Vietcong style of rural guerrilla warfare pursued by flexible strategy in a terrain familiar to the insurgents became increasingly obvious after an initial period of American military success. US forces were drawn into the jungle on 'search and destroy' missions. Attempts at hunting guerrillas from helicopters killed civilians as well as the Vietcong. Meanwhile the paddy fields provided the Vietcong with an ideal location for building up and training their guerrilla network which was also supported by an extensive system of supply bases in Laos and Cambodia.

The Vietnamese war brutalized a demoralized American army, divided a traumatized American society, and undermined national, as well as international, confidence in the efficiency and probity of US institutions. Military discipline broke down in the village of My Lai on 16 March 1968 when American soldiers under the command of Lt William Calley massacred 109 women, men and children – an outrage which the high command then tried to conceal. This was the first major war of the television age and the medium's influence on public opinion was a major element in eventual

US defeat. At the end of January 1968 the Vietcong and their North Vietnamese allies launched a major offensive on over a hundred cities and military bases in the South and were rebuffed. But the heavy casualties inflicted by US air power, horribly visible on the news bulletins, turned the 'Tet Offensive' into a political victory for the militarily defeated. By 1968 it was obvious that, despite such heavy casualties, Vietnamese nationalism was a resilient force which could not be defeated by the conventional methods of US fire power and the bombing of the North was having little effect on the Vietcong supply lines.

Television also demonstrated the profound divide between the army's rank and file, who were mostly blacks escaping from poverty, and an overwhelmingly white officer class. By the beginning of 1969 the number of American soldiers killed or injured in the Vietnam war had risen to 222,351 – and most of them were blacks. College deferment meant that university students, a mainly white grouping, could avoid conscription until the end of their studies. A wave of campus demonstrations rejected not only the war but also the interpretation of 'American values' which were used to justify it. Vietnam therefore helped to produce the politics of 'youth' and also contributed to the spread of a disillusioned 'counter culture'. By a savage irony the 'Great Society' reform programmes of President Johnson were now trying to heal the social divisions of the US but their budgets and, therefore, their effectiveness were undermined by war expenditure.

On 31 March 1968 a broken president announced his decision not to seek re-election. The Democratic Party's convention in Chicago was besieged by protestors seeking an end to the war and nominated Vice President Hubert Humphrey to contest the presidency. Johnson, seeking to help Humphrey's campaign, announced on 31 October an end to all air and naval bombardment over the whole of North Vietnam. But Humphrey, a figure central to the war policy, could not galvanize a party divided by that policy. Richard Nixon, the new Republican president, continued the war while starting a process of troop withdrawal. Nixon bypassed Congress when, in March 1969, he ordered the bombing of Vietcong bases in the east of Cambodia and also when he followed this up with a land invasion of the region in May 1970. The two illegalities were among the first of his subversions of the constitution. But the Vietcong had already retreated to the west and the American action only aggravated the Cambodian civil war. Communist forces based in the country refused to be bound by the terms of the January 1973 peace accords and were therefore subjected to intensive American aerial bombardment. The Cambodian collapse prefigured an even worse nightmare – the genocidal regime of Pol Pot whose paranoia killed a million Cambodians between 1975 and 1979.

At the end of the twentieth century Robert McNamara, US defence secretary in the 1960s, said that Vietnam showed the complexity of modern warfare and that human understanding was simply not up to the job of mastering that complexity. But it was a collective governmental delusion, subsequently corrected, which led to America's involvement and McNamara was closer to the mark when he said that in Vietnam the US had seen what it wanted to believe in: a vast conspiracy against itself. The names of those sacrificed in the service of that delusion are now inscribed on the wall of black granite which serves as their sombre and profound memorial in Washington DC.

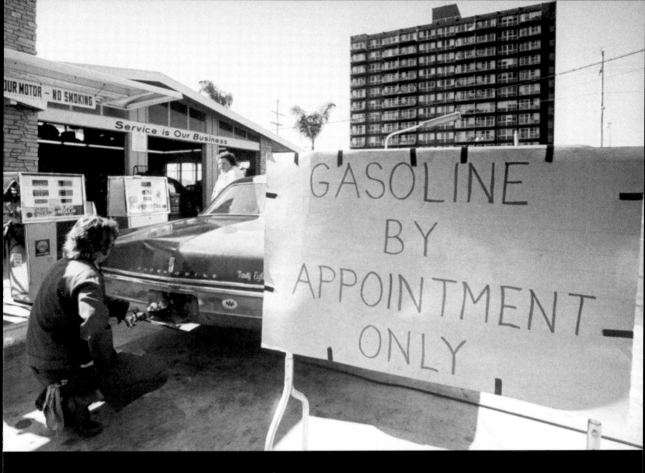

16 October 1973

OPEC Raises the Price of Oil

Recession Hits the West

'*This was the first time that major industrial states had to bow to pressure from pre-industrial ones.*'
International Institute for Strategic Studies, *Strategic Survey 1973*

It was an autumn of Middle Eastern battles. Israeli tanks had divided two invading Egyptian forces in the sands of the Sinai desert and on 16 October Egypt's 3rd Army was trapped. In the north, Syria's attempt at regaining the Golan Heights had been repelled. The Yom Kippur War (6-26 October) demonstrated Israel's successful defence of the territorial gains made in the Six Day War of June 1967. Oil would be the means of retaliation. Meeting in Kuwait on 16 October, Saudi Arabia, Iran, Iraq, Kuwait, Qatar and the United Arab Emirates – all of them OPEC members – decided to raise the price of a barrel of oil from $3 to $5.12. The following day a related body, the Organization of Arab Petroleum Exporting Countries (OAPEC), came out in support. This mattered since OAPEC included not just all of OPEC's Arab state members but also Syria and Egypt who, although not oil producers, had the state strength to make a policy bite. OAPEC announced that its members would no longer ship petroleum to countries that were pro-Israeli. A programme of embargos and of cuts in both the export and production of oil followed. These were designed to hit 'unfriendly states' – notably the US and its west European allies. For the first time in their history the Middle East oil producers were setting their own prices and operating a cartel with a political purpose. They could also rely on the support of OPEC's wider membership of countries with their own history of anti-western resentment: countries such as Venezuela, Indonesia and Nigeria brought into play the protests of Latin America, South-East Asia and West Africa. Algeria and Libya ensured the intrusion of a North African fury. By the beginning of December OPEC had quadrupled world oil prices to $11.65 a barrel and the Arab oil states had cut their output by twenty-five per cent. The US, having tried and failed to create a consumers' cartel to combat this shortfall, was resorting to price controls. The western dependency on oil was so great that its demand for the commodity was proving inelastic. Higher prices followed inexorably. Global economic interdependency, a suddenly apparent western instability, and a coalescence of Middle Eastern anger were all being demonstrated in a combined effect that was immediate, shattering and enduring. On 16 October the western world's politics of contentment ground to a halt.

OPEC had been trying, and failing, to influence the low-price policy of the British, Dutch and American oil companies ever since its establishment in 1960. Cheap oil had fuelled western economic growth and the west was increasing its energy use by five per cent annually. The engines of vehicles powered by oil, diesel and petrol ran along new roads and motorways transporting goods to the suppliers and buyers whose consumerist demands had grown remorselessly in the 1950s and '60s. Personal spending, increasingly sustained by credit, also responded to government plans and demands. Those same governments themselves borrowed on a new scale supposing that economic growth would, eventually, be self-financing. The automobile was no longer a luxury and its possession enabled millions to live in the new suburbs. Western European governments had nationalized many of their key industries as they negotiated their way out of the immediate post-war debris into an era of planned capitalism structured within a mixed economy. Expansionist government schemes had underpinned new welfare systems, extended state education and promoted better health care. As a result some class divisions seemed less excruciating than in the past – even in Britain. US prosperity was particularly prodigious and in the quarter of a century from 1950 onwards the country doubled its oil consumption. Europe might be dangerously divided but life in the continent's western half was more entertaining and less laborious for more people than at any stage in its history. 'Full employment' seemed a reasonable goal for governments led by politicians haunted by memories of the 1930s. Few questioned this democratic consensus as old ideologies yielded to new materialism. There had been protests that this age of satisfaction was turning into one of self-satisfaction. Student riots in May 1968 spread from Paris to other European cities but were easily dismissed as the incoherent noise of pampered youth.

Crude oil (petroleum) was paid for in a denominated currency of US dollars (petrodollars) and the west was selling its exports to the Third World petroleum producers at the inflationary price levels which were beginning to affect western economic systems. These exports included the petrochemicals derived from petroleum. Together OPEC held about two-thirds of the world's oil reserves and tried to get a slice of the oil companies' profits. Nationalization was one solution and in 1973 Saudi Arabia, which owned thirty per cent of all the world's oil, was moving towards full state control of its local industry. But inter-state co-ordination was fitful in the Middle East and the failure of pan-Arab nationalism was keenly felt – especially after the death of that movement's great figure Gamal Abdel Nasser in 1970. With its headquarters in Vienna, and a secretariat which convened ministers for regular meetings, OPEC offered an instrument for combined action.

The world economy had been vulnerable ever since President Nixon ended the international monetary system based on the Bretton Woods agreement of July 1944. Under the agreement's terms the International Monetary Fund was established to administer a system of fixed but adjustable exchange rates using the dollar as the fund's reserve currency. The system's effectiveness was based on the convertibility of US dollars into gold and as a result the dollar became the world's primary reserve currency. Countries expressed their exchange rate in units of dollars and they maintained that rate by buying and selling a dollar currency which they knew would be gold-convertible. But western governments' trade imbalances were becoming acute because of poor export sales and their expenditure programmes had created inflationary pressures. Britain devalued in 1967; Germany and France followed in 1969. In 1971 the US balance of trade went into deficit for the first time since the nineteenth century and its inflation rates were soaring as well. Germany allowed its mark to float in that year and gained in value. As a result there was a flight from the dollar. Nixon decided to imitate the mark. On 15 August 1971 he announced that the US government would no longer sell gold and the dollar was allowed to float in the world markets. The falling dollar was good news for US exports but OPEC members were now being paid in a depreciated currency.

The architect of the OPEC policy was Saudi's oil minister Sheikh Ahmed Zaki Yamani, a Harvard-educated lawyer who co-ordinated the initial response and then opposed further increases since he feared the danger of a global economic collapse. On 17 March 1974 progress on Arab-Israeli disengagement led to the formal end of the OPEC oil embargo and Yamani faced down subsequent Iranian demands for a price of $20 a barrel. By July 1977 prices were stabilizing at around $12.70 a barrel. The gains had been huge. In 1972 oil exporters received $23 billion for their oil and five years later the figure had shot up to $140 billion. The outbreak of the Iranian revolution in 1979 led to a further crisis in oil production. Western panic buying caused an oil glut followed by a price war and then a price fall. Yamani, increasingly out of favour with the Saudi theocracy, was blamed for this reversal. His policy of moderating the oil price rise had also won him the enmity of fanatics and OPEC's tactics were contributing to a new climate of aggression which could threaten the organization's own members. On 21 December 1975 'Carlos the Jackal' (Ilich Ramirez Sanchez), a Venezuelan terrorist working for the Popular Front for the Liberation of Palestine, led his armed gang into an OPEC meeting at Vienna. Yamani was seized and flown by his captors to Algiers where he was released after narrowly escaping execution by 'the Jackal'.

OPEC's campaign proved the catalyst for a prolonged British crisis marked by economic recession, unemployment and high inflation. A Conservative government, elected in 1979, promised sound money, an end to inflation, and less government. Margaret Thatcher, the prime minister, had been converted to monetarism, a doctrine which stated that the supply of money was the sole determinant of inflation. Like any economic theory pursued to extremes it proved destructive until her government abandoned the doctrine – by which time Britain's manufacturing industry had been undermined by high interest rates. 'Thatcherism', however, continued and achieved government expenditure cuts which had been attempted more half-heartedly by the Labour government of 1974-9. Having faced issues which were merely postponed in Continental Europe, Britain's economic future lay with various 'services' among which the supply of financial services would become predominant.

OPEC's actions helped Canada and the USSR, giving them, as oil-producing countries, new markets. The Soviet economy may well have been given an artificially long lease of life because of the decisions arrived at in Kuwait but Third World countries which were not oil producers became heavily indebted to western banks and this created a prolonged crisis in north-south relations during the 1980s. The American economy went into a further inflationary spiral just as the Watergate scandal revealed that President Nixon had used state security to spy on his opponents. The US became very distant from Continental Europe in the post-1973 period. The European Community responded to the oil crisis by siding with OPEC and demanding an Israeli withdrawal from the occupied Arab territories. This strengthened the increasingly common American view of Europe as a defeatist civilization.

The global search for renewable and alternative energy sources started in earnest as a result of the new cost of oil. OPEC, on US government estimates, succeeded in transferring $7 trillion from American consumers to oil producers over three decades after 1973 by keeping oil prices above their market-clearing level. Meanwhile the new money of the Middle East swelled the bank accounts of potentates, reinforced the power of the region's undemocratic elites, and thereby ensured an endemic instability. In 1974 Israel agreed to withdraw from the west bank of the Suez Canal and by the terms of the Camp David Accords of September 1978 Egypt gave Israel diplomatic recognition. However, this promise of a more equal balance of power in the Middle East collapsed when Egypt's president Anwar al-Sadat was assassinated in 1981 and Lebanon descended into civil war in the early 1980s. The new power of oil had turned impotent fury into armed resilience.

3 February 1976

The Rise to Power of William Henry Gates III

The Impact of Microsoft

'There is no such thing as a global village. Most media are rooted in their national and local cultures.'

Rupert Murdoch, Australian-American media mogul,
Business Review Weekly, 17 November 1989

The twenty-year-old who had recently abandoned his Harvard course was angry. Bill Gates told his fellow enthusiasts in an open letter on 3 February 1976 that although they accepted the fact that computer hardware had to be bought, 'most of you steal your software', and that therefore 'the thing you do is theft'. Specifically, he was cross that users of Altair Basic, a software program he had recently developed with his friend Paul G. Allen, were not paying royalties. His response ensured that the information revolution's initial stage would be dominated by a monopoly. Gates' Microsoft company turned to a 'Closed-source' policy, refusing access to its computer programs' source code and therefore stopping users from modifying the software. By the early twenty-first century Gates would be worth some $50 billion and Microsoft's market dominance had transformed conditions of work as well as patterns of leisure throughout the world.

Gates was a computing 'hobbyist' since childhood and in 1975 he started to work with Allen, a friend since high school days in Seattle, on developing software programs for the microcomputers which were then starting to be sold. Containing a single chip which brought together informational, logical and arithmetical processes, these microcomputers grew in sophistication and in their capacity to process information. By the 1980s they were the basis of personal computer systems and of work-stations as well as operating in a variety of other applications ranging from video games to military electronics.

Creativity, innovation and enterprise were the attributes preached by the advocates of an 'age of information' and invoked by the management gurus whose textbooks became the period's sacred texts. But Gates and Allen started their paths to billionaire status by developing a system rather than inventing one. They took BASIC, a programming language previously used on large computers, and adapted it for use on microcomputers. The next step involved the politics of American corporate life since Gates and Allen were approached by the International Business Machines Corporation (IBM) which had decided to build the hardware for its new desktop personal computer, the IBM PC, but needed to find an operating system for it. Microsoft leased its disc operating system, MS-DOS, to the company. The new computer's success meant that IBM became increasingly dependent on Microsoft for its software. By the early 1990s Microsoft had sold more than 100 million copies of its program and seen off its market rivals. Its dominance was further strengthened by its new operating system, the Windows program designed for computer interfaces. By the mid-1990s nearly ninety per cent of the world's personal computers ran on a Microsoft operating system and the company, a publicly owned corporation since 1986, was earning profits of twenty-five per cent on every dollar of sales. Gates' personal wealth was running into tens of billions of dollars and, by some counts, he was the world's richest individual. He had shown extraordinary acumen in grasping the opportunities of his time and a consistent determination to crush any competition. Microsoft was now illustrating two classic truths of capitalism: as a system it thrived on competition but individual capitalists were keen on monopolies which stifled competitive challenges. Ever since the late nineteenth century the US Congress had been alert to the dangers of such monopolies and many successful suits had been brought under the Sherman Anti-Trust Act (1890). Gates was accused by the US Department of Justice of being yet another monopolist. Previous investigations had forced Microsoft to change some of its sales' techniques but the case of US v Microsoft (1998), a result of the company's move into Internet technology, was altogether more serious. The company had developed its own, free, 'browser' program, Internet Explorer, which enabled its users to explore the 'World Wide Web'. Aggressive marketing had persuaded many Internet service providers and computer makers to distribute the program on an exclusive basis. In 1999 the trial judge ruled that Microsoft had violated the Sherman Anti-Trust Act and ordered the break-up of the company. Microsoft appealed, and in 2001 the break-up order was annulled, but the company was still found guilty of trying to maintain a monopoly. American law had rebuked an American giant.

The idea of computing long preceded its consumer development. In 1813 Charles Babbage, a British inventor, became the first to conceive of a machine which could calculate mathematical tables by mechanical means. But organized modern science was slow in developing this idea of 'artificial intelligence' for mass application. Alan Turing, a British mathematician, was the great twentieth-century pioneer in the field and a prime mover in the breaking of German intelligence's Enigma code during World War II. Subsequently, he designed a program for the Ferranti Mark 1, the world's first commercially available electronic digital computer. Turing believed that the human brain was in effect a digital computing machine which, having been born in an unorganized state, was then trained by experience as it evolved into an effective calculator. Unease at some of the mechanistic aspects of this suggestion may explain the slowness of computing science's development for daily use. The large and cumbersome computers of the 1950s and '60s, mostly isolated in research laboratories, were as far from daily experience as the abacus invented for calculation purposes by the Babylonians of the first millennium BC.

California's Silicon Valley, where a concentration of electronics and computer companies centred around Stanford University had developed since the 1950s, first showed the powerful synergy which was possible between academic research and the business development of computing. The location also became synonymous with a new view of economic development, human labour and national wealth. By the 1980s the western economies, most notably Britain and the US, were emerging from a painful period of adjustment after the decline of their 'heavy industry' – especially in coal, iron and steel – once the basis of their economies but now grown uneconomic. The bargaining power of trades unions had been reduced and the vogue was for a different kind of worker, technologically trained and de-unionized. Information technology was part of this new, and highly individualized, world of work in which employees sat at different work stations while operating their screens. This also encouraged the emergence of a highly specialized worker – stereotyped as the 'computer nerd' uninterested in any aspect of life save computing systems. Gates was himself an advanced example of the type with his talk of 'the enduring magic of software' although his charitable foundations spread the founder's reputation for human sympathy.

Ability to access information and then deploy it, especially through the Internet, became the most important quality of a flexible and ambitious workforce. This was, initially, a first world truth but it also had a dramatic impact on the emerging economies – especially in South-East Asia whose 'tiger' economies, such as Singapore, South Korea and Malaysia, were roaring ahead throughout the 1980s on the basis of low labour costs and quick technological minds. The development of this 'Pacific rim', including coastal mainland China, showed an historic shift away from the Atlantic economy as did Microsoft's own location in Washington State on the US western seaboard. The new economies of scale in production meant that old business hierarchies were fast dissolving. Traditional job security might have gone, but in its place arrived new opportunities as businesses concentrated on their core competences and 'outsourced' other areas of their work to specialized companies.

The economic liberalization of the 1980s also encouraged people to start their own businesses, to work from home and to be generally more self-reliant in their attitudes towards work – as long as they were armed with a personal computer and possessed nimble minds. Most people still worked for others and the corporate organization remained a massive truth of life. But human attitudes had changed with the idea of 'life-long learning' supplementing and challenging the older idea of professional knowledge as a competence which, once mastered, entitled the professional to a secure career and social standing. The impact of the computer, along with such liberalising measures as the City of London's deregulatory 'Big Bang' in 1987, also transformed financial services and the international money markets. The flow of capital now moved in seconds between Wall Street, the City of London and Tokyo.

Within this newly individualized democracy the traditional representative institutions suddenly seemed stuffy and irrelevant. They were, after all, founded on the fact of geographic distance between parliaments and the electorate as well as on the superior knowledge of the elected representatives. But the computer and the Internet gave access to immediate knowledge wherever one lived, and that fact led many to view party politicians as members of a remote and impotent tribe. Voter participation in many national elections plummeted accordingly. The power of governments, already much reduced in terms of economic management, was also affected by the new technology. There was talk of how computing power would reform 'bureaucracy', making it 'leaner' and 'fitter', this was the age of the personal trainer as well as of the personal computer and such metaphors were much in vogue. Computing capacity, however, gave governments fresh opportunities to demonstrate their incompetence as systems costing billions frequently crashed, were subject to human error or proved incompatible with other systems. Some new superstitions emerged, such as the conceited idea that the new technology was a development different in kind from other similar shifts of knowledge like the invention of printing in the fifteenth century. Computing was a technique of organizing knowledge rather than a change in its content, but what was original was the scale of its impact in a globalized and interconnected economy.

The initial prospect of greater human freedom through computer technology faded in the 1990s with the recognition that it could also promote new concentrations of power such as that of Gates. Economic liberalism was not equivalent to political liberalism – as China showed. Invasion of privacy, as a result of data stored without individuals' consent, became a problem as did the gathering of false information. Gates had protected his own company's product but protection of intellectual property rights became a widespread difficulty with the copying and reproduction of books, films and music. A classic dilemma of competing human freedoms had recurred as the information revolution's first phase drew to its close.

9 November 1989

The Breaching of the
Berlin Wall

The Berlin Wall started as a basic wire fence raised around the western, and democratic, part of the city in August 1961. West and East Berlin had therefore been separated from each other by the communist-run government of the German Democratic Republic (East Germany). The encircling fence ensured that now, more than ever, the whole of West Berlin formed an enclave within East Germany. Further refinements of containment followed. Between 1962 and 1965 a much improved wire fence was installed a hundred yards in from the first, creating a mined no-man's land in which escapees could be observed and shot. By stages a ninety-six-mile-long concrete wall was raised between 1965 and 1975. To this was added another border wall built between 1975 and 1980 – a technically sophisticated affair with twenty bunkers and 116 watch-towers. The Wall also went underground dividing the city's subway system. Just over 200 in all were killed trying to cross the Berlin Wall during its grim history and some 5,000 people managed to cross it illegally. The structure was designed to stop not only defectors but also the daily migration of those East Berliners who had found work in the western part of the city. This massive drain of professionals and skilled workers covered in all some two and half million people between 1949 and 1962 – a figure which was dramatically reduced to just 5,000 migrants from 1962 to 1989. East Germany's leadership feared an economic collapse and the USSR, to whom the country owed substantial war reparations, was therefore happy to support the Wall for economic as well as political reasons.

A mass exodus had started in the late summer of 1989 as East Germans made their way to an increasingly porous Austro-Hungarian border and then to West Germany. Thousands more crossed the border once the Hungarian government opened it officially on 10 September. That autumn the German Democratic Republic was celebrating its fortieth anniversary and Erich Honecker, the official in charge of building the original Wall, had been the country's leader since 1971. The Soviet leader Mikhail Gorbachev, a guest at the celebrations of 6-7 October, told him that there would be no USSR help if he tried to crush the pro-democracy protests which, from 4 September onwards, spread from Leipzig across East Germany. That spring the Chinese government had ruthlessly suppressed the reformist protesters assembled in Tiananmen Square, Beijing. Gorbachev did not want a bloody imitation to take place in eastern Europe. On 18 October Honecker was replaced by Egon Krenz who opened the border with Czechoslovakia which then became another exit route. Apparatchik panic had set in and the new government decided to allow East Berliners to apply for visas enabling them to visit West Germany. On 9 November this policy change was due to be announced by Gunter Schabowski, the propaganda minister, at a broadcast press conference held in the early evening. But Schabowski was inadequately briefed. The new regulations had been drafted in the course of the day of the 9th and were meant to take effect on the 10th once the border guards had been informed. An official note was handed to Schabowski just before he started speaking. As drafted, this simply stated that East Berliners would be allowed to cross the border as long as they had permission. Schabowski now read out the note. It was interpreted, correctly, as meaning that all East Germans would now be allowed to travel abroad. At 6.53 p.m., Schabowski was asked by a journalist when did this new law come into effect. He replied: 'Well, as far as I can see, immediately.' Tens of thousands of East Berliners who had watched the broadcast now rushed to the various checkpoints on the Wall where guards, armed only for regular duties, were overwhelmed. Only a large military force could have dispelled the crowd and the government was not keen on mass casualties since it knew its own life was going to be short. The checkpoints were opened and the crowds flowed through. In the days that followed the East German authorities created ten new border crossings and from 23 December both East and West Germans were allowed visa free travel. The Wall itself remained in place until 13 June 1990 when the East German army started the job of demolition. Within its rubble were interred the last consequences of the Second World War.

The West had been able to outspend the Warsaw Pact since communist regimes were financially as well as morally bankrupt. In the 1980s a new generation of weapon systems had arrived as Soviet SS-20s opposed US Pershing 2 and Cruise missiles. This of itself was a burden beyond the economic capacity of the USSR. But the US's Strategic Defence Initiative (SDI), announced in 1983, was beyond any Soviet capacity to respond. The SDI programme ('Starwars') took deterrence into space where President Reagan now proposed to build a defence system against intercontinental ballistic missiles. There had, however, been years of uneasy co-existence before then and sometimes the two sides almost seemed ready to agree to disagree. West Germany's Chancellor Willy Brandt developed an *Ostpolitik* or eastern policy which thawed diplomatic relations between the Federal Republic and her communist neighbours in the 1970s. At other times tensions would increase as happened after the crackdown on Czechoslovakia in 1968, the Soviet invasion of Afghanistan in 1979 and the imposition of military law on Poland in 1981. Supporters of deterrence could point to forty years of peace in Europe and link it to the vast programme of military expenditure. Sceptics doubted whether Soviet Russia was intent on a pan-European domination. The USSR after all had not expanded its western borders ever since its defeat in the Polish-Russian war of 1920. Nonetheless, its satellite states constituted a huge imperial buffer zone and a vast area of influence. Optimists, joined by some cynics, predicted that the two systems would 'converge' and that hawks would learn how to be doves. But eastern European societies, while economically feeble, were run by entrenched office holders who lacked the incentive to cease their autocratic ways. Liberals and human rights activists pointed to the repression of anti-communists in Warsaw Pact countries. All could agree that it was a good time for those who wanted a long career as disarmament negotiators. Treaty negotiations went on for decades and achieved little.

At a diplomatic and non-military level *détente* produced the Helsinki Conference on Security and Co-operation in Europe (CSCE) which ran from 1973 to 1975, recognized the fact of Soviet dominance in eastern Europe, and sought to build security by confirming Europe's present borders. Polish and Czech dissent took particular heart from the conference's agreement to protect human rights. Karol Wojtyla, the archbishop of Warsaw who was elected Pope in 1978, was a powerful witness against totalitarianism with his insistence that Europe's division disrupted an historic intellectual and spiritual unity. But the longer that division lasted, the greater the temptation to regard it as justified - especially for those born since 1945. Pope John Paul II, Margaret Thatcher and Ronald Reagan, however, were all figures formed by World War II and regarded communism as an unnatural system of government. They formed a climate of moral opinion which proved as important a solvent of communism as the more obvious failures of a command system of economic management in which the government pretended to be able to pay the people's wages while the people, in return, pretended to work. The first sign of an extraordinary change came in December 1987 during the US-Soviet summit held in Reykjavik to discuss a treaty on reducing intermediate-range nuclear forces (INF). Mikhail Gorbachev suddenly proposed that all nuclear weapons be cut by fifty per cent. Reagan rejected the idea and then regretted his refusal. Gorbachev, whose 1985 appointment as general secretary of the Soviet Union's Communist Party had been secured by the usual insider deals, was a new version of Soviet Man. He was a reforming communist rather than a democrat and his talk of *perestroika* (restructuring) was meant to make Soviet communism more efficient by introducing market reforms. Reducing the arms budget would, he thought, help the USSR survive. But the method threw the system into internal contradictions and the aspiration was unrealistic. Gorbachev discovered that any touch of his cautious reform simply made the economic crisis worse. *Glasnost*, another aspiration, meant a more public policy but in the light of day Marxist-Leninism withered to a quick death.

The events of 1989 in central and eastern Europe, together with their consequences, meant the collapse of an empire. Poland was in the lead. A national election on 4 June led to the formation of a coalition government led by representatives of the dissident movement *Solidarnosc* (Solidarity). On 23 August a human chain of protesters spread right across the Baltic states, absorbed within the USSR since 1939, and demanded their independence. Hungary proclaimed itself a democratic republic on 23 October. Communist rule was over in Czechoslovakia by the end of November and in Bulgaria two months afterwards. A military court shot Rumania's leader Nicolae Ceausescu and his wife Elena, a true mobster's moll, on 25 December. Honecker was placed under house arrest on 5 December and free elections were held in East Germany in March 1990. This led to the formal reunification of Germany in October. Eighty million Germans were together again in their *heimat*. But the one-to-one parity hastily agreed between the deutschmark and the ostmark would cause major economic problems in the 1990s.

The emergence of Serbia from the dissolved Yugoslavian federation proved to be a genocidal disaster since the country's former communist leadership sustained its authority by reviving Serb nationalism. This led to the bloody Balkan wars of the early 1990s as an expansionist Serbia waged wars and engineered massacres of Muslim Bosnians as well as of Catholic Croatians. Gorbachev became a victim of the process he unwittingly launched. The coup of 19 August 1991 tried to stop the dissolution of the USSR. Gorbachev was detained by the plotters and, since the Soviet system could no longer even run a successful putsch, was then released. In December 1991, Gorbachev, his authority diminished, resigned as president of the USSR – a title he had greatly coveted and held since 1989. The Union had simply dissolved. Four days earlier the former republics of the USSR had created a new organization, the Commonwealth of Independent States, with the Russian Federation as just one among eleven. Ex-communist states now tried to become capitalist. Poland, Hungary and the Baltic States succeeded and built on their pre-communist past. But Russia, bereft of an empire, faltered. Berlin's Wall meanwhile, fragmented into tourist gifts, survived only in the European memory.

11 February 1990

Nelson Mandela is Released from Prison

The End of Apartheid

*'Out of the experience of an extraordinary human disaster...
must be born a society of which all humanity will be proud.'*

Nelson Mandela, inaugural address as president of South Africa, 10 May 1994

Victor Verster prison, located in the Dwars valley near Cape Town, was the scene of Nelson Mandela's detention during the last fourteen months of his twenty-seven-year captivity. Here he entertained visitors in the house allocated him inside the compound and negotiated the details of his release. Jack Swart, his guard, was also his cook and all the warders now called him 'Mr Mandela' – a far cry from the unremitting coercion of Robben Island where, from 1964 onwards, he had worked in a limestone quarry under daily conditions of hard labour. But the chains of imprisonment had eventually shamed Mandela's captors and become the means of his freedom.

A tumultuous weekend had started with a Friday visit to F.W. de Klerk who had succeeded the intransigent Pik Botha as South Africa's president in the previous year. Knowing that the release was imminent Swart left work that day not expecting to see Mandela again. But the prisoner was still there on Saturday morning when Swart returned. 'Did you then not leave?' he asked. Mandela replied: 'They are going to release me the way I want to be released, not the way they want me to be released.' He had argued for six hours with de Klerk and won. The thirty-year ban on the African National Congress, Mandela's organization, had been lifted days previously and the prisoner was insistent that his own choreography would have to be followed before the cameras of the world. Five years earlier Botha had offered to release him as long as he denounced the ANC. Mandela had refused since: 'Until my people are free, I can never be free.' Right to the end of his sentence therefore he was asserting control over his destiny.

On the Sunday Mandela sat down after breakfast to make his daily cuttings of political stories from the newspapers. The former lawyer was always a man of method. He lay down after lunch in the large bedroom he used in summer months but rest must have been difficult since helicopters were now circling the house and raising dust. The arrival of ANC colleagues was the cue for departure. Mandela, hand in hand with his wife Winnie, walked down the drive, past the bushes and beyond the prison perimeter into the waiting crowds of thousands. He then raised his right fist in salute. It was the gesture which had marked over a generation of black activism. 'I had not been able to do that in twenty-seven years,' he wrote later, 'and it gave me a surge of strength and joy.' He was then driven to Cape Town for the victory parade at which he would speak. But in the drama of the moment he had left his speech behind in the prison house. Swart worried but need not have done. Mandela's ANC colleagues had a master copy as they sped on their way through the valley of the River Dwars – a sylvan scene first colonized three centuries previously by those other followers of conscience, the Huguenot Protestants exiled from an intolerantly Catholic France.

In 1910 the Cape Colony, Natal, Transvaal and the Orange Free State combined to form the Union of South Africa as a self-governing dominion within the British empire. Afrikaner farmers and settlers, originally called Boers, had already fought a war against the British (1899-1902) and their rhetoric of national self-determination expressed in their own Dutch-derived language of Afrikaans would predominate in the new country. Meanwhile, the Dutch Reformed Church of South Africa provided a Calvinist assurance that God was, somehow, supportive of Afrikaner intentions.

Afrikaner generals led a rebellion in 1914 against the decision that South Africa, as Britain's imperial ally, should attack the then adjacent German colony of South-

West Africa (subsequently Namibia). This resistance, though defeated, indicated a future of Afrikaner dominance whose political expression was the National Party, established in 1914. Racial segregation spread in the workplace, schools and hospitals. Gold-mining was the bedrock of the country's economy and much of the original race legislation was designed to support the structure of compounds, reserves and migrant labour which had become basic to that industry. Economic dislocation, as a traditional and rural society became more urbanized, meant that 'poor whites', predominantly Afrikaners, identified segregation as a way of protecting their jobs. At the same time Afrikaners promoted by government patronage were raised to a status equivalent to that of the white English-speaking elite.

After the election of a National Party government in 1948 *apartheid* or separateness became a fully conscious state policy. Inter-racial marriage became illegal. Public transport, cinema seats, beaches and wash-rooms were all segregated. Blacks had always been denied the vote and mixed race 'coloured' voters were removed from the electoral rolls in 1956. Urban areas were racially separated for both residential and business purposes. Each individual was racially categorized by the state and enforcement required the creation of a huge and costly bureaucracy. But the administration was implacable. When the country's Supreme Court declared in 1952 that the recent racist legislative package was illegal, the government got its way by making parliament the Supreme Court. Africa's whirlwind of decolonization was ignored and this isolationism was typified in the 1959 decision to keep television out of the country – a policy followed until the mid-1970s. In 1961 South Africa became a republic and left the British Commonwealth.

Residence requirements reflected the state view that Africans were inherently tribal. Those who were not working for whites were therefore gathered into 'reserves' where they were ruled by pliant chiefs. Between 1976 and 1981 these reserves were then gathered together to form four territories whose 'independence' of the Pretoria government was entirely fictitious and unrecognized by any other country. The Pass Laws now stopped Africans from remaining in towns for more than seventy-two hours unless they were working for whites. By these means over three and a half million Africans were expelled to the reserves.

Riots recurred in 1950s' Johannesburg despite detention without trial and a preposterous Suppression of Communism Act (1950) which interpreted most protest as 'Communist'. On 21 March 1960, 20,000 blacks gathered outside the police station in the Johannesburg suburb of Sharpeville to protest against the Pass Laws. Police fired at the crowd, killing seventy-two and wounding 146 others. Days afterwards the ANC was banned and the Sharpeville massacre proved to be the start of an organized anti-apartheid movement. It was during this new phase of protest that Mandela was sentenced in June 1964 to life imprisonment for espionage and subversion after he had renounced his earlier non-violence. Walter Sisulu, his great ANC mentor, was imprisoned for life at the same time and would only be released in October 1989. World opinion at the level both of governments and of popular protest became increasingly outraged after the carnage in the township of Soweto when, in June 1976, 176 were killed and over a thousand injured during the protests against the compulsory teaching of Afrikaans. And the death in September 1977 of Steve Biko, an African activist, while in police custody led to international condemnation. South Africa's position became critical internally as a result of the long and financially disastrous attempt to stop the independence of its colony Namibia whose war of liberation was being supported by Cuban troops and also by the neighbouring state of Angola. South Africa's withdrawal from Namibia in 1988 prefigured the regime's collapse. UN sanctions also had an economic effect, African Christianity was consistently eloquent in opposition, and morality began to affect money markets. In July 1985 Chase Manhattan Bank of New York recalled a $500 million loan to the South African government and other banks followed a similar policy of disengagement. Pik Botha talked tough throughout the 1980s and declared a state of emergency in July 1985 but economics as well as demographics were moving against him. Apartheid was proving unenforceable because there weren't enough whites to fill the jobs reserved for them. Meanwhile, blacks were becoming urbanized with the repeal of the Pass Laws in 1986. South Africa's collapse, like that of the USSR, was a political reflection of an economic failure.

The transition to a multiracial democracy took four years during which a power-sharing administration was formed, and in 1992 a whites-only referendum gave a comfortable majority for ending apartheid. International sanctions were lifted in 1993 and the ANC won the national elections of 1994. Mandela brought a gracious touch to the presidency of South Africa from 1994 to 1999. He was, after all, the son of a chief and had been raised among the royal household of the Thembu tribe in the eastern Cape. South Africa rejoined the Commonwealth and Mandela turned out to be a fan of the female chief who headed it. His multi-party government included representatives from all ethnic groups and, in 1995, Mandela established the Truth and Reconciliation Commission in order to investigate human rights abuses in as non-partisan a way as possible. Botha refused to testify. But state building in a nation without a shared history was desperately difficult. Labour disputes and criminal violence were endemic. Black solidarity was dented by the Inkatha Freedom Party (IFP) which expressed Zulu ethnic interests and led to violent conflicts, especially in Natal, between Zulus loyal to the ANC and those who supported the IFP. The political instability kept foreign investment away despite the ANC's abandonment of its earlier socialism. South Africa was still living with the isolation and the divisions which had been the explicit aims of apartheid.

Mandela was the greatest single figure to emerge from the late twentieth-century movement towards a multiracial society – a development which established new links between Europe and Africa as the decolonized migrated northwards. Legislation against race discrimination had enforced greater toleration in European societies and shown how laws could improve human conduct. Although racial prejudices persisted, a climate of 'political correctness', designed to show sensitivity to the cultures of the previously marginalized, had now spread from American universities to the western world. This sought to show a greater understanding of the varying cultural contexts in which the human spirit could flourish. It drew mocking responses such as the American novelist Saul Bellow's query 'Where is the Proust of the Papuans and the Tolstoy of the Tahitians?' But the dethronement of an automatic superiority showed a readiness to empathize, which was new in western culture. An enlarged human sympathy now asked whether western societies were right to impose their interpretation of reason and progress even within their own national domains.

11 September 2001

Nine Eleven

The Destruction of the World Trade Center

'We do not let fear make our decisions for us. We choose to live in freedom.'

Rudolph Giuliani, Mayor of New York, United Nations General
Assembly, New York, 1 October 2001

On the morning of 11 September 2001 nineteen men affiliated to al-Qaeda, an Islamic terrorist network, seized the controls of four US commercial jet aircraft. Two of the planes, which had been flying from Boston to Los Angeles, were crashed into the northern and southern towers of New York's World Trade Center at, respectively, 8:46 and 9:03 a.m. Fully fuelled for a long journey the two planes were now effectively incendiary bombs and both towers, which had stood 110 floors high, collapsed in flames. A third plane, deflected on its flight from Washington DC to Los Angeles, crashed into the southern side of the Pentagon in Arlington County, Virginia by 9.40 a.m. Another plane seized on its journey from New Jersey to San Francisco was probably intended for a similar attack on the US Capitol in Washington DC. Passengers resisted the flight's takeover and the terrorists crashed this fourth plane into a field in southwest Pennsylvania at 10:03 a.m. Almost 3,000 people died as a result of the attacks including approximately 2,750 in Manhattan. The bodies of over a thousand of the New York dead could not be identified because of the destruction's intensity. Black smoke billowed over the world's most cosmopolitan city in a scene emblematic of sophistication's vulnerability to barbarism. But if the context of this outrage was novel the savagery of its motivation was already familiar. By late afternoon, the al-Qaeda training camp in eastern Afghanistan could acclaim nineteen dead warriors as martyrs.

In July 2004 the official US Commission report on the atrocity named Khalid Shaikh Mohammed as the attacks' co-ordinator. Born in Pakistan and partly educated in North Carolina as a mechanical engineer, he had fought in Afghanistan alongside the local rebels supported by the US during the war (1979-89) which had followed the country's invasion by Soviet forces. Anger at America's pro-Israeli policy led to Mohammed's involvement in an earlier al-Qaeda attack on the Trade Center in 1993 when his nephew, Ramzi Yousef, planted a bomb in the underground garage of the north tower, killing six and injuring over a thousand. Until his March 2003 capture in Pakistan by local intelligence forces, Mohammed was a central figure within the international network of Islamic organizations whose interpretation of *jihad* (struggle) legitimized civilians' murder. In 1995 he had visited operatives in Brazil, Sudan, Yemen and Malaysia before travelling to the Tora Bora area of eastern Afghanistan where al-Qaeda ('the base') were being protected by the country's austerely Islamic government, the 'Taliban'. At a meeting in mid-1996 with the organization's leader, Osama bin Laden, Mohammed described details of the plan which was subsequently implemented on 11 September 2001. The al-Qaeda bombings of US embassies in Nairobi and Dar es Salaam on 7 August 1998 killing some 220 and injuring over 4,000 convinced Muhammed that the group was now committed to an attack on US territory and he therefore became a senior member of the organization.

By the time of the sea attack on the USS *Cole* on 12 October 2000, killing seventeen and injuring thirty-nine, the US was facing an al-Qaeda attack which was co-ordinated and global rather than random and local. But the CIA had a poor understanding of this aggressive force, first established in the late 1980s, and its long-term goals. Accepting responsibility for '9/11' in a filmed statement broadcast in the autumn of 2004, a figure claiming to be bin Laden stated that he had first conceived of such an attack after seeing the 'destroyed towers in Lebanon' during the 1982 Israeli bombing campaign which expelled the PLO from the south of the country. As a result the lesson was drawn that: 'the tyrant should be punished with the same and that we should destroy towers in America, so that it tastes what we taste...'

With his wealthy family background in Saudi Arabia, bin Laden showed how Islamic fundamentalism and Arab anger were no longer confined to the impoverished and marginalized 'Arab street'. Mohammed Atta, the Egyptian pilot of the first plane to hit the Trade Center, was a lawyer's son who had studied architecture in Cairo University. As a specialist in urban planning he was especially critical of the skyscrapers which he thought had ruined the centre of ancient Aleppo and his thesis subject at Hamburg's Technical University in the mid-1990s discussed the conflict between modernity and Arab civilization. Such a resentment against the alienating shock of the new had echoes beyond the Middle East.

Religious fundamentalism was a late twentieth-century phenomenon underestimated by a largely secular media, especially so in Europe, where secularisation was most advanced and fundamentalism least vigorous. The political support of an evangelical 'Christian coalition' which opposed multi-culturalism had helped to secure the election of a 'born-again' US president, George W. Bush, in 2000. Orthodox Judaism, rejecting the faith's liberal and reformed traditions, supported Israel's Likud party and opposed any concessions on the issue of national borders. Islamic fundamentalism's first great political success came in 1979 with the expulsion of Iran's Shah and the Ayatollah Khomeini's return from exile to Tehran. Islamic *Sharia* law became the state law of an Iranian theocracy. Literalist interpretation of sacred texts, whether of the Bible, the Hindu scriptures or the Koran, along with mass emotion and comradeship through ritual, typified all forms of fundamentalism. Fear of change dictated the movement's opposition to modern secularity, sexual emancipation and individualism. It also condemned established religious leaders for betraying 'truth'. Not all of the new enthusiasts were ignorant but fundamentalism invariably tried to recreate an idealized, largely imaginary, past of universal and unquestioning faith. Osama bin Laden's particular aim was a return of the mediaeval caliphate which would then provide unity in the Middle East. In order to achieve that goal he gave a murderously novel twist to fundamentalist politics.

US military bases in Saudi Arabia provided al-Qaeda with a particular focus of anger and were condemned by bin Laden in the 1998 *fatwa* he had issued against America. The installations had been there ever since the 1990-1 First Gulf War when a US-led coalition had expelled Saddam Hussein's invading Iraqi army from Kuwait – an invasion initially condemned by bin Laden. Since the cities of Mecca and Medina were on Saudi territory the bases were widely seen by Muslims as a violation of their holy land. US governments, bin Laden thundered, were consistently supporting decadent Middle Eastern regimes which abused their own peoples' rights. By 2001 there were, ironically enough, Washington policymakers who agreed with him on this last point.

9/11 strengthened the position of those 'neo-conservatives' within the US administration who thought that the Middle East would never be peaceful while its undemocratic governments remained in power. Democratization, imposed militarily if necessary, was the solution to a regional instability. In 29 January 2002, as part of this newly adopted policy, George W. Bush named Iraq, Iran and North Korea as part of an 'axis of evil' bent on destabilising democratic order through violence. The US government's foreign policy was, at least, now consistent with its democratic values. Previous administrations' support of conveniently anti-communist, but manifestly despotic, regimes was rejected. The proclaimed 'war on terror',however, was globally diffused and its critics thought the goal of US security guaranteed by a universal democracy was utopian and an open-ended guarantee of unending conflict.

The US attack on Afghanistan dislodged al-Qaeda from its bases by the end of 2001, despatched the Taliban, and led to an Afghan democracy. But pursuit of al-Qaeda was now secondary to conflict with Iraq whose president, Saddam Hussein, was a tyrannical despot who had waged one of the century's bloodiest conflicts in the Iran-Iraq War (1980-90) and remained in power despite his defeat in the First Gulf War. Both the US and Britain believed that Saddam was capable of providing terrorist groups with chemical and biological weapons. The Iraqi leader's hindrance of UN weapon inspections confirmed them in that view. Britain's PM, Tony Blair, persuaded the US that ideally a UN resolution was needed to authorize an invasion of Iraq. But the explicit US aim of 'regime change' contravened the UN charter as well as much of international law and no resolution was forthcoming. Britain justified its participation in the 2003 Second Gulf War on the grounds of an immediate threat of Iraqi attack. But the government's claim that Iraq could unleash weapons of mass destruction (WMDs) within forty-five minutes of an order being given was false and a result of over-enthusi-astic British intelligence. After the invasion no such weapons were found in Iraq.

Saddam's government and army had been easily defeated and, following an American-dominated interim administration and then a UN one, a democratic government was elected. Libya's renunciation of WMDs and nuclear weapons in 2003 along with Syria's troop withdrawal from Lebanon in 2005 seemed to vindicate US-British policy. But the spread of an Iraqi insurgency attacking the occupying forces also witnessed intense conflict between the majority Shiites and the Sunni Muslim minority whose members had formed Saddam's ruling elite. Meanwhile both British and US governments had introduced legislation which curtailed civil liberties in their own countries in order to help prosecute their campaigns against terror suspects.

Evidence of US soldiers torturing Iraqi prisoners, at the Abu Ghraib prison in 2004 undermined US moral authority while Islamist fanaticism continued to frighten and destroy. The bombs that exploded on the transport systems in Madrid (11 March 2004) and London (7 July 2005) were a retaliation against countries whose governments had supported the Iraqi invasion. Traditional Republicans in the US lamented the policy's financial burden and questioned the war on terror's relevance to domestic interests. A 'New Labour' administration, however, had provided further proof of the depth of Britain's commitment to its American ally. In September 2005 the Gaza strip and parts of the West Bank came under Palestinian control following Israel's withdrawal from those areas, but the 2006 democratic elections in the Palestinian territories elected to government the avowedly terrorist Hamas organization on a new and violent wave of Arab solidarity. The Middle Eastern powers, collectively and unanimously opposed to the policies adopted by the US government in its response to 9/11, were now more united than at any stage in their modern history. It cannot be known if this was the result desired by al-Qaeda while calculating its strategy and planning the horror unleashed on the innocent that September morning.

INDEX

FOR FRANK AND VIRGINIA JOHNSON

Quercus Publishing plc
21 Bloomsbury Square
London
WC1A 2NS

First published 2006
Third trade edition published 2006

A catalogue record for this book is available from the British Library.

ISBN
Cloth case edition 1 905204 76 0
Printed case edition 1 905204 38 8
Paperback edition 1 905204 94 9

Printed and bound in Great Britain.

Picture Credits
The publishers would like to thank the following for permission to reproduce illustrations and photographs: Corbis, cover images and pages 17,21,40,45,47,57,61, 73,77,89,113,117,125,129,133,137,141,149,153,157,165,173,177,181,193,197,201; Japan Archive p.65; Mary Evans Picture Library: pp. 5,9,13,29,33, 37,49,53, 81,85, 93, 97,101,105,109,121; Getty Images: pp. 25, 41,69,145,169,185

Edited and typeset by Windrush Publishing Services, 12 Adlestrop, Moreton in Marsh, Gloucestershire, GL56 0YN
Picture research by Victoria Huxley
Index by Ingrid Lock